Stories of

ROARING
FAITH

• COMPILED AND EDITED BY
DONNA SKELL
LISA BURKHARDT WORLEY
BELINDA MCBRIDE

Stories of Roaring Faith
Copyright © 2017 by Roaring Lambs Publishing

All Scripture quotations, unless otherwise indicated, are taken from the Holy Bible, New International Version®, NIV®. Copyright ©1973, 1978, 1984, 2011 by Biblica, Inc.™ Used by permission of Zondervan. All rights reserved worldwide. www.zondervan.com The "NIV" and "New International Version" are trademarks registered in the United States Patent and Trademark Office by Biblica, Inc.™

AMP: Scripture quotations are taken from the Amplified® Bible, Copyright © 2015 by The Lockman Foundation. Used by permission. www.Lockman.org.

CEV: Scripture quotations are from the Contemporary English Version Copyright © 1991, 1992, 1995 by American Bible Society. Used by Permission.

ESV: Scripture quotations are from the ESV® Bible (The Holy Bible, English Standard Version®), copyright © 2001 by Crossway, a publishing ministry of Good News Publishers. Used by permission. All rights reserved.

MSG: Scripture quotations are taken from THE MESSAGE, copyright © 1993, 1994, 1995, 1996, 2000, 2001, 2002 by Eugene H. Peterson. Used by permission of NavPress. All rights reserved. Represented by Tyndale House Publishers, Inc.

NCV: Scripture taken from the New Century Version®. Copyright © 2005 by Thomas Nelson. Used by permission. All rights reserved.

NKJ: Scripture taken from the New King James Version®. Copyright © 1982 by Thomas Nelson. Used by permission. All rights reserved.

NLT: Scripture quotations are taken from the Holy Bible, New Living Translation, copyright ©1996, 2004, 2007, 2013, 2015 by Tyndale House Foundation. Used by permission of Tyndale House Publishers, Inc., Carol Stream, Illinois 60188. All rights reserved.

TLB: Scripture quotations are taken from The Living Bible copyright © 1971. Used by permission of Tyndale House Publishers, Inc., Carol Stream, Illinois 60188. All rights reserved.

No part of this publication may be reproduced, stored in a retrieval system, or transmitted—electronic, mechanical, photocopy, recording, or any other way—without the written prior permission of the copyright holder, except as permitted by U.S. copyright law.

Published by:
Roaring Lambs Publishing
17110 Dallas Parkway, Suite 260
Dallas, TX 75248
Email: **info@RoaringLambs.org**

Dedication

To God,
Thank You for the difference
You make in our lives.

To Garry Kinder,
Founder of Roaring Lambs Ministries,
Because of you, this book is possible.

To all the contributors of this book,
Thank you for sharing your personal testimonies
With the world.

To all the readers,
May your relationship
With our Lord Jesus Christ grow.

Introduction

About thirty-five years ago, I had the opportunity to attend a small class that taught me how to confidently and effectively share the gospel against the backdrop of my life experiences. **It changed my life.** I learned the importance of sharing how God had proved Himself real to me.

Come and hear, all you who fear God; let me tell you what he has done for me. — Psalm 66:16

For the last several years, Roaring Lambs has been encouraging and equipping believers to effectively compose their testimony. Whether sharing one-on-one, speaking to a group, or just putting it in writing as a legacy for future generations, it is beneficial.

We will tell the next generation the praiseworthy deeds of the Lord, his power, and the wonders he has done, so the next generation would know them, even the children yet to be born, and they in turn would tell their children. — Psalm 78:4, 6

Our testimony is our opportunity to let God use the circumstances He has allowed in our life for His glory. When you can take a difficult time, show how God used it for His good and yours, then you can give Him glory for that very hardship.

When he heard this, Jesus said, "This sickness will not end in death. No, it is for God's glory so that God's Son may be glorified through it." — John 11:4

Putting your faith story together will prepare you for many opportunities to share your faith. Each day, you are more likely to realize just how many there are.

But in your hearts revere Christ as Lord. Always be prepared to give an answer to everyone who asks you to give the reason for the hope that you have. But do this with gentleness and respect. — 1 Peter 3:15

The world needs to see how real Jesus is. Times are short. Your story matters; it is the living water that others need.

Then he said to his disciples, "The harvest is plentiful but the workers are few." — Matthew 9:37

Are you ready to be used by God and be richly blessed? Tell your story of what He has done for you.

Then I heard the voice of the Lord saying, "Whom shall I send and who will go for us?" And I said, "Here am I. Send me." — Isaiah 6:8

Donna Skell, Executive Director
Roaring Lambs Ministries

Acknowledgements

My sincere thanks are extended to Frank Ball for his gracious help turning this manuscript into a book. You are a kind, generous, God-loving man, and very appreciated by this ministry.

To Dan Thompson, our graphic designer from T-Bone Designs, many thanks for all your work with Roaring Lambs, to give us such a great look. You are talented and have established our visual image. Thanks especially for a great cover for this book.

Thank you, Sherry Ryan, for your work editing the testimonies. I know you were blessed by reading them, but we are blessed by all your spelling, punctuation, and grammar corrections.

To my co-compilers and editors, Belinda McBride and Lisa Burkhardt Worley, without the two of you, this book would have never been completed. Thank you for your endless hours of reading and re-reading the stories. Thank you for your attention to the small details.

Thank you, again, to all who contributed their personal testimonies. This book is not about you, but is all about our great and awesome God we serve.

The Power of a Testimony

There is no better witness than a personal testimony, and I never tire of reading how God has reconstructed people's lives. I had the privilege of editing *Stories of Roaring Faith* and *Stories of Roaring Faith, Volume 2*. Through working on these books, my own relationship with God was strengthened as I saw how our merciful Father never discards the broken pieces of His children's lives. In His eyes, we are all salvageable, and in our brokenness, He does His best work.

Our Maker is in the business of redeeming problems and life issues. In *Stories of Roaring Faith, Volume 2,* you will see how the Lord healed both men and women after childhood sexual abuse. You will read how powerful prayers helped a child conquer addictions. You will be drawn into a woman's testimony about forgiving the father who abandoned her as a child. Illness, divorce, prostitution, terrorism, and recovering from a traumatic robbery are all topics addressed. What is the common thread in each of these faith stories? It is God's outstretched tender hand beckoning people to draw near to Him so He can touch their lives with compassion, healing, and love.

As you read the accounts of those who have overcome the most horrific of circumstances, you will know that God still performs miracles. He is a relational Creator who desires to re-write our story for His glory.

Lisa Burkhardt Worley, Director of Special Projects
Roaring Lambs Ministries

Table of Contents

The Speeding Bullet
by Nancy Shore

I am a hopeless romantic.

I love talking about engagements, weddings, and marriage. As a young adult, I had a cake business based out of my home. I even made the groom's cake for our wedding. The enjoyment of this type of work led me to employment as a wedding/event coordinator for a short season.

Before computers and blogging, we had newspaper columnists and a lady named Ann Landers, who gave all kinds of advice about life, love, and marriage. She wrote a column that ended with a poem that has been used in many marriage ceremonies, including mine in 1983. It reads: "Love is friendship that has caught fire. It is quiet understanding, mutual confidence, sharing, and forgiving. It is loyalty through good and bad times. It settles for less than perfection and makes allowances for human weaknesses." That's the life I had always dreamed of, being married, having a family, and growing old together. FH was the love of my life.

FH and I raised three awesome children, and we were a family that placed God and His Word as a high priority. We attended our church regularly. We both sang in the adult choir, and our children were in children and youth choirs, along with all the other church activities. Each of the kids played a sport, so we spent a lot of family time together.

In decisions on how we would raise our children, we wanted to instill such traits as serving, giving, and loving beyond our family and church. We served on a mission trip to Mexico, and the kids were encouraged to volunteer. When the oldest entered high school, we decided to host an exchange student from Brazil and another one from Germany. It brought a new worldview to us as we welcomed them into our family. It was an exciting season.

Our oldest daughter and son were both in out-of-state colleges, and our youngest daughter was in high school as we began nearing the new season of empty nesting. One night at our church, they spoke about all the mission trips that were planned and encouraged people to stay and see if God might impress upon their hearts to serve. So I decided to listen to information about several of the

1

trips. I went over to the group that talked about serving in Zambia, Africa. I wasn't going to go. I just wanted to hear about it. What they shared was very interesting, but both the cost and the thought of making a trip of that kind were too much. After all, I had been diagnosed with fibromyalgia, an autoimmune disorder that left me with excruciating pain and chronic fatigue. I left the meeting with an unsettled feeling, so I decided I should seriously pray about this ridiculous possibility that God might indeed be calling me to Africa.

At home, I briefly discussed the meeting with my husband and asked him if he had any interest in going, to which he replied no, but he quickly suggested that I approach our youngest daughter about her interest. So after some prayer and finding out more details, I spoke with our daughter, and she promptly said, "Yes, I would love to go." Apparently, that instilling of serving, giving, and loving had taken deep root in her heart.

The trip required attendance at numerous planning and preparation meetings. The first meeting was another "level of interest" session where we learned more details about the trip. I had been praying fervently about my involvement and kept asking God to let me know if He *really* wanted me to go. In other words, I still didn't want to go and was begging for an escape route. Instead, God was clear and showed me that it was my year to go, that I could no longer wrestle with uncertainty.

Each year, this mission organization creates a new theme and focus, with activities and music prepared around that theme. That year's theme was God's amazing love and John 3:16. They wanted to focus on how much God the Father and Jesus the Son loved us. In the explanation of the plans, one of the items the children in Zambia would receive was a certificate with their picture taken with us. On the back was "The Father's Love Letter," written straight from scripture passages that tell of God's love, Jesus' love, and the plan they have in wanting the children to know this love through a personal relationship.

Through this "love letter," God spoke to me. Ten years before this mission planning meeting, my earthly father had passed away suddenly on Christmas day. It was a shocking and painful experience that shook my faith. I grieved and mourned his loss, trying to understand how a loving God could take my daddy so suddenly, and on Christmas day. In response to this grief, I felt led to write myself a letter straight from scripture. I have carried that letter in my Bible ever since. It was a secret, and I did not share it with anyone for many years, not even my husband or children. So this was a very personal call God was placing on my heart. I finally submitted and found peace about the trip.

During my time of service in Africa, I learned the amazing power of the name of Jesus. In my group of twelve young girls, there were two that I sensed needed to be delivered from demons and curses. Leaders directed them to the prayer room for deliverance. During this intense time of prayer, I didn't know what to do except call on the name of Jesus, along with the head pastors who knew how to pray, and to ask God to intervene in their lives. I saw God free those children, and the next day, one of them prayed with me to receive Christ as her personal Savior. Our God is a very personal God, not some far away untouchable spirit, and I praise Him for showing Himself to me so vividly. After the week came to an end, my daughter and I boarded a plane to return home, forever changed.

When we arrived at the airport, we joyfully ran to FH, who was waiting to pick us up. On our trek home, I felt something was not right with FH, but I couldn't put my finger on it.

As our younger daughter left for college, FH and I officially entered the season of empty nesters. We were both trying to "find ourselves" as this season moved further along in our lives.

On August 18, 2012, FH was out of town on business for the weekend, and I was preparing to host a women's tea at our church. I spent time with the Lord reading my Bible and praying for our speaker and that event. I felt led to share a scripture with our speaker and have found it to be a significant life verse: "The Lord your God is with you, he is mighty to save. He will take great delight in you, he will quiet you with his love, he will rejoice over you singing" (Zephaniah 3:17). The Tea was a wonderful time of fellowship and encouragement.

That evening, I went back to church to witness the baptism of a longtime family friend. On my way home, I stopped by Taco Bueno to get supper and then proceeded home. I drove into my garage as usual, then got out of my car and took a step toward my house. Suddenly a man had his arm around my neck, with a gun to

3

my head, demanding my purse. I wrestled away from him, turned around, and faced him. He demanded my purse again, and in my flustered state I promptly handed him my Taco Bueno bag. Well that didn't go over very well, and he demanded my purse a third time, this time with expletives. I was within an arm's length of him as I stared down the barrel of his gun. I shoved my purse into his chest and cried out, "Jesus save me!" as the robber shot me. I went down, alone in the garage, and bled profusely. My God, who is more powerful than a speeding bullet, spoke to me. "Get up, get up!" With these words, He also gave me the physical strength to pull myself up onto a metal stand. About halfway up, my knees buckled, and I landed facedown on the garage floor. I was unable to pick myself up. So I began to "army man" or belly crawl to my car to push the emergency button to get help. But the button didn't work. God gave me the strength to push myself up and out of the car. Holding on to my car, I shuffled back through my own blood to make the excruciatingly painful journey into my home. I turned the house alarm off, paused at my bathroom to see my horrifying self, and stumbled to the kitchen counter to dial 911. I described the shooter and gave all the needed information to send help.

The investigation led police to discover that FH, my husband of twenty-nine years and father of our three children, had been involved in a three-year affair. Within a few days, he was sued for misappropriation of funds by his employer. Two weeks after the shooting, FH was arrested for "criminal solicitation to commit murder." Yes, that's murder for hire.

After seeing all the evidence from the investigation, I realized that FH was not just having an affair. He was living a double life. My longtime dream of growing old together ended in divorce in June of 2013.

God often uses a song to speak to me and impress upon me something He wants to teach. At my lowest point, God messaged me through a song whose lyrics challenged me, and my conversation with God went something like this: "Really, Lord? You want me to *ask* you to make me broken, make me lonely, and make me empty? I have nothing. I am nothing. My past, present, and future have all unraveled and are one big loss." But over the next few weeks I did what He asked. I prayed those things and completely surrendered my shreds to Him.

4

While my story is one of complete loss, betrayal, grief, fear, depression, and excruciating physical pain, I praise God that He didn't leave me there to find my own way out. A few months before the trial, God took me through an agonizing journey of facing the horrible emotions I had felt since the shooting. God impressed upon me the need to pour out my anger, rage, bitterness, and feelings of betrayal at His feet. I confessed all of that and was given merciful forgiveness and freedom. This was clearly in preparation for the jury trial ahead. During the two-week jury trial in August 2014, evidence of God's sovereignty was overwhelming as testimony revealed numerous failed attempts on my life. God was in control and did not allow it to happen *until He* was ready. "He thwarts the plans of the crafty, so that their hands achieve no success. He catches the wise in their craftiness, and the schemes of the wily are swept away" (Job 5:12–13).

After an hour-and-a-half jury deliberation, my former husband was found guilty of attempted capital murder and sentenced to life in prison. God gave me the peace and strength in open court to publicly forgive him. I must say, other than the gift of my own forgiveness and salvation, there is no greater gift than to forgive someone else. A sure reminder of this is found in Isaiah 42:16: "I will lead the blind by ways they have not known, along unfamiliar paths I will guide them; I will turn the darkness into light before them and make the rough places smooth. These are the things I will do; I will not forsake them."

The man who shot me was tried in a two-week jury trial in August 2015. Facing this man in court was overwhelming. The last time I had seen him in person was when I stared down the barrel of his gun. ML was convicted of aggravated robbery and sentenced to sixty years in prison. With previous felony convictions, he could not be eligible for parole for thirty years. In my victim-impact statement, I told him that I forgave him, and I prayed that he would someday come to know the Jesus, whose name he heard me call on the day I was shot.

Many have asked, "Why did you turn off the alarm? Why didn't you just let it call the police?"

God had a plan.

He showed Himself by giving me the strength and breath to provide the details to the 911 dispatcher, along with the ability to pray and call on God and Jesus to help me and save me.

He showed Himself by leading me to speak on NBC Dateline, where many people would hear that 911 call and be encouraged by the outcome of those prayers.

He showed Himself by giving me the opportunity to honor my 911 dispatcher with an award for "Telecommunicator of the Year" for the State of Texas. I was the first survivor to do this. I also got to pray over 600 first responders and police officers at that award gathering.

The injuries I sustained required a year of brain retraining and physical therapy, as well as numerous surgeries to rebuild my face and eye socket. In the repair process, God provided a world-renowned ocularist to create and paint a beautiful prosthetic eye to match my God-created blue eye. I'm forever grateful that he is such a kind doctor, passionate about helping his patients to feel normal again. God always turns bad things for good for those who are called according to His purpose. During one of my many visits to Dr. T's office, he sent me out to lunch while I waited for him to work on my prosthetic. Wearing my white eye patch, I stopped at a local restaurant. Business was a bit slow, and my waitress was curious about my eye patch. I told her how God had saved my life during the shooting, but I had lost my left eye. She asked about my faith, which led to a clear presentation of the gospel. This young woman was searching for Christ. Our divine appointment ended with her praying to receive Jesus as her personal Savior. I was overjoyed to be God's vessel that day.

In my journey with the Lord, I struggled with being convinced of His all-sufficient, never ceasing, never-changing love. As a child, I prayed to receive Jesus as my personal Savior and was baptized. I was one who tried to faithfully follow Jesus, but I waffled with doubts about whether I had truly received Him. I couldn't remember the prayer I had prayed, and I worried that I didn't say it right or do everything right. I persistently asked God for assurance. It wasn't until I was an adult that I finally put all those doubts to rest. Through much seeking and searching, I understood that it wasn't about what I had said or if I had "done it all right." It was about God and what He had done by sending His Son Jesus to die on the cross for me. Jesus had done it *all* right. I was thankful when I accepted that fact. The bottom line is this: there's no doubt, no sin, no secret, and no pain so deep that God can't pull us out.

While I believed that He loved me enough to send Jesus to die for me, the concept of the daily personal relationship and the love and care for me each moment of the day was something that I couldn't grasp. Therefore, any pain or loss in my life was viewed as "I deserved it," and/or because "He didn't really love me." But God's Word is alive and active, and once again I didn't have to continue believing the lies. Neither do you. "This is love: not that we loved God, but that he loved us and sent his Son as an atoning sacrifice for our sins" (1 John 4:10).

Until I became convinced of *this* kind of love, I struggled with trusting God's promises, whether His heart was for me. If we cannot believe that God's love is about shaping us to look more like Jesus, we will struggle when the storms of pain and loss come.

Spending time alone used to be a form of punishment for me. I'm a people person, and I hated being alone. But through various situations, God taught me. I began to understand that being alone, feeling lonely, and solitude were different. Through times of solitude, I learned how to rest in His presence. As I sat and listened to music, read my Bible, and prayed, the Holy Spirit spoke to me and taught me, healed me and comforted me, and refueled me. Surrendering to this form of self-discipline has transformed me. Now, I crave solitude and this special quiet time of focus. It has also prepared me for my new life alone with my little dog. Sometimes I feel lonely, but God is always there, providing His presence and often providing a person who checks on me. I call it "Jesus with skin on."

"God is our refuge and strength, an ever-present help in trouble. God is within her, she will not fall; God will help her at break of day. Be still and know that I am God" (Psalm 46:1, 5, 10).

I'm grateful that God didn't choose to just save my life, but He has also continued to heal me so I can live and care for myself. Early in my recovery from the shooting, I worried about what the long-term ramifications of my injuries would be. But God. Yes, He's always there for the pause and consideration of His plan. As I continued through my surgeries, therapies, and testing, improvement was always evident.

I'm thankful that after many stepping stones of working small jobs, I am now working my first full-time job in twenty-five years.

It's not just *any* job. After a sixteen-month job search, God opened the door to a secular job with a Christian culture. I go to work every day knowing that I'm allowed to ask for prayer, or I can offer to pray for someone. I can read and talk about scripture. My natural abilities and spiritual gifts are played out daily, and joy and thankfulness are present, even in the rough days.

Last year, I felt led to tell my story in a book titled, *The Shooting of Nancy Howard: A Journey Back to Shore*, written by Alice Mathews. We both hope it will draw others to Christ.

I hope you can see the many times God has acted on my behalf or has prepared me for the path He has laid.

Since the year of the shooting, I prepare for the year ahead by praying and asking God to show me an area where I need to grow and to give me focus on a specific verse. My 2017 focus words are strength and courage, based on Joshua 1:9: "Haven't I commanded you? Strength! Courage! Don't be timid; don't get discouraged. God, your God, is with you every step you take" (MSG).

Thank you for sharing my spiritual journey. May you find new strength and courage in your life too.

Nancy Shore *is the mother of three married children and speaks publicly about her faith in Jesus Christ after surviving an attack at her home in August 2012. She lives in Plano, Texas, and is an active, longtime member of First Baptist Church, Carrollton. Nancy's story was written by Alice Mathews and published in May 2017.* The Shooting of Nancy Howard: A Journey Back to Shore, *can be purchased at*
AliceMathewsNancyShooting.com *or on* ***Amazon.com.***

Thoughts to Ponder
from The Speeding Bullet

1. God can protect us supernaturally.

2. Even during crisis, God is always good.

3. When people betray us, God will help us forgive them.

> **How has the Lord
> protected you in a crisis?**

Deliver me from my enemies, O God; be my fortress against those who are attacking me. — Psalm 59:1

Where Do You Run?

by Jennifer McAlister

You may remember the movie quote, "Run, Forrest. Run!" It's one of my favorite lines from *Forrest Gump* because it reminds me to run when I need to. We live in a world that demands we run to the latest fad, worldview, or deception—anything that draws us away from God. Every time we give into temptation, give up on ourselves, or give up on God, we can rest assured we are running in the wrong direction. God gives us the ability to choose what direction we will run. As Dr. Seuss says in his book, *Oh, The Places You'll Go*, "You have brains in your head. You have feet in your shoes. You can steer yourself any direction you choose."

So where do you run?

Years ago, I read a story of a hunter who was surprised by a frightened bunny that frantically jumped out of the bushes and ran straight toward him, seeking shelter between his legs. As he was puzzling over this, out of the same bushes that delivered the bunny came a hungry weasel that wasn't happy to see his potential lunch sitting at the feet of a man with a gun. The weasel froze in its tracks as he stared at the hunter. The hunter looked down at the rabbit, still squeezed between his hunting boots, heart racing, completely spent, and realized that the poor thing must have run as fast as it could and was close to death before running to him as its last source of refuge. The hunter didn't disappoint the defenseless rabbit as he raised his gun and shot at the ground sending the weasel scurrying away.

"Where did he go, little one?" the man tenderly asked the frightened rabbit. "Where did he go?"

I think of this story every time I make the mistake of not running to God first. Like the rabbit, we too have an enemy who would love to destroy us. The Bible says the devil roams the earth like a roaring lion, seeking someone to devour (1 Peter 5:8). Like the bunny, in our own strength we would be defenseless, but if we run to Jesus for protection, the enemy is only able to roar.

Many years ago, I found myself in a place where I wanted to run far, far away to a problem-free oasis and hide forever. I was sixteen years old, sitting in a women's clinic, frantically awaiting the test results. The nurse walked in, looked at me, and nonchalantly told me my test was positive. I was overjoyed. I needed something positive to happen in my life. My parents had recently divorced, I was living with my grandma, and I was struggling to fit in at my new school. I told the nurse, "Thank you for the good news. I was worried I was pregnant."

"You are" she said with irritation. "That's what a positive test means."

My heart sunk as I tearfully let her know that her news wasn't "positive" at all. It was very negative. I cried and couldn't stop repeating to myself, *I can't be pregnant, I can't be pregnant, I can't be pregnant,* as I tried to change my past decisions with my present declarations. She handed me information on my options and told me I was free to go. But I wasn't. I wasn't free at all. I felt trapped, defenseless, and fearful. How could I tell my mom, my grandma, or the rest of my family? I didn't want to let anyone down, and I knew I would. I didn't see a light at the end of the tunnel and was sick that I wasn't going to finish high school. I felt like my life was over.

It's been said that we all need hope to cope, so when I found out there was a school where I could go while I was pregnant and later take the baby with me, I had a glimmer of hope. That glimmer was what I needed to give me the strength to take the next step and try to figure out a way to tell my family, but how? I felt shame and embarrassment as I anguished over telling them that I was pregnant. I was over three months along, and I still could not muster the courage. Keeping this secret to myself was making me physically sick and in a constant state of anxiety, but I just couldn't bear the thought of letting everyone down. So I kept it to myself. I was scared of being an embarrassment, I was scared of the future, and I was ashamed that I had thought I was invincible. This type of thing happened to bad girls, not me. Looking back now, I see that God in His mercy had to intervene and help me peel the bandage off and share my secret.

On Thanksgiving Day, the whole family was gathered around the table when I began to feel nauseous. I had gone to my grandma's room to lie down when my mom came in.

"What's wrong with you?" she asked.

"Nothing, Mom. I just don't feel good."

"You're not pregnant, are you?"

I couldn't believe she asked me that. Even though I was terrified of saying yes, I knew I had to. So I sheepishly responded with, "What if I was?"

She walked out of the room, and I heard her crying. Then I heard my grandma crying, followed by my uncle's yelling. I ran to my grandma's car, where I hid on the floor, praying the earth would swallow me up. Again I wondered how any good could come from this—I was such a disappointment. Yet in spite of all this, a heavy weight had been lifted from my shoulders. Finally, they knew. Thankfully, grace and mercy were extended after the shock wore off, and they realized that what was done was done. When my daughter Marissa was born, all the sad tears turned to happy ones. Everyone adored her and thought she was theirs. The pain of that day of truth was overshadowed by the joy and love felt when she entered the world.

I loved my daughter, and it didn't take long before the reality of adult life set in. When Marissa was six months old, I was driving home with her on a dark, cold night that perfectly represented my outlook on life. I despaired over Marissa's dad, who had chosen a path of drinking and partying that wasn't good for my daughter or me. I knew, if I didn't leave him, I would be the one responsible if anything happened to her. I was so insecure in myself and so afraid of being alone that I had forgiven him time and time again. But on this particular night, protecting her was more important than my fear of being alone, even if that meant being alone for the rest of my life. I couldn't see a light at the end of the tunnel, I didn't have a plan, and I was tired. Physically, mentally, and emotionally drained, I pulled to the side of the road and whispered a prayer. "Lord, if You love me and have a better plan for my life than the one I have created, then I give it to You, because my way isn't working out very well. I'm so sorry. I can't do this on my own anymore. I need You."

I needed to know God had heard my prayer. I needed something to hold on to, so I asked Him for a particular song to come on the radio, the only Christian song I knew. God didn't disappoint as He met me in my pain. I turned on the radio, scanning through the stations, when suddenly I heard the most beautiful sound in the world—the song "Here We Are" by Dallas Holm, the very one I had asked for. From the speakers of my barely functioning radio, I heard that I was in his presence, lifting holy hands to him, praising Jesus for all he had brought me through.

At that moment, I knew with everything in my heart that God had a beautiful plan for my life. But more importantly, I knew I wasn't alone and never would be again. If the God of the universe took time to meet me in my pain, if He heard my prayer from an old, beat-up Honda Prelude on the side of a dark road, then He was with me—and He was big enough to trust. When I had entered my car on that evening, I was beaten-down and depressed, but when I got out, I was a brand-new person with a newfound faith. No matter what life brought or what my circumstances were, God would never leave me, and He had a better plan for my life. I had a confidence in the future that I never had before. Knowing that I would never be alone again, I finally had the courage to leave a bad situation and start working on the life I envisioned for my daughter and me.

Things didn't all-of-a-sudden become easy for me. In fact, the next few years were very hard. Being a single mom, working and going to school full-time isn't a walk in the park, but I knew I was never alone. I had to depend on God for everything, and I realize now what a blessing in disguise that was. He was training me to trust Him. I could endure and persist when I would remember His words from Jeremiah 29:11: "For I know the plans I have for you, plans for good and not for harm to give you a future and a hope."

Faith in the future is important if we are to have power in the present—and that is what His Word and His presence did for me. Looking back on my life today, I can say that God has been more than good to me. He did have a better plan and has blessed my life far more than I deserve, even more than I could have asked for or even imagined. When my daughter was three, while going to school at the University of Nevada, Reno, I met an amazing man who became my husband of almost twenty-four years. Jason, as well as the two other daughters God has given me, are proof of Jeremiah 29:11. His plans for me were good.

In appreciation for all He has done for me, I wanted to give back, so I volunteered as a counselor at a pregnancy center. For the past twelve years, I have had the privilege of being a voice for the unborn, to offer hope to young girls and women who are faced with an unplanned pregnancy, and to love and encourage women who have been emotionally wounded by abortions. Most importantly, I get to share the gospel to all who want to know where my hope comes from. They listen to me because they know I have walked in their shoes. I have genuine compassion for them, because I know how they feel. It is a great day when a mother chooses life for her unborn child and prays to receive eternal life for herself. I thank God for entrusting me to play a part in this and allowing me to work alongside Him.

All those years ago, when I first heard that my pregnancy test was positive, I didn't understand how God could turn things around for good for those who love Him. His ways are so much higher than ours, and He sees around corners that we don't. I didn't understand that He allowed me to have a baby because He was preparing me to someday be on the front lines of a life-and-death battle for the unborn. In His goodness, He had me go through trying times so I wouldn't put faith in my own strength but rather in His. He rescued me so I could join His team and help rescue others. He transformed my life, and because of that, I am not ashamed to share the gospel. I can boldly tell you which direction to run and that is to Him.

Fast forward to 2013, where I am running again, but this time I am racing toward the finish line of the Boston Marathon. Qualifying for and completing in the Boston Marathon had been a goal, dream, and prayer of mine for years, and I was about to see my dream become a reality.

Overwhelmed with emotion, I stared down the street leading to the finish line. The joy of seeing a dream become a reality, the relief of finishing, and the excitement of greeting my husband Jason there kept my feet moving. I normally sped up when I saw the finish line, but on that day, my legs could barely shuffle. All I wanted was to be done, to get my medal, and to sit down. I was exhausted, and I couldn't wait for the relief. At mile twenty-six, close to the finish, I heard a loud boom. I didn't stop running. I saw smoke, but I wasn't close enough to the finish line to understand what it was from. Patriot's Day fireworks, perhaps? The building in front of me shot into flames, and thick smoke billowed into the street. The loud blast, fire, and screams of bystanders made it clear that we were under attack.

As I watched people frantically running away from the finish line, I felt paralyzed and helpless. The finish line was where my husband and friends were.

A police officer yelled at me, "Run, run. Run!" When I saw the panic in his eyes, I realized that this was serious and braced myself for the next blast. Yet in this moment, I also discovered that I was not afraid to die. I didn't want to be separated from my family, but I had a peace that God was in control. Because I had accepted Jesus as my Savior, I knew I would immediately be with Him if He chose to take me home. What I was afraid of was the pain of getting there.

Silently I prayed that if another bomb went off and hit me, it would be quick, painless, and complete. After a few moments when nothing happened, I tried to reach the finish line. True panic now started to set in. Jason and my friends were all supposed to be there. Was my husband alive? Was he hurt? Were my friends okay? My mind raced, and my heart pounded. As I tried to get to them, I was turned back by police officers who were not allowing anyone near the devastation.

At mile fifteen, I had given my cell phone to Jason, so I was without means of communicating with him. I frantically ran to the first person I saw.

I cried out to a spectator on the route. "Please, can I use your phone?"

I phoned Jason, but all I heard was "beep, beep, beep." My heart jumped into my throat. "Please Lord, let him be okay. Please Lord. Please!" I hit redial twice before I heard the beautiful sound.

"Hello."

"Oh, thank God," I cried into the phone.

"I got stuck in traffic," he said. "I couldn't make it to the finish line."

I vowed to never complain about traffic again.

Panic and confusion reigned as emergency workers pushed us away from the finish line. In less than five minutes, I had experienced so many emotions: exhaustion, euphoria, joy, confusion, fear, panic, terror, relief, and then nothing.

I was numb.

Life has a way of doing that to us, doesn't it? You are in your lane, running your race, when out of nowhere the enemy strikes.

Again I found myself in a place where I couldn't understand how any good could come from something so evil—a terrorist attack on innocent spectators who were there for one reason, to encourage others. I was very grateful that God had spared my life, but I still tearfully asked Him why He chose to have me so close to the finish line that I could see it but couldn't cross it. He gently spoke to my heart and said, "You will cross the Boston Marathon finish line, but when you cross the eternal finish line, you will have many souls with you because of your testimony." The following year, I did exactly that.

Here we are in 2017. For four years, I've shared my story with clients at the pregnancy center. The realization that we aren't promised tomorrow opens the door for me to share the good news and introduce them to the only One who has conquered death and the only One who can save eternally.

Evantell produces tracts to share the gospel. They recently interviewed me because an entire class at the Pregnancy Center put their trust in Jesus after I shared my story and the gospel. I am not saying this to brag, but to confirm that only a God as big as ours can take what the enemy meant for harm and use it for the saving of many lives (Genesis 50:20).

Two of the most distressing times turned into the biggest blessings in my life. My baby girl is now twenty-eight years old with two kids of her own, another generation of blessings. Week after week, I get to share my story at the Pregnancy Center. I have such joy in seeing people who had been running in the wrong direction change course and run to their Savior. What the enemy intended for evil, God has used for good.

So where do you run when the predator of worry is about to overtake you? Where will you run when your past pursues you? Where will you run when temptation pounds on your door? Where will you run when your fear feels stronger than your faith? What will you do when your energy is spent and all seems lost? I pray that from this moment on, you will immediately run to your Savior—not as a last resort but as your first reaction.

Remember that He is your protector, your hiding place, and your victory. In the light of His presence, darkness has no choice but to flee. Yes, we are weak, but He is strong. Through Him, we are more than conquerors. When you run to God, you can boldly tell the enemy to pound sand, sending that predator scurrying away in fear. In the face of whatever trouble, attack, or sin you're experiencing, run away from evil and instead, run to Jesus. Run while you can. Don't walk, because we never know when a bomb may blow.

If you would like to make the best decision you can ever make, please don't waste another moment. Pray this prayer with me:

Dear Lord, I know I am a sinner. I know I deserve the consequences of my sin. However, I am trusting in Jesus Christ as my Savior. I believe that His death and resurrection provided for my forgiveness. I trust in Jesus and Jesus alone as my personal Lord and Savior. Thank you, Lord, for saving me and forgiving me. Amen.

Jennifer McAlister is an author, graphic designer, and founder of *Witness Thru Fitness. Her book,* Press On – Stories of Endurance, Faith and Trust *was published in June 2017. She is a fitness enthusiast and has completed seventeen marathons, as well as two full IRONMAN triathlons. As part of the John C. Maxwell Team, she is a certified speaker, trainer, and coach. Her passion includes empowering young women to make healthy, life-affirming decisions as a counselor at a pregnancy center.*
JenMcA@mac.com
Press-OnBook.com

Thoughts to Ponder
from Where Do You Run?

1. God can transform our mistakes into ministry opportunities.

2. It is important to have faith in the future if we are to have power in the present.

3. God determines the course of our race.

> **Where do you run when all seems lost?**

Let us throw off everything that hinders and the sin that so easily entangles. And let us run with perseverance the race marked out for us. — Hebrews 12:1

Who Do You Want to Be?

by Ray Biggs

Think back to when you were a child. For just a moment, rewind to a more "innocent" time. Back to your Hot Wheels and Barbie dolls. As a little girl or boy, do you remember the first time you were asked, "What do you want to be when you grow up?" Depending on *your* environment, you might have said something like "a fireman" or "Miss America." Sadly, had I considered *my* environment to answer that question, I might have said "pedophile" or "womanizer" or maybe an "angry drunk." In those younger, more *innocent* years, our limited frame of reference was comprised of the things to which we were exposed.

Go back to the question that was being asked. Was that person really asking, "What do you want to be?" No, not really. Not *what*, but *who* do you want to be when you grow up? As we grew up, our environment influenced our list of possible character candidates. Only time would tell who we would choose as role models, people worth imitating.

For me, changing that one word in the question, from "what" to "who" caused me years of confusion and great frustration. Most children relate to the noun, the inanimate attractive playthings with which their parents allow exposure. But in my life, the things I was exposed to weren't found in toy stores or comic books. I was not inanimate, yet like so many other victims, I was a human plaything for someone else to enjoy.

Helpless and alone. Afraid to say something. Afraid not to say anything. Guilty, shameful, dirty, and somehow, I thought I must have done something terribly wrong for this to be happening.

With innocence obliterated, memories of fire trucks and cap guns were blurred by dark closets and tool sheds. The desperate need for basic childhood affection was forever stolen and pawned off for sadistic acts of counterfeit love. The question of "what" I wanted didn't exist. The "who" that brought such darkness over me was mysteriously called "a friend of the family." And unbeknownst to her, my mother literally drove me to the home of the hunter every other week or so for two years. At the age of five, I didn't know much, but I knew who I *didn't* want to be when I grew up.

With the first role model "candidate" in my life being a slithering predator, one might ask, "Where was your father?" As the first-born son in the early seventies, all we knew of our father was a large map of Southeast Asia taped to a closet door down the hall. In fact, for six of the first eight years of my life, my father carried out special operations in the Viet Nam war. At least that's what his letters told my mother and his three children. Later though, through the Freedom of Information Act, my sister discovered my father living in a second marriage, with a family in Michigan during his "extended tour of duty."

Fast forward to a few very loud and scary years and to the old brown couch in our living room. The three of us children sat at attention, watching our father carry armloads of clothing out to his car. On his last trip, he abruptly stopped, looked down at me with the face of a Drill Sergeant, and barked, "You're the man of the house now. Don't screw it up."

With that, he was gone.

I was only eight years old. But what was I to do but take up my new field promotion and lead, protect, and provide for my family, a mother and two siblings? On that day; as much as any eight-year-old boy could comprehend, I discovered "what" I was going to be when I grew up. In my little mind, I had been promoted to Captain America.

At age ten, I had only one real friend. Kurt lived a few blocks over and was five years older than me. Once, while we were hanging out in his bedroom, he handed me a magazine from his father's stash. "Open it up to the middle page and unfold it," he said.

Shocked and mesmerized by the pictures, I had lost my innocence all over again. Once by the first "man" in my life, who forever twisted my boyhood frame of mind, next by the "man" I perceived to be my protector, and now by my best friend, "who" I looked up to like a big brother.

Scratch them off my list of possible character candidates.

Coupled with the sexual abuse from a few years earlier, the effects of that first image was forever seared in the deepest parts of my soul. I was a ten-year-old boy who was instantly engulfed in a full-blown addiction to pornography and acting out, consuming my every thought for two decades to come.

A few years later, my mother felt the need for a father-figure in our lives and married someone she'd known from years past. But all too soon, she was asking herself, *Who was this person she'd brought into our home, a weak shell of a man who hid behind expensive suits and cheap bottles of liquor?* My mother was devastated, and I had yet another example of "who" I didn't want to be when I grew up. At sixteen, I physically removed him from our home. Once again, I was recommissioned to the "man of the house" status where I proudly served as my mother's keeper until she passed at the age of seventy-two.

By sixteen, "who" I had become was best described by a popular TV show, "The Incredible Hulk." Mild mannered on the outside; raging binge drinker, bent on self-destruction on the inside. Desperately misunderstood by others while knowing all too well who I really was in the dark annals of my mind. Angry at the world and the air I breathed, I drank myself into the hospital at the age of eighteen; still wondering "who" I wanted to be when I grew up. All I knew were examples of "who" I *didn't* want to be. My anthem became a song by Simon & Garfunkel that said I was a rock that felt no pain, an island that never cried. In my mind and in most relationships, I built a stone wall around myself where few were allowed access.

A dozen years later, it's late June on the morning of my thirtieth birthday. With my head still on the pillow and my eyes refusing to open, I heard a voice. Not like the voices I'd heard after a night of heavy drinking. This voice was clear as a bell, direct and concise.

"Ray, if you don't get rid of this anger, it's going to kill you."

I knew the messenger was right. I was on a fast track to prison or death—or both. However, by now I had found a few men "who" I had been emulating. Country & Western singers at the top of their charts. All drunks, all womanizers, and just like the men in my past "who" I swore I'd never become. The toll on the life that had gone awry was a heavy tax.

I did make another close friend in my twenties. Raul was a co-worker and my wingman when we cruised from one bar to another on weekends. But Raul began to pull away from the friendship. In truth, though, I was the one pulling away. I was seeing a change in my friend. It was a mysterious change, a slow softening sort of change, but I was too consumed with my own life to ask Raul about his transformation.

One night a year later, it happened. I called him up to see which bar would be our starting block for the night. To my surprise, he suggested we meet at a local IHOP. I thought he wanted to grab a bite before hitting the streets.

I slid onto my seat in the green vinyl booth, across from Raul. For a moment, I thought I had sat at the wrong table. Who was this person? It looked like Raul, but he looked so different, so much at peace. After hearing my friend explain how his life had turned a different way, I realized just how out of control mine was. Raul had traded his old life for a relationship with Jesus Christ, and though he had extended the same relationship to me before, this night was different.

He said Jesus Christ was the *only* Son of God and the son of man. God with skin. Along with His Father God, He created this world perfectly, for us to live together with Him forever. But the devil poisoned this world and the people God had placed here. Sin caused a divorce-like split between God and His people. But Jesus came to this broken world to save me from my sin and the curse in which I was born. The penalty for sin required the death of all those who lived as their own god. But Jesus had good news for those who chose to believe Him. The Bible tells the story that Jesus told everyone: "Believe in Me and believe in My Father, and you will live with Us forever." But His message went against the rulers of His day, and they crucified Jesus on a cross as a heretic. In reality, it was all part of Father God's plan.

When Jesus hung on that cross, He was hanging there in place of me. He became the substitute prisoner who paid the death penalty for the sins of everyone on earth, including mine. He died and was buried in a nearby tomb. But three days later, Father God raised Him from the dead. Brought back to life, Jesus walked out of that tomb alive forever. His good-news message is that I am forever forgiven of my sins if I believe that Jesus Christ is the Son of God.

Because I've received this act of God's grace, it's important to tell others in the same way that Raul shared Jesus with me. His offer is available for us right now. One day, we can stand side-by-side with Jesus in His Father's heaven forever. We can be freed from our sins and the shame they create. Set free to live in peace and perfect acceptance by our Father God, through a personal relationship with His one and only Son, Jesus Christ. But this offer is only good for a limited time. We are not guaranteed tomorrow.

That night; November 23, 1990, my life changed forever. As I listened to Raul talk about all that Jesus had done for *me* on that cross, all for the purpose of showing His love for me, I felt my stone walls crumbling. I finally understood that overwhelming sense of peace that surrounded my dear friend. It came from His own personal, intimate, and growing relationship with Jesus Christ, which was something I desperately wanted. As I left the restaurant, for the first time in my life I felt what I could only describe as hope. I somehow realized that I was no longer walking alone in this messed-up world.

As my own relationship grew with my adopted Father, I came to realize the depth of what Jesus went through to forgive my sins. By His example, and over time, He helped me completely forgive those who had caused me so much pain—and the pain I had caused others in my wake.

While every word from God's Bible is precious and beneficial, two significant milestones have anchored my faith in the loving grace of Jesus Christ. Early in my journey with Him, and to help me with my past, He gave me good counsel from Isaiah 43:18–19. "Forget the former things; do not dwell on the past. See I, [God] am doing a new thing, [in your life] will you not perceive it?" And in more recent years, God rocked my world when He showed me how He takes all things in my life and turns them into good.

"Praise be to the God and Father of our Lord Jesus Christ, the Father of compassion and the God of all comfort, who comforts us in all our troubles, so that we can comfort those in any trouble with the [same] comfort we ourselves receive from God" (2 Corinthians 1:3–4).

Looking back on my life, I see where God has used the difficult times in my past to display His compassion and to comfort me. In my life now as a Christian counselor, I can relate to those I talk to in their troubles. I can confidently offer that same compassion and comfort I myself received from God.

Closer to home though, it is my goal to be a living example, someone worth imitating, a role model candidate for my four grandsons. For their good and God's glory.

Ray Biggs *is a passionate men's minister getting his start in 1994 with Promise Keepers. His education began in 1999 at Criswell Bible College in Dallas. His primary focus has centered on helping men and their families. This led to his training in Biblical Counseling at Southwestern Baptist Theological Seminary in 2013. In the same year, he helped launch Compass Health Counseling Ministry at his church: The Community at Lakeridge, Arlington, Pastor Paul Mints. Ray can be reached at* **Ray@MyDaysman.com.**

Thoughts to Ponder

from Who Do You Want to Be?

1. Children deserve protection.

2. How you start has nothing to do with how you finish.

3. Role models are important influencers.

Who are your role models?

*Therefore, if anyone is in Christ, the new creation has come:
The old has gone, the new is here! — 2 Corinthians 5:17*

Aftershocks
by Sherry Ryan

At 6:01 in the morning, the ground began to shake. I was eleven years old, fast asleep in my bed—until our trembling house woke me up with a start.

Mom screamed, "Sherry, get up. Go to the hallway." The terrazzo marble hallway in our middle-class suburban home outside Los Angeles was the most stable part of the house, so I attempted to make my way there. The glass doors on the bookcase in my bedroom clattered. Since the ground was moving, I stumbled, trying to keep my balance. When I finally reached the hall, I saw the chandelier in our dining room swinging wildly, touching the ceiling in one direction and then the other.

The 6.6-magnitude earthquake was centered in Sylmar, about forty miles from my home. It was felt as far away as Las Vegas, 280 miles away. The quake left 58 people dead, more than 1,000 injured, and property damage of over $500 million, including 62 freeway bridges, 5 dams, and 30,000 homes.

(http://metroprimaryresources.info/40-years-ago-today-san-fernando-earthquake-topples-freeways-prompts-seismic-retrofitting-plan/773 – Accessed 8/24/2016.)

My world was shaken. Literally. But fortunately, our family was spared. However, there was another time my world was shaken. Like an earthquake, this shaking rocked my world, taking me by surprise.

My hands and face tingled and were sometimes numb, especially first thing in the morning when I woke up. I decided to see the doctor. This was just the beginning of a "shockwave."

"Stress," the doctor said. "Your symptoms are most likely due to stress. Let's put you on some medication, and come back to see me in a month."

Stress, I thought, *What an understatement.* Three-and-a-half years earlier, I left my job at IBM and went back to school for my Ph.D. in Information Systems. My kids were five and eight, and I wanted to spend more time with them. What a joke. That didn't turn out like I had planned.

I was accepted in the Ph.D. program at the University of Texas at Arlington. I wanted to teach at the college level, but found you couldn't excel at a university without a Ph.D. My mom was a teacher. She taught every grade from kindergarten through high school during her career. I never wanted to be a teacher, but somehow, after being a Systems Engineer at IBM, I ended up as a database instructor. I discovered that I liked teaching adults. They asked interesting questions. I enjoyed figuring out problems and learning new things when I didn't know the answers. It seemed like teaching college would be fun too.

At the start of my Ph.D. program, I was a bit naïve. I had done a lot of things at IBM and felt like I was a capable person. Heck! Just weeks after I completed my undergraduate degree from a Christian university, I tested out of six master's level classes for my MBA at the University of Southern California. So when I started the Ph.D. program, I thought, *I can handle this*. But it was more difficult than I ever dreamed. Instead of spending more time with my family, I was consumed with studies. I was torn between school work and enjoying time with my family. I tried to compensate by staying up late and working while the kids were asleep.

After everyone else had gone to bed, I moved my computer to a card table in the bedroom so I'd be out of the way and have some quiet during the day. My husband, Doug, said it wouldn't bother him if I continued to work, although he was going to sleep. As I clicked the computer keys, Doug twitched in bed. He was able to sleep, but unfortunately, I stayed up for hours finishing my paper.

Now in my mid-thirties, I found that my body didn't hold up the way it had in my twenties. I "hit the wall" when trying to finish a project for class. After being up for three days without sleep, I was "losing it" from both ends of my body. Ugh.

Besides being physically demanding, the program was psychologically difficult. While undergoing Ph.D. work, people feel as if they are the lowest form of life, and I was a perfectionist. After several years of the program, I felt like life had been beaten out of me. Although I had made a 4.0, I was frantically trying to stay on top of my grades.

I learned that as an academic, you could not just teach. You had to research, write, and publish as well. While I was still working on my degree, I submitted my first article to an academic journal and was horrified when the editor said I "wrote like a foreign student."

He offered countless words of criticism and corrections. I always had done well in English and writing classes, plus my mom was an English teacher. I showed the review to one of my professors and he said, "No, this is good. He likes it. Just make the changes that he suggests, and it will get published." I thought, *If this is what the editor says about a paper he likes, I wonder what he says about the papers he doesn't like?* I made the changes and got published. In the publishing process, you need "thick skin," because reviewers and editors tear your work apart. You must be persistent and not take rejections personally. After so much time, effort, and thought put into your work, that's easier said than done.

God was my strength and strong tower. He could get me through. I always thought I didn't have much of a testimony. I came to know the Lord as my Savior when I was a child and had been a "good girl" all my life. I never rebelled against my parents, was active in my youth group, and ended up going to a Christian college. As I look back, I find my testimony has become the sustaining power of Christ through difficult times. I wish I could say God delivered me *from* difficulties (and sometimes He has), but what I learned was how God would sustain me *through* difficulties.

I told one of my professors about my numbness and tingling. Although the doctor said it was probably stress, the medication wasn't helping. My professor said, "You've got to get that looked at." He went on to tell me about his wife who had multiple sclerosis (MS) and that those are sometimes the symptoms. Because there were drugs now available that worked to slow progression of the disease, it was important to get diagnosed early and get on medication.

When I went back to the doctor who prescribed the medication, he sent me to a neurologist. Sometimes MS is a hard disease to diagnose, because it affects people differently. Some people might have trouble moving their legs while others might have double vision. The symptoms can come and go. The doctor sent me through a battery of tests. I had a spinal tap (also known as a lumbar puncture) in which they stuck a needle into the spinal canal in my lower back and collected the cerebrospinal fluid that surrounded the spinal cord. Next was the evoked potentials test in which the nerves of my arms and legs were stimulated by an electrical pulse to see how long it would take for my nerves to

28

respond. I also had a Magnetic Resonance Imaging (MRI) test. The cylinder that surrounded me was about three inches from my face.

When I opened my eyes, I became claustrophobic and panicked. My husband, Doug, was in the room with me, touching my leg, to give me some sort of external anchoring and comfort. I was so scared. I don't think I would've made it through if he had not been there. When the tests started, there was a deafening banging. As they were taking pictures of my brain, neck, and spinal cord, they told me how long each test would last: five minutes for one, two minutes for another. Halfway through, they rolled me out of the tube, gave me a shot of dye, and put me back in. The whole thing lasted about an hour and a half.

Later, I went to the neurologist to get the results. As an educator, I would not give him an "A" for "bedside manners." He looked off to the corner and told me the tests confirmed I had MS, an autoimmune disease in which the body attacks itself and eats away at the protective coating around the nerves, so the signals don't pass correctly from the brain to the muscles. For example, my brain may say, "Lift your leg," but it gets lost along the way, so I can no longer lift my leg to walk, leaving me in a wheelchair. They don't know for sure what causes MS, and there is no cure.

The doctor drew a bell curve and said most people diagnosed with MS fall somewhere in the middle in terms of functional disability. People on one side had almost no disabilities while the other side had severe disabilities. Of course, I felt sure I would be one that had little or no disabilities. Unfortunately, I wound up on the other side of the scale.

Two-and-a-half years later, the disease was progressing rapidly. I went to kids' camp as a counselor at our church. In one of the evening services, I felt the Spirit of the Lord so strongly. Kids were praying for other kids. Some kids, when they were prayed over, fell on the floor, knocked down by the power of the Holy Spirit. Maybe that sounds weird or scary, but it really wasn't. It was awesome. My pastor's seventeen-year-old son came up and prayed for me. I fell on the ground under the weight of the Holy Spirit. I felt like God told me that He healed me. He also said something about Abraham, but I really did not understand. That night, I told the girls in my cabin that I believed God had healed me.

After camp, I called my neurologist and asked for another MRI.

I was still feeling numbness and tingling, but I believed what God had told me. The MRI results said I still had lesions on my spinal cord.

I was devastated. I thought God had lied to me. If the Bible was true, why had He healed other people but not me? After that, I still went to church some, but I left the service partway through, angry and crying. I had a real crisis of faith.

One Sunday evening, my husband *dragged* me to church. A visiting minister spoke that night on the Holy Spirit, then invited people to come for prayer. When he prayed for me, the power knocked me to the floor for the second time, and I heard God say, "My love for you is everlasting." Maybe God knew I was too analytical and logical, so much so that I would not have had the faith to stand for my healing had something miraculous not have happened. Since that time, I have had a lot of hard things happen, but I know that He is with me, loves me, and helps me through.

Much later, I began to understand the word about Abraham. I met a woman who was a missionary from Guatemala. She was stricken with polio when she was three years old and had used crutches ever since. God called her at the age of thirteen to the mission field. After marriage, she and her husband applied to become missionaries, but they were rejected because of her physical condition. Finally, forty years later, she made it to the mission field. She told me of other promises that God had made to her but had taken years to be fulfilled.

God's timing is not our timing. Since God is eternal, what He views as a short time can seem like forever to us. One example in the Bible is Abraham. God promised him a son, but it took twenty-five years before Isaac was born. Romans 4:18–24 says that Abraham did not give up hope, even though his body was "as good as dead." Picture one-hundred-year-old Abraham bouncing baby Isaac on his knee and laughing. How ridiculous it would seem. God kept His promise, although to Abraham it seemed like it took forever. Isaac's name means "laughter."

Throughout the years, God has confirmed the promise of my healing and has sent people to encourage me along the way. Not too many years after my diagnosis, a woman at my church called me on the phone and said she felt impressed to share a verse with me:

But this is what the Lord says: 'Yes, captives will be taken from warriors, and plunder retrieved from the fierce; I will contend with those who contend with you, and your children I will save.' — Isaiah 49:25

This verse is about restoration. I felt like my body was taken captive by Satan, but God promises to take back the captives. Satan is a fierce warrior and does not want to give back what he has stolen. The verse goes on to say that plunder will be retrieved. It is not just the poor naked captive who will be retrieved, but riches that were taken too. Satan has stolen a lot more from me than just my physical capabilities. I cannot wait to see the "plunder" that is retrieved.

While there have been many encouraging instances, I'll share three additional stories: 1) the word I was given by a man at McDonald's, 2) a dream, and 3) circumstances around the Year of Jubilee.

I was early for an appointment to see my neurologist at UT Southwestern in Dallas, so I decided to stop at McDonald's for lunch near the clinic. (That alone was a miracle, because I am almost never early.) A large African-American man said he was a pastor and felt the Lord told him to pray for me. When he said he never went to that McDonald's but felt led to stop, I laughed. I don't think I had ever gone inside to eat at that McDonald's before, and I don't think I have since then. Apparently, God had made arrangements for us to meet. He said God wanted me to know He was going to heal me. With a small flask of oil, the man anointed me and prayed for me. That was many years ago, but it still encourages me.

One night I had a dream where I was driving a car, and some "bad guys" were chasing me. I stopped the car and jumped out. The bad guys ran after me and threw something like acid all over me. Then I saw my deformed face in the mirror. I didn't look like myself. My face was like a deformed cartoon character. I heard a voice say, "No weapon formed against you shall prosper." This was a promise I had heard on a healing CD several years before:

'No weapon formed against you will prosper, and every tongue which rises against you in judgment you shall condemn. This is the heritage of the servants of the Lord, and their righteousness is from Me,' says the Lord. — Isaiah 54:17 (NKJ)

This was a verse the Lord wanted me to quote, mediate on, and stand on. Multiple sclerosis had disabled me, leaving me in a wheelchair and limiting the use of my right hand so much that my writing was hardly legible. Multiple sclerosis was the weapon Satan used to debilitate me. This verse assured me that ultimately MS will not prosper, but I needed to speak out and condemn it. At times, I still lack the boldness. However, I know we are in a battle and that the Word of God is our most powerful weapon.

I occasionally have a home health worker help me shower and get into bed. One night, Ruby came. I had never met her before, and throughout the night we chatted, getting to know each another. Toward the end of her three-hour shift, she felt the Spirit of the Lord saying, "God is going to heal you." I told her, "I know." We talked about it a bit. She believed restoration would happen within a year. She also said, "You've got a book in you too." Many people have said I should write my story. I am finally doing it.

A few weeks later, I went to my church's monthly special Sunday evening service. I sat next to a couple I did not know. At the end of the service, the man handed me a folded yellow sticky note.

The note said: "Get Excited! This year is the year of restoration, the Year of Jubilee. God is restoring your land."

He attached a $100 bill.

According to the Old Testament book of Leviticus, the Year of Jubilee comes every fifty years. Property is returned to the original owner. Slaves and prisoners are set free. Debts are forgiven. And God pours out His blessings.

A few weeks later, a visiting pastor talked about restoration. His text was:

As for you also, because of the blood of my covenant with you, I will set your prisoners free from the waterless pit. Return to your stronghold, O prisoners of hope; today I declare that I will restore to you double. — Zechariah 9:11–12 (ESV)

There were three different instances of being told about restoration within a month. "Okay Lord, I get it."

On the evidence of two or three witnesses a matter shall be confirmed. — Deuteronomy 19:15 (NASB)

I have my three witnesses.

Isn't it interesting that after so many years, God used the same language of restoration to confirm His promise to me?

For years, I felt like my story would not be considered legitimate until I was physically healed. I now believe God wants me to share with others even while I am still going through my battle. God has been my strength and continues to sustain me. If He had not, I would have given up, or maybe even committed suicide.

I truly believe I will be healed and restored physically in this life. However, I realize that when God answers our prayers, it is not always what we expect. Even if I am not physically healed on this earth, I will be healed in heaven. This is not a cop-out as some may say. He gives me strength for today and the ability to go on tomorrow. As the apostle Paul wrote:

Therefore we do not lose heart. Though outwardly we are wasting away, yet inwardly we are being renewed day by day. For our light and momentary troubles are achieving for us an eternal glory that far outweighs them all. So we fix our eyes not on what is seen, but on what is unseen, since what is seen is temporary, but what is unseen is eternal. — 2 Corinthians 4:16–18

One of the other scenarios that shook my world was when my husband, Doug, was diagnosed with Non-Hodgkin's Lymphoma in 2011. Since Doug was such an incredible athlete, this news was a shock.

Over the years, he had run over two dozen marathons, including the prestigious Boston marathon before "graduating" to ultramarathons, which are anything over 26.2 miles but usually 50–100 miles. In 2006, Doug ran his fastest ultra, a 100-mile race in nineteen hours, twenty minutes and nineteen seconds. (Yes, they run straight through with only short breaks at rest stops, and no, they don't stop to sleep.) Doug finished seventh in the race which was the forty-sixth fastest time in North America that year. So we couldn't believe it when he was diagnosed with Stage 4 Follicular Non-Hodgkin's Lymphoma, the most common blood cancer. The doctor said Doug had twenty-five tumors and that the cancer had spread to his bone marrow. This type was slow growing, so his oncologist recommended a "wait and see" approach. Doug connected with a group that recommended a lifestyle approach— eating healthy and exercising. While the first oncologist said the average life expectancy for that number of tumors would be six to eight years, some people in the group had lived past twenty years and were going strong. So after his diagnosis, he said, "We plan to live life abundantly and trust God."

Doug was doing great. In the fall of 2013, he decided to ride his bike across the United States, a journey of over 3,200 miles. The forty-day ride began at the Pacific Ocean in Santa Barbara, California, and passed through the Grand Canyon, across the United States, and finished in Charleston, South Carolina, where he and thirteen other riders dipped their bicycle wheels in the Atlantic Ocean. After the ride, he experienced a "spontaneous" regression, which meant that his largest lymphoma tumor disappeared without drugs. This was unusually good news.

But seven months after he finished that cross-country bike ride, Doug took a turn for the worse when the Lymphoma transformed into Acute Lymphoblastic Leukemia, which is much more aggressive. This kind of transformation was especially rare. UT Southwestern and the Mayo Clinic had never seen it before. They found only two other cases in the literature. Doug had chills, nausea, weight loss, and fatigue. His kidneys and liver were shutting down, and he had internal bleeding. The doctor said if Doug had not come in that day, he would have been dead in twenty-four hours.

He had several rounds of very heavy chemo. He lost his hair and had the nausea and pain associated with it. They rushed him for a bone marrow transplant because this was the best chance for survival.

Seventy days after his transplant, the leukemia came roaring back. It affected his nerves, so he had problems lifting his right arm. It also affected his esophagus, so he couldn't swallow properly. His lungs were contaminated and he developed pneumonia. Doug said he wasn't afraid to die, that he was ready to continue his adventure with God.

Doug passed away on November 10, 2014. He was the love of my life and my caregiver. At times, being a disabled widow has felt overwhelming. But God has been with me through the "aftershocks" of his death. Several years before Doug passed away, he and I visited Mount St. Helens in Washington state. In 1980, an earthquake had struck below the north face of the mountain, triggering a landslide and a volcanic eruption, spreading volcanic ash over eleven states. Thirty years later, some areas still showed significant devastation, looking something like "the moon."

34

However, beautiful signs of regeneration were also present.

Just like the earthquake and volcanic eruption, God is bringing beauty out of ashes in my life. Isaiah 61:3 says God will *provide for those who grieve in Zion—to bestow on them a crown of beauty instead of ashes, the oil of joy instead of mourning, and a garment of praise instead of a spirit of despair.*

It is still so hard, but God has brought people alongside me to help. I met a Christian friend with MS, who lost her husband to cancer about eight years before Doug passed away. What are the odds of me meeting and becoming friends with a person who had such similar circumstances? She had walked through what I was going through. She's helped me out a lot. Friends and family have been so supportive. I have a new grandbaby. But most of all, I have the Holy Spirit, who has promised never to leave me or forsake me. God does not say He will always deliver us *from* difficulties, but God does promise to be with us *through* difficulties.

He has done it for me.

He can do it for you as well.

Dr. Sherry D. Ryan is a retired Associate Professor of Information Technology and Decision Sciences at the University of North Texas. Prior to earning her doctorate in Information Systems, she worked for IBM, teaching courses and speaking at national conferences. She has published numerous academic journal articles and conference proceedings. Sherry has two children and one granddaughter.

Ministry@RoaringLambs.org

Thoughts to Ponder
from Aftershocks

1. God's timing is not our timing.

2. God is in control, not man.

3. Don't give up on God's promises.

**Through what difficulties
has God brought you?**

---

*Never will I leave you;
never will I forsake you —Hebrews 13:5*

Cracked ... Not Shattered
by Grace Burke

"In every single thing you do, you are choosing a direction. Your life is a product of choices." — Dr. Kathleen Hall, International Stress Expert

My oldest daughter—smart, beautiful, athletic, and a talented dancer—made a series of very bad choices. At the age of twenty-five, she met "the love of her life," not knowing the depth of his involvement in the drug culture.

"He's smart and very caring," she said. "I can see us being together a very long time."

Lamentably, she soon discovered her "dream" man was unemployed—on occasion doing a few odd jobs around the apartment complex where she lived. He had no money, no fixed place of abode, staying here and there with relatives and friends.

When my daughter shared information about this man with me, red flags flew in every direction.

"I don't think this is the person for you," I said. "You might want to think carefully about this and make a better choice for your life."

By then, though, she'd fallen hopelessly in love. "I'm totally happy with him. He's the best thing that's ever happened to me."

As their relationship continued, I found out that the man both sold and used drugs. I was most disheartened that she'd allowed him into her life. Although intelligent and streetwise, she ignored the fact that he had little to offer her in terms of a future. To my knowledge, she'd never hung out in the drug world before, and I was certain she wasn't a user. She was a member of a church, but not a regular churchgoer. I hoped the spiritual foundation she received as a child would help her discern how risky her association with this man was. I prayed desperately that his influence on her wouldn't cause her to experiment.

"Dear God," I said, "please open her eyes and let her come to her senses. Help her realize the dangerous path she's walking on."

My prayers were to no avail. She was first introduced to marijuana, then to methamphetamines. Gradually, that damnable fellow, named Mr. CrackCocaine, pulled her into his grasp until he dominated her life.

I asked myself, *What can I do to help her? Is there anything I can do to stop this?* I was completely at a loss for answers. Even more upsetting, my sweet and caring daughter didn't seem to *want* my help.

You might wonder what it's like being the mother of a drug addict. To put it bluntly, it's a hellish nightmare. Not only does your child suffer unspeakably, but you and the rest of the family are greatly impacted as well. Although my daughter was an adult, and I was no longer responsible for the choices she made, I was still extremely concerned about her welfare. I desperately wanted to rescue her from the quagmire that engulfed her.

I read everything about crack cocaine that I could get my hands on. As a registered nurse, I had clinical knowledge about the effects of narcotics on the brain, the changes in the body, and in one's behavior when one became addicted. The effects of crack cocaine were another story—a frightening revelation. Crack can take a person down almost immediately. Even after the very first "hit," the person seldom survives unscathed. The addicted soul craves more and more and can't stop smoking the drug, even with a strong desire to do so. Simply put, crack assumes the highest priority and overtakes finances, relationships, and all other important areas of one's life.

As I contemplated what could happen to my lovely daughter as she danced with this horrible drug, I felt physically ill. Being face-to-face with it within my family made me even more determined to interrupt the cycle of drug abuse she had entered.

Exactly as my research warned, my daughter's life spiraled out of control under the influence of crack. She moved her boyfriend in with her, and he took charge of everything. She lost her job and her car. He began cutting hair in her apartment to earn a few dollars, and she became his assistant. When I visited her on one occasion, she appeared to be in a twilight zone. "Please get rid of this man," I said. "This can't end well for you. Go into rehab and get help for yourself before it's too late."

My daughter glanced at me and mockingly said, "Mom, I'm just fine. Go home, and stop worrying about me. I'm a big girl now."

Tears filled my eyes as I noticed her glazed, vacant look, which said, *I'm just waiting for my next fix.*

I was in a fight for my daughter's life. I had to wage war on her behalf, and I couldn't let the devil win. I frantically assembled a few close friends of mine, women who knew how to pray and touch heaven for desperate situations. We formed a prayer chain, and they became my go-to source of encouragement and support as I gave them updates and lived through the nightmare. My prayer partner carried the burden of my situation with me. Later I learned that she also had children who were battling addiction. I believed God would turn my daughter's overwhelming predicament around.

One day, I received a disturbing call from my younger daughter, asking me to go with her to her sister's apartment. "I was there yesterday," she said, "and she looked worse than ever. Somehow, we've got to help her."

Her boyfriend answered our knock at the door, annoyed that we'd come. He didn't invite us in, but we entered anyway. Three of his cronies were sitting in the living room, obviously under the influence of something. My daughter was nowhere in sight.

"Where is my daughter?" I asked.

"She's asleep."

"Please let her know we're here to see her."

While waiting, I glanced around. The apartment was a pigsty. Dirty dishes filled the sink. Trash everywhere. I cried inwardly, remembering the tidy and beautifully decorated apartment in which my daughter once took so much pride. Although it was almost noon, the drapes were still pulled shut, making it dark and gloomy inside. A musty odor prevailed.

When the man realized we'd be there for a while, he quickly grabbed a revolver from the coffee table, zipped it inside his jacket, and made a hasty exit with his buddies.

As her mother and as a Christian, I struggled not to hate this man. Not only had he introduced my daughter to crack, but he also had become her supplier. She'd become his servant, asleep at home while he negotiated their drugs in the street.

A cry escaped my lips as my daughter stumbled out of the bedroom. I couldn't believe this was my child. She was unkempt and mumbled distractedly. She'd lost a considerable amount of weight.

I hugged her and held her close. "What's happened to you?"

"Hello, Mom. I'll be all right. I wasn't feeling well, so I was lying down."

My daughter, obviously, was heavily into drugs. She appeared dazed and secretly scanned the room. Her eyes darted back and forth as if she was fearful of something or someone.

"Please come with us," I said."

"I'm just fine. I'm not going anywhere. My man's a good man. He takes really good care of me."

"You're high on drugs. Don't you want to get help?"

"I only smoke weed occasionally. I don't do the hard stuff."

My heart bled for her. I was overwhelmed by a keen sense of hopelessness. My child might die in this environment. I could stand it no longer. I had to get out of there. As we turned to leave, her eyes brimmed with tears. "I think I'm pregnant," she said abruptly. "I'll call you soon to let you know for sure."

One week later, she phoned to say she was pregnant with twins. Words can't express how I felt when she gave me this news. First, a deep sadness engulfed me. This was followed by a feeling of rage. "What's she going to do with twins? How's she going to manage? She's using drugs and can hardly care for herself. She's barely hanging on by a thread."

I had to pray and ask God to help me become more tolerant toward my daughter and her man. It was beyond my comprehension that she might bring two drug-addicted infants into the world. Worse, how would these babies survive in their parents' disordered life?

After a time of real soul-searching, I reached a place of peace. I developed greater compassion for my daughter and prayed earnestly for my two grandchildren in her womb. I asked for a healthy road ahead of them and for her safe delivery. At her request, I became actively involved in her prenatal visits and was there for her delivery. When she declared to me she'd stopped taking drugs, I wanted so much to believe her. I prayed this was so.

Two beautiful infants—a boy and a girl—were born to my daughter that late-December morning. I was thrilled that my granddaughter appeared to be normal. However, my grandson needed care in the neonatal intensive care unit and seemed to be battling the effects of his mom's drug addiction. He cried constantly, taking only catnaps. His body was extremely irritable. Many prayers went up for him. Thank God, after treatment, he was discharged to go home.

Shortly after the twins' birth, my daughter married their father. "We want to raise the babies the right way," she told me. "He's working now, and things are going well."

A few months later, her husband got into a street fight and nearly lost his life. Both he and my daughter had returned to using drugs, again addicted to crack. The fight had resulted from a drug deal gone bad. What troubled me most was the fact that their responsibility for two young children was not enough to keep them away from that awful drug scene. I became extremely concerned for my grandchildren. I reactivated my prayer chain and prayed for direction on which way to go.

In the wee hours of the morning, I was called by my daughter's neighbor, who expressed concern for the children's safety. "Your daughter is outside, as high as a kite. She's screaming at the top of her lungs. Somebody needs to do something."

I dressed hurriedly and rushed to the apartment. My daughter was sitting on the ground, speaking incoherently, with fresh bruises on her face and her arms.

"Who's the snitch who called you?" she said angrily. "I'm just fine. I don't need your help."

I guided her back inside and asked about the children. She collected her thoughts and told me they were asleep. "Their father and I had a dreadful argument today," she said. "We fought with each other, and he beat me up. The neighbors heard my screams and called the police. They came and carted him off to jail."

"I'd like you and the kids to come home with me right now."

"No. We'll be all right. All is well. He'll be fine once he gets home. I only need to do what he says, and everything will be all right."

I couldn't get her to budge. She stubbornly refused to go with me. Dejected, I left with great concern and resolved to stay in touch often.

Not long afterward, another call came—this time from Child Protective Services (CPS). They'd received a call from another neighbor, who reported the children as being neglected. They asked me if I'd take the twins temporarily.

"Of course," I said. Within a few minutes, they brought my precious grandchildren to me.

"There's another problem," the CPS worker said. "Their father is out of jail, but he overdosed on drugs. He became wild, was hearing voices, and went completely out of control. An ambulance took him to a mental hospital for evaluation and treatment."

"What about my daughter?"

"Will you take her to the lab for drug testing? We've mandated this for her, but we're not sure if she'll go. If she tests highly positive, we'll have to make serious decisions about this family."

I was heartsick and very upset to realize that for the twins at eighteen months, the outlook was dark and dismal.

"I'll take her for the drug test."

I was totally aghast, when I went to pick her up. She looked awful. In the few short weeks since I'd seen her, she'd deteriorated completely. Her body had wasted to skin and bones. I could see the blood vessels in her head, arms, and legs. She told me her weight had gone down to seventy pounds. At the sight of her, I silently screamed inside.

The trip to and from the laboratory was unbelievable. My daughter was angry and belligerent. She smoked constantly, used much profanity, and was extremely rude to the lab personnel. The crack she smoked had morphed her into a most ungrateful and intolerant person. My efforts to calm her were to no avail. In fact, she contradicted me loudly. However, she finally did the test.

When we returned to her apartment late that afternoon, I was totally exhausted. Worse yet, I was mortified to observe her house had turned into a drug-infested den. The front door was open, and several unsavory-looking characters moved in and out. Dilapidated cars were parked out front. I cringed at the thought of leaving her at their mercy.

A few days later, the CPS worker gave me the results of my daughter's drug test. I was flabbergasted and felt totally sad and broken. Her results were so highly positive, she was required to immediately enter a drug rehabilitation program. They offered her one in which she could take the children with her. I agreed to take them to the rehab.

When I went to my daughter's apartment on that hot July morning, a man was there with her and the children.

"I'm not ready, and I don't know when I will be," she yelled. "My neighbor here has come to do some repairs, and I'm not leaving until they're done. You can leave if you want to."

Quite exasperated, I threatened to let CPS know what was going on. She exploded and angrily grabbed me by the wrists, shaking my arms as if she wanted to fight. My daughter had never accosted me in that manner before. I immediately went to my car and called CPS.

The worker gave her an ultimatum: "I will take you and the kids to the rehab program myself. If you aren't ready by 2:00 p.m. when I return, your children will be placed in foster care."

She and the children entered rehab that afternoon.

The man in the apartment that morning was a drug dealer who'd come to supply my daughter with her last hit of crack before she went to rehab. Her plan was to go there "tanked up" with drugs. I'd interrupted the deal when I arrived, and she hadn't had time to smoke it. This had made her absolutely livid.

After only three weeks in rehab, my daughter returned with the children to her drug-infested neighborhood. She refused to talk to me, still angry that I'd called CPS. However, her neighbor kept me informed, especially about the children.

My daughter seemed to be in the hands of Satan himself. Her apartment became a crack house with drug dealers and users in control. The children were frequently left by themselves and foraged for food among the neighbors.

CPS intervened, removed the kids, and placed them in a foster home. Finally, my beloved daughter was evicted from her home. All her worldly goods were put out on the street. People took everything. She was then homeless with nowhere to go. My heart bled to know she was living on the streets.

Where is she sleeping?

What is she eating?

Who might be taking advantage of her?

I went on a mission to find my child—my single obsession. The first time, my prayer partner went with me, and we located her. We prayed with her, gave her food and clothing, and begged her to turn her life over to God. I told her how much I loved her and how important it was for her to enter another rehab program. She refused, wanting me to leave her alone. She and her husband had separated. The members of my prayer chain didn't give up on her, however. We fervently believed a change would come.

Later, I tried again to find my daughter, but my search was unsuccessful. I drove up and down those mean streets, but she was nowhere to be found. Looking became too painful for me, so I stopped. If she wanted help, she'd have to reach out for it. All I could do was pray and trust God to perform a miracle in her life.

Days turned into weeks, then months to years. Two years went by without a word from my daughter. I didn't know if she was alive or dead. During this gut-wrenching time, I refused to give up on her. Every day, I prayed for the Lord to watch over her and bring her back to us. Meanwhile, my husband and I took the twins out of foster care and became their legal guardians.

After two years on the run, my daughter called me. I could hardly believe she was on the phone. She was in the county jail and wanted me to visit her. I felt a tremendous surge of relief. She was alive, safe, and off the streets. She was better off in jail than on the outside. I didn't know what the future held, but I had finally found my child. When I told her that her twins were safe and living with us, she was overcome with joy. She had to spend time in prison because, while on the streets, she had committed both misdemeanors and felonies. However, she vowed to do her time and take back her kids when released. About that time, she received word that her husband had been brutally murdered.

My daughter served her time in prison and walked a rocky road after her release. She went in and out of rehab programs and was arrested several times. She remained in touch with me, however, and tried hard over several years to get her life in order. My husband and I joined a support group for family members of addicts, which became a real lifeline for us.

At the age of thirty-two, my daughter declared she was finished with the street life forever. "I'm tired, Mom. I want to clean up my life and start over."

My family was amazed when she returned to church and rededicated her life to God. Tears rolled down my cheeks when she came. My prayer group rejoiced.

My testimony has a happy ending. Due to continuous and fervent prayers, my daughter recovered completely from drugs, has remained sober, and has transformed into a new person. She has her kids back, has a new home, and has started her own business. I'm one grateful mother who has proven that prayer really changes things.

God can take the pieces of our shattered lives and can make us whole again. We must be willing to persevere and never lose hope.

Dr. Grace Allman Burke, *a freelance writer who lives with her husband in Dallas, Texas, has published five books.* Broken Pieces: Mending the Fragments Through Adoption *(2017), is an inspiring story of one family's joyful, albeit traumatic, adoption journey. She received the 2016 Christian Literary Henri and Reader's Choice Award for* The Stranger's Son. *An ordained minister, Dr. Burke does premarital counseling and performs marriages. Her hobbies include scrapbooking, ethnic dining, and home decorating.*

GraceBurkeBooks.com
GBurke333@gmail.com.

Thoughts to Ponder
from Cracked ... Not Shattered

1. Prayer fuels hope.

2. God hears our prayers even when we do not see immediate answers.

3. Prayer partners are powerful.

Who are the top five people on your prayer list?

Pray without ceasing. — 1 Thessalonians 5:17

Shipwrecked
by Debbie Stuart

One of the top ten shipwrecks of all time occurred in 1628. The Swedish Warship, *Vasa*, with great anticipation, was making its maiden voyage. After only twenty minutes at sea, strong winds and flooding sank *Vasa*, only one mile from the start of its journey. This shipwreck was considered an embarrassment for the King of Sweden. None of several salvage attempts were successful.

Shipwrecks are never expected. We don't sail into life's waters expecting to crash or overturn. But occasionally, a doozy of a storm blows in out of nowhere, our lives capsize, and the situation seems unsalvageable.

For some time now, the Lord has been leading me to share a very personal story, a word of encouragement and practical application of God's Word to those experiencing a "shipwreck." And if perchance there is no storm or signs of a storm on your horizon, I pray this will prepare you to share with someone who is struggling through the waves of disappointment, despair, and shattered dreams. I pray His Word will be "an anchor, steadfast and sure" (Hebrews 6:19).

There is a boy who stole my heart. He calls me Mom.

I am the mom of a former prodigal, our son Jarrad. Thus far in my life, parenting a prodigal has been the most painful experience I have lived through. I have buried my mom, my dad, my brother, a nephew, and have grieved over great losses of various kinds. I miss my daughter terribly, as well as my son-in-law and grandsons who live 2,500 miles away. But nothing has compared to the pain of loving and trying desperately to save a prodigal, only to watch him self-destruct by his own choices, leaving a storm of pain behind.

I am some fifteen years into this journey and have finally come to the place where I can genuinely thank the Lord for this season of my life. After much crying, complaining, begging, and pitching hardheaded fits, the Lord finally broke me of my unwillingness to yield to His plan. He also relieved me of my determination to "fix this." I broke because I was unwilling to bend. Please don't let that happen to you. To prevent your repeating my mistakes, let me share with you how the Lord made our shipwreck successful. "You will be sorrowful, but your sorrow will turn into joy" (John 16:20 ESV).

For twenty years, I have served on two church staffs as Director of Women's Ministry. I also worked as the Church and Leadership Development Director for "Women of Faith." Currently, I'm on staff as Director of Ministry Initiatives at "Hope for the Heart." I say all that so you will know I love serving the Lord, and I love His church. My husband and I raised Jarrad and his sister, Haley, in church from birth, and we loved everything about it. However, that did not exclude us (as I thought it should) from the Lord's assignment: parenting a prodigal.

Early on, Jarrad was an absolute joy to parent. He was tenderhearted and compassionate—always willing to give and helps others—including every stray animal he could find. However, at age thirteen, "the perfect storm" came into his life, including the unexpected death of his beloved grandfather, affectionately known as "Pappaw." That pain propelled him on a journey of full-blown rebellion and self-medication.

I began this journey kicking, screaming, whining, and complaining.

My first word of encouragement: Don't waste your time and God's time screaming, whining, and complaining. Once I got my mind and heart right with the Lord about parenting a prodigal, I had to accept the fact that this *was* the assignment God chose for me. I went "all in." I made up my mind, because I am hardheaded, to be the best mom of a prodigal that ever walked the face of the earth. I fought fearlessly for my son because I loved him passionately, and I believed the Lord completely. The warring was mostly done in prayer, but it also included personal Bible study about parenting a prodigal.

In addition, I also had a support group of faithful friends in the fight, who have talked me off a cliff on more than one occasion. Do not suffer in silence. I discovered this journey was more about what God wanted to do in me than in my son. I also sadly discovered, in my own way, that I too was a prodigal.

When Jarrad was a little boy, his T-ball number was 17. That number stuck. He acquired the nickname J-Stu 17. He loved the number 17. On all his birthday cakes, he wanted a 17 instead of his true age. Jarrad was born five weeks before my mom lost a battle with cancer at age forty. Her birthday was September 17.

It makes you wonder.

During a particularly difficult time with J-Stu 17, I was out browsing garage sales with my husband to get my mind off things when I came across a big baseball jersey with the number 17. On the back, in big red letters, it read: WILDCAT. I thought, *He's my wildcat, all right,* and something about it made me feel close to him. I wore it for the rest of the day. Late that night, as I was weeping and praying for my "wildcat," I slipped out of bed, put the jersey back on, and knelt by his bed, even though I had no idea where he was. I spent hours interceding for my Wildcat-17 (and I still wear that jersey to this day).

The next morning during my Bible study time, I read from the *Streams in the Desert* devotional, which had a passage from Romans: "God calleth those things which be not as though they were." I loved that verse. I quickly looked for the reference, and it took my breath away when I saw it was 4:17. How sweet and personal of the Lord to say to me that morning, this is for *your* 17. Since then, the Lord has given many more verses to encourage me with the reference 2:17 (to Jarrad) and 4:17 (for Jarrad).

Let me give you a few that I hope will encourage you as well:

The Lord has done what he has purposed. — Lamentation 2:17

Our present troubles are producing an immeasurable great glory. — 2 Corinthians 4:17

Blessed are those who trust in the Lord and have made the Lord their hope and confidence. — Jeremiah 17:7

No one gave him a thing. — Luke 15:17, the prodigal story when the son came to his senses.

Jesus rebuked the demon, and it came out of the boy, and he was healed at that moment. — Matthew 17:18

Be sure to carry out the work the Lord gave you. — Colossians 4:17

God gave these young men an unusual aptitude for understanding and every

aspect of literature and wisdom. Knowledge and skill in both books and life.
— Daniel 1:17

This is a scripture I constantly pray for Jarrad:

Precious One, don't allow pain, sorrow, shame, and regret to keep you at a distance from the One who loves you most. I know it hurts because we know He could change things instantly. But, sometimes He doesn't, and you must continue to live in it. His Divine intervention is in play, whether we see it or not.

Do you have a promise for your prodigal? If not, ask the Lord for one. Here's mine: "I have seen what they do but I will heal them anyway! I will lead them and comfort those who mourn" (Isaiah 57:18 NLT).

The Lord has comforted me through this journey. He will do the same for you if you take time to meet with Him. We know we can't fix or change a prodigal. If it could be done, I would have done it. But the truth is, you cannot make another person walk with the Lord. You can only make one person do that, and it's you.

We watched through tears and unimaginable pain as our son defiantly walked the dark road of rebellion until he was out of sight.

Lost in darkness.

Our lives were shipwrecked.

The Bible talks about an important shipwreck in Acts. 27: "We took such a violent battering from the storm that the next day they began to throw the cargo overboard. On the third day, they threw the ship's tackle overboard with their own hands. When neither sun nor stars appeared for many days and the storm continued raging, we finally gave up all hope of being saved."

Paul was being faithful and obedient, yet he shipwrecked. Seems to me that people serving the Lord, being faithful and obedient should be successful, not shipwrecked. But the Lord didn't ask my opinion. Now let's unpack the whole story so we can see the Lord was preparing to do a great thing in Paul's life. Good thing that didn't stop at the tragedy. Take some time to study through this the story to see what personal lessons you can pull out and apply to your life.

Here are some I found:

Lessons for Successful Shipwrecks:

- God appoints shipwrecks. God wanted Paul shipwrecked for His own good reasons.
- Sometimes, although we are faithful, obedient, and trying to do what is right, we will be shipwrecked.
- Do you need to alter your course?
- There are things we need to throw overboard that are delaying our progress.
- The storm is not hindering your destiny, it's helping it.
- Don't give up. (verse 15)
- Don't abandon hope. (verse 20)
- Faith will make you calm. When everyone else wanted to "jump ship," Paul remained calm because he knew to "Whom he belonged". Paul knew who he served. And God was beside him (same for you) (verse 23)
- Anchor yourself to God's Word. (verse 24)
- Allow God to encourage you; then go and encourage others.
- It's not what you know, but what you obey that determines your destiny.
- Pray for providence. Providence: God's divine care, control, and guidance over a life, situations, and circumstances; making you ready for future events. (Definition from an 1812 dictionary)
- Take courage; believe God. (verse 25)
- It was just as God said: They were shipwrecked, and they survived (as will you) (verse 26)
- You might have to *be* shipwrecked, but you don't have to *stay* shipwrecked.
- This shipwreck set into motion a series of circumstances that changed the lives of many, many people.
- Your shipwreck is for a purpose you cannot see while the winds are raging and your ship is battered.

How brave and inspiring Paul's behavior was in the midst of a storm. God caused extraordinary ministry to come from his extraordinary tragedy. The storms in your life have made you what you are today.

Are you winner or a whiner?

A champion or a complainer?

If you want to be used by God, and if you are asking God for a greater degree of usefulness, then prepare for a greater storm.

When God wants to drill a man,
And thrill a man,
And skill a man
When God wants to mold a man
To play the noblest part;
When He yearns with all His heart
To create so great and bold a man
That all the world shall be amazed,
Watch His methods, watch His ways!
How He ruthlessly perfects
Whom He royally elects!
How He hammers him and hurts him,
And with mighty blows converts him
Into trial shapes of clay which
Only God understands;
While his tortured heart is crying
And he lifts beseeching hands!
How He bends but never breaks
When his good He undertakes;
How He uses whom He chooses,
And which every purpose fuses him;
By every act induces him
To try His splendor out-
God knows what He's about.
— Anonymous

Don't waste your shipwreck. Wait on God's purpose to be fulfilled. "Let your hope make you glad. Be patient in time of trouble never stop praying" (Romans 12:12 CEV).

One morning while praying through our devastating shipwreck, I didn't listen to my own advice. My prayers turned from praying to whining. I was so overwhelmed with all that was happening, I didn't even know how to pray. I could not find words to articulate what I felt, needed, and believed. I begged God to intervene and end this living nightmare. I would do anything, for storms will make you desperate. While studying several passages, I heard the Lord clearly speak in my heart and memorized the words so I could quote them whenever I found myself overwhelmed: "When you pray to be delivered from your difficulties, you are only being rescued, not victorious. I am trying to train you to be armed, equipped, and disciplined for the adversary, but you keep trying to end the training process. I want you to win this, Debbie, not be excused from it."

Think on that for a moment. Read it again.

That is notecard worthy, my friend. It's a Word that I believe He is speaking to anyone who has ever begged for His intervention to end the nightmare. To beg the Lord to rescue you from pain and distress will only make you weak, spoiled, and spiritually unresponsive. I can't promise that in this storm everything will be okay. I can promise that *you* will be okay, if you will anchor yourself to the Word of God.

Here are some scriptures that became anchors for me:

This hope we have as an anchor for the soul, both sure and steadfast. — Hebrews 6:19 (NKJ)

You are a refuge from the storm and a shelter from the heat. — Isaiah 25:4 (NLT)

He who sows righteousness will have a sure reward. — Proverbs 11:18 (NKJ)

God has made me fruitful in the land of my affliction. — Genesis 41:52 (ESV)

I will . . . transform the Valley of Trouble into a gateway of hope. — Hosea 2:15 (NLT)

The Lord your God in your midst, the Mighty One, will save; He will rejoice over you with gladness, He will quiet you with His love, He will rejoice over you with singing. — Zephaniah 3:17 (NKJ)

So what can *you* do for your prodigal? Here is what I have found to be "best practices" for dealing with a prodigal:

Prayer

Meet with the Lord every day, and consult with Him on the matter. Pray scripture instead of spending time "second guessing God's purposes, ignorantly confusing the issue and mudding the water" (Job 42:1–4 MSG). Stop the what-if questions and start with what-next?

Pray for divine intervention at all cost.

Pray for a spiritual awakening. I found it helpful to fast on the 17th day of each month and spend extended time in prayer for Jarrad.

Preparation

Get into God's Word. There you will find help, comfort, strength, direction, and revelation to face the self-destructive behavior of the one you love. Start with Luke 15, the story of the prodigal. Pay careful attention to verses 16–17, which describe the prodigal in the pigpen—sad, hungry, and in need. The Bible says, "yet, no one gave him a thing. . . . and he came to his senses." For me, the Lord clearly indicated that those two things were connected. At the Lord's direction, my husband and I stopped the flow of money, second chances, and phone calls to get him out of trouble, all enabling things parents do to "help" their kid out of trouble. Jarrad had to experience the full brunt of the consequences for his choices, which landed him in jail. It was there that he came to his senses.

Purpose

Your prodigal's behavior is not a reflection of you as a parent. This is not a waste of time or useless. It's beneficial to the ultimate plan of God. There is a plan in play, so don't forfeit *the win* because life has not turned out the way you had planned. I remember one morning when I was grieving deeply about even more destructive choices Jarrad had made. There seemed to be no stop in his downward spiral. I said to the Lord, "I hate the way he is turning out." I felt great disapproval from the Lord as He said in my heart, "He hasn't turned out yet."

The Lord says, "For you shall know that I have not done

without cause all that I have done" (Ezekiel 14:23).

Perseverance

Don't you dare quit! Love your prodigal, but stop the enabling and start setting healthy boundaries. Start thanking the Lord for what He is doing, whether you can see it or not. Stop any negative thinking, and pray for homecoming. Remember, "What the enemy intended for evil God means for good." Be brave and very courageous. I am named after Deborah in the Bible, and Judges 5:21 challenges me to "March on, my soul, in courage."

"The Lord is not only mighty to save from sin, but He is mighty to save from blinding tears of rebellion against your fateful circumstances." — Frances Roberts

In 2 Kings 8, there is a story of a woman who lost everything because of a famine. She had to leave her home and land to go where she could get food. When the famine ended, she returned home. In those days, you could petition the king to get your land back. After hearing the woman's story, the king declared that not only would she get her land back, but she also was to be given the value of the crop that would have been harvested had there not been a famine. She received the value of what had been lost.

The King of kings, our Lord Jesus Christ, can restore the value of what you have lost. Start thanking the Lord for salvaging the shipwreck in your life. Praise him for the rebuilding process and for creating a more beautiful vessel than before.

Debbie Stuart is Director of Ministry Initiatives at Hope for the Heart and is a certified Life and Ministry Coach. She has served in women's ministry for over twenty-five years as Leadership Director for Women of Faith, Director of Women's Ministry at Prestonwood Baptist Church, and Willow Point. She has also been a LifeWay Trainer/Consultant. Books: 20 Minutes a Day for the Rest of Your Life and 20 Lessons Learned (available on E-Bay). She is a conference/retreat speaker and Bible teacher.
DStuart@HopefortheHeart.org

Thoughts to Ponder
from Shipwrecked

1. Although we are faithful and obedient, we can still be shipwrecked.

2. Pray for whatever it takes to bring your prodigal to the Lord.

3. Setting healthy boundaries is better than enabling your prodigal.

What has God taught you through your shipwreck?

God is our refuge and strength, an ever-present help in trouble. — Psalm 46:1

When Tomorrow Is Maybe
by Jack Bush

Tomorrow is a very important day in your life if it is only a "maybe."

I discovered this truth at a hospital in, of all places, Belize City, Belize. It's not a good place to be if you might not see tomorrow.

Before we get into the details of this untimely situation, I must tell you that I have been in communication with God since age seven. I am very blessed that God and the Holy Spirit have been with me all along the way, guiding me through great highs and great lows. This day would qualify as one of my greatest lows and biggest tests.

So what's the story? What caused this uncertainty?

Two days earlier, Dr. M, the Belize physician in charge, told my wife, Mary, that he did not know what was wrong with me. "He is in critical condition," he said. "As soon as possible, he must be moved to a major hospital in the United States that has the ability to treat him. In his condition, I believe he has only three days left."

It was unsettling news for my wife, but the doctor's next comments were worse. He explained that he didn't know how to get me back home in a hurry. There were no evacuation planes in Belize. He said he'd try to find a plane somewhere in the U. S. "If I find a plane," he said, "where would you like to take him?"

Mary said, "I want him to go to Mayo Clinic in Rochester, Minnesota."

According to my wife, the doctor almost flipped out over that reply. Gently, yet professionally, he explained his doubts about her choice. He was not sure if I could make that long of a trip, and we didn't have that much time.

But she was determined. Mary has tremendous inner strength and faith. She had already survived five cancers, and it was her deep faith that helped pull her through. Today, she will tell you that God helped her make this very big decision concerning my health crisis. On top of that, she can be as stubborn as a Missouri mule.

Still, Dr. M. did not want to give in. He finally asked, "Do you have a doctor to call?"

Mary gave him the Mayo switchboard operator and the name of

my doctor.

"Do you realize it is 4:00 p.m. on Saturday afternoon? I don't know of many doctors in the states who are available on Saturday afternoon. Getting into the famous Mayo Clinic is not going to be easy. But I will try." He clearly was a "Doubting Thomas." He went into another room to place the call.

He came back astonished. "I cannot believe this. I called and asked for Dr. C., and he answered in about a minute. I told him you were determined for Mr. Bush to go to the Mayo Clinic, and he actually told me to send him on. He will take care of the arrangements when your husband arrives." In shock over the ease of the process, there was still a hurdle to cross. "Now we have to find a plane."

Unlike the phone call to Mayo, that wasn't an easy task. But praise God, some of the staff people in that little hospital suggested an air evacuation service in San Antonio, Texas. They gave Mary the number to call.

She explained the situation and that she could pay them on our American Express card. They could be there the next morning, but it was a very long flight. They would have to stop for fuel on the way to Minnesota.

With the "maybe" looming overhead, time marched on.

Precious time.

Early the next morning, after flying most of the night, my emergency transport arrived at the airport, met the waiting ambulance, and wheeled me onto the plane.

Most of what I am sharing is what I have heard. I was out of it and did not have a clue as to what was going on. My strong-willed wife, with all her inner faith, was in charge.

Our 2,915-mile journey to Minnesota began. The medics on board were great, but my vital signs were not. My oxygen was very low. My heart was beating extremely fast. My sediment rate was 128 instead of a normal 1–18. And worst of all, I was spitting up blood into a big jar.

The medics attending me must have been wondering if I would make it. My wife told them, time after time, that I had the constitution of a bull with tremendous inner strength. I would make it. As strong as my betrothed is, I imagine her faith was running on fumes about this time.

We landed in New Orleans and refueled as quickly as possible, but the clock was winding down. Based on Dr. M's opinion, little more than a day was left. We still had about 1,200 miles to go in a small plane.

As I hung on, defying the projected timeline, we finally reached the Rochester skies, but there was a big problem concerning our landing. Fourteen inches of snow had already fallen, and more was coming. Landing in this mess would be a challenge, requiring significant pilot skills. They had never faced a situation like this before and were in a dither. Rather than lose a patient, they must have decided they had to go for it.

We landed in one of the worst snowstorms ever recorded in Minnesota. Ten years later, the local folks still recall the great snowstorm of February 2007. Talk about coming in on a "wing and a prayer." These guys pulled it off with amazing skill and determination. But maybe, just maybe, God and the Holy Spirit were helping them out just as they had helped me about a jillion times before.

The ambulance was waiting in snow up to its hubcaps, and the snow was still dumping by the bucket-loads. They wheeled me onto a cart and began the trek to the hospital. I can only remember that it was awfully cold. Mary remembers the cold part *really* well. She was still wearing tropical clothes.

I have no recollection of what happened in the critical care wing of St. Mary's Hospital, part of the Mayo Clinic. However, I do know a team of doctors worked on me throughout the night, and tomorrow did arrive.

At some point the next day, a group of doctors came in and tried to explain what had happened. They had managed to stop the bleeding of my collapsed lung. I was still in bad shape, but there was good news.

I call this one of the "bad news/good news" parts of my story.

The diagnosis and medical tests showed that I had Wegener's Disease. This was probably not good news. I just nodded because I could not talk. Not a peep could come out.

I wondered, *What is Wegener's?* I thought this must be named after Honus Wagner, the famous old-time baseball pitcher. My next thought was, *Oh my, this is probably like Lou Gehrig's disease.* I knew that didn't turn out well for the "Iron Horse."

The doctors explained that Wegener's Disease is very rare and affects only about 1 in a 100,000 or so. No one really knows the cause or trigger, but for some reason your immune system goes haywire and attacks parts of the body. In my case, my lungs were the target. It could be treated but not cured. This did not seem like very good news to me.

Finally, they got to the good-news part. The world's greatest authority on the disease worked at the Mayo Clinic. "Dr. S. will be your doctor as soon as you are stabilized," they said.

I felt a lot better. I was now certain that God and the Holy Spirit had been with me this far, and somehow this was going to turn out okay. I felt very, very blessed, but I was in bad shape.

I could hardly breathe. My voice was gone. I didn't know much, but I did know this was definitely not good, especially since my family was gathering. My daughter flew in from California, and my other daughter was coming from Charleston. My Minnesota-based sister-in-law arrived. And of course, my wife, Mary, was by my side. I silently wondered if a preacher was about to show up for final comfort.

By the grace of God, I made it. After I felt better physically, I looked out the window into the parking lot. After twenty-eight inches of snow, the cars were covered up to their tops. I wondered how in the world I ever made it to the hospital.

I was put in a hospital room for what the doctors called "recovery," which started slowly and went badly from there. To add to my health fragility, I developed a blood clot. Once again, I was not in good shape.

A couple of days later, Dr. S., "the great authority on my disease," arrived. I couldn't return home after I had recovered. After I got out of the hospital, the treatment would include very heavy doses of Prednisone, chemotherapy, and antibiotics. I also needed to find an oncologist in Dallas. A lot to do to erase the "maybe."

Much time passed, but eventually I was healthy enough to go home.

Chapter two of this story is coming up, but I think I should first explain how I ever got into such shape that tomorrow would be a "maybe."

In December 2016, I was having sinus difficulties and went to a doctor, who prescribed Levaquin. Three weeks later, I was in Mexico on a business trip and became extremely sick. The medication I had been prescribed was too harsh, and I had a reaction. I needed to stop the medication and get back to Dallas as soon as possible. So I did. My new Dallas doctor diagnosed my problem incorrectly and placed me on Prednisone. He said it would be all right to go on our scheduled eighteen-day cruise from Los Angeles to Miami. That turned out to be very bad advice. Even worse, we took his advice. But in defense of stupidity, we had planned this great trip for a long time and really wanted to go.

After getting on the ship, I was in terrible shape, with night sweats so bad the sheets had to be changed. I could not sleep. All I could eat was ice cream. The ship doctor diagnosed my problem as pneumonia. That prescription was the worst possible for my situation.

By the time we made it to Panama, I was so ill that the ship stopped in the middle of the canal locks so an ambulance could take me to a hospital in Panama City. The hospital doctor again diagnosed my problem as pneumonia and believed, with the new medications he prescribed, I could get back on the ship, which was now eighty miles out to sea.

We boarded a taxi and drove around the isthmus, then chartered a speedboat to take us to the ship, which was anchored, waiting for us in the middle of the ocean. We made it. There were a lot of people looking out the balconies as we boarded through the little opening.

I started spitting up blood. My vital signs were erratic. We arrived in Belize, where I was forced to disembark for good. The captain and the head of housekeeping helped Mary pack our things. I was carted off to the hospital. I really didn't know what was happening, but years later we visited Belize and the historic hospital. By American standards, it was "modest."

Now we get to chapter two, when I was finally discharged from St. Mary's.

I flew home on American Airlines. My wheelchair carried two oxygen tanks. This was the hardest flight I ever experienced in my countless frequent-flyer miles.

Home at last, I was supposed to be recovering, taking the Prednisone, chemo, and other drugs. The high dosages of

Prednisone had bad side effects, with extreme highs and very dismal lows, which made it difficult to sleep. After six weeks, I was in serious condition. This time my kidneys were bleeding. Not good, so we were off to Mayo again.

Dr. S. said the treatment was not working. We had figured that out already. I wondered how this whole mess was going to turn out. And I must admit, I had to question whether Dr. S. was really "one of the greatest authorities on this disease."

What comes next is another "bad news/good news" story.

"We are conducting an experimental study," Dr. S. said, "which uses Rituxan to kill the patient's B cells and hopefully bring remission. The patient will then have no immune system. So far it has worked, but the trials are limited. We are not sure about the long-range side effects or how it will work with different patients. This is still very experimental."

This was a time when a lot of faith and inner strength was needed. I felt blessed to be at the right place at the right time. So I volunteered for this test with Mayo Clinic in collaboration with some other well-known hospitals. I became "Number 51."

I had four large infusions over a five-week period. What happened?

It worked.

When I think of all the great blessings in my life, this was certainly the best, because it eliminated the "maybe," at least for now, and gave me the gift of tomorrow.

Today, I am healthy. I still have infusions every nine months and have no immune system. But I am fortunate. I know the Holy Spirit was with me during this incredible experience, or I wouldn't be around to tell my story.

The story is not quite over. Ten years later, I still participate in the study. Once or twice a year, I participate in numerous interviews, extensive blood tests (twenty-one different ones), and a lot more. Two six-inch-wide binders full of interviews and test results are on file at Mayo, and a lot more information is stored in Mayo's big data cloud.

We are finally coming to the best part of the story.

The study and the experimental group went very well. Dr. S. and others spent years trying to the get the Washington FDA bureaucrats convinced that this really worked. Three years ago,

Rituxan was approved for this disease.

Thanks to this experiment, a lot of people are going to be treated properly. Best of all, great strides have been made in finding the causes and effects of Wegener's Disease. Thousands worldwide are about to live good lives instead of wondering if they will see tomorrow. I feel good about being part of this. Really good.

So what is the point of this long and complicated story?

We learn a lot about life when we are not certain if there will be a tomorrow.

Mary, the pilots, and Mayo Clinic saved my life, but there is more. Without a doubt, when the Holy Spirit is working within us, He is the inner strength of hope and faith that pulls us through, even during the toughest of times.

God can turn what appears hopeless into good, and because of that, as Roaring Lambs, we need to amplify our faith by telling our stories, no matter how difficult they are.

Every day I count my blessings and thank God for all of them, but this blessing stands out, for God extended my life to glorify him.

Thanks be to God! Praise be to God!

Jack Bush is a Roaring Lamb and feels the need to amplify God's love about his and his wife's faith during some very difficult times. He is now retired and has published seven books and numerous articles. During his business career, he was President, CEO, Chairman, Director and Founder of several different large companies. JBush4421@aol.com

Thoughts to Ponder
from When Tomorrow Is Maybe

1. No one has a promise of another day.

2. God can instill courage and determination in others to help us in time of need.

3. We can use the difficulties we face today to help others in the future.

> **Tomorrow is a maybe for all of us.
> How will this reality shape
> your thoughts and actions today?**

Jesus looked at them and said, "With man this is impossible, but not with God; all things are possible with God."— Mark 10:27

Even Miracles Need Help

by Jack and Mary Bush

My wife's oncologist at the Mayo Clinic in Rochester, Minnesota, is a soft-spoken, southern gentleman. His voice is like an expensive moisturizing lotion—very soothing. He has other notable attributes. Smart as well as realistic. Extremely knowledgeable about cancer. In fact, he is one of the nation's top oncologists.

Over the years, I've gotten to know my wife's physician pretty well. Sometimes we just visit for a while about my wife's physical condition. Last November, I asked, "How many people do you know who have had six cancers like Mary?"

He said, "Quite a few, actually." He paused. "But hardly any are still around. You see, Mary has an extraordinary inner spirit."

Mary has extraordinary faith—never wavering in face of extremely difficult times—not ever. This faith in God and the Holy Spirit has translated into hope, strength, determination, grit, and a spirit that has pulled her through six cancers and even worse times.

Dr. B. explained that Mayo can do great things, and at times, he has seen miraculous results. In his career, he has seen people with extraordinary inner spirits survive the toughest and worst situations. On the other hand, those who feel sorry for themselves, or do not have confidence and faith, generally have a very difficult time—or worse. "Even miracles need help," he said.

I started thinking about this a lot.

After a mulling over what Dr. B. had shared, I came to understand how this applied to Mary. First, you have to talk to God about problems as well as possibilities. Next, the Holy Spirit is willing to help, but if you reject Him or don't have faith in Him or don't do your part, miracles might not happen. It seems to me, it's a "partnership."

A lot of people said that it was a miracle that Mary "just happened to be at the right place at the right time" during her cancer experiences, but she's the first to tell you that God can only do so much. You have to "buck up" and do your share.

Mary will also tell you that the prayers of many, along with her personal faith, give her "inner strength" with hope, spirit, strength, and determination.

The Mayo Clinic may have saved Mary's life several times, but it has been her faith that provided the extra push to pull her through each time. The Holy Spirit was with her, and she knew it. She's had a "good partnership" with God all her life.

But on with the story.

How did this cancer stuff start with Mary?

In the fall of 1994, the Chairman of the Board of the company where I worked insisted that I take Mary to the Mayo Clinic for a physical. "This is a great place," he said. "You must get up here." We tried every way possible to weasel out of going, but he had already made the reservations. I had "important meetings" coming up. Mary was launching a new women's choral group, the *Mary Notes*. Neither of us was eager, and we contemplated cancelling. But a little voice told us we really needed to go, so we went.

At 8:00 a.m. during my first exam, I was called into where Mary's tests had started. There, we were told she had a very serious and aggressive colon cancer. They needed to operate the next morning.

Good grief! That bad? Why so soon? This was shocking news.

We wanted to know more about the doctor, so I was "delegated" to have a talk with him. He called me into a conference room with a team of doctors and asked what I wanted to know.

"Well," I said, "Tell me about your qualifications."

He pulled a book off the shelf that contained the procedure for my wife's operation. He had written the book. After that, I couldn't think of any other questions to ask.

The next morning when we checked in, Mary said, "Don't worry. I will be okay." She seemed assured. I think her faith was at work, but was probably standing on shaky legs.

And she was right.

The doctor successfully completed a very long and difficult operation and was confident of the outcome. After the surgery, he talked like a player on a winning team celebrating in the end zone. "Mary will be okay," he said.

We certainly were at the right place at the right time. A miracle? Well, I don't know. I do know Mary is a strong believer in God's angels.

After a difficult recovery, she was again going full blast. The

Mary Notes volunteer choral group that Mary still manages and directs was finally organized. They practiced a lot and gave four outstanding performances the next May. That took a lot of her "inner strength."

The *Mary Notes* consisted of forty ladies, with about thirty who sang. They performed a mixture of songs: contemporary, old, patriotic, and spiritual. Many times, I looked around at the audience and saw tears in people's eyes, especially when they sang, "I Believe" or "He Lifts Me Up." The audience always stood and sang along when they performed the "Hallelujah Chorus" during the Christmas season. I think their voices brought God joy too. The group performed for thousands over the last twenty-two years. The *Mary Notes* just kept rolling on, even when the next big cancer occurred.

But there is more to the story.

A year later, a little voice told us that a return trip to the Mayo clinic was a good idea. I believe God wanted Mary to keep on singing, but maybe it was her overwhelming belief in angels from above that were calling. I am not sure.

So we went, and the news was not very good. In fact, it could not have been much worse.

There were three liver cancers, and they were thriving. The doctors said there could be no operation this time, because of the number of growths. There could be no transplant. Cancer-patient liver transplants were taboo. The best news they could offer was to treat the cancer and hope for the best for a year or two. We knew what that meant.

But Dr. B. had an idea. He told us there was a Mayo doctor, Doctor N., who was not afraid to try new approaches and might be interested in this case. Unfortunately, he was not there and would be in Europe for another week. We waited for him to return and consulted with him.

"You know," he said, "I think I can do this. I have a new procedure I could try if you don't mind taking a big chance."

"I am okay with that," Mary said. There was a lot of faith in that *okay*.

I recently read a faith comment that I think describes what was going on with her. "Faith is not about everything turning out okay. Faith is about being okay no matter how things turn out."

During this time, I had frequent conversations with God about our situation and got the distinct impression that my calling was to retire early from work and support what might be a much-shortened life together. We did not know what would happen, but we'd be in this together.

Thanks be to God. It was the best decision I have ever made. The new procedure happened as planned. Dr. N. used a laser on the two little guys and operated on the big-guy cancer. This was a very difficult operation for him back in 1995. I think it was the first time it had been tried.

The procedure seemed successful. However, recovery would be long and hard: fifty-two weeks of chemo infusions and a lot of struggles. Things continued to be uncertain. We went together to chemo and other treatments for a full year—not my idea of "dinner and a movie." Definitely a good time for me to be retired. Help was needed. Mary's inner strength kept her going. She was doing her part. I needed to do mine.

A lot of folks, some of whom believe in angels, said this was really a miracle and that we were at the right place at the right time. Maybe so. But as I said earlier, miracles sometimes need help.

Her choral group of forty wonderful ladies, the *Mary Notes,* kept right on going, even though their Director was terribly sick. There were four performances in December and four more the next May. Meanwhile, Mary's faith kept directing her. She knew she would be fine. But I knew she was breathing on the fumes of faith and her inner spirit.

A couple of years went by, and guess what. Once again. a little voice said, "You need to go to Mayo, and you better hurry." I was convinced God wanted Mary to keep on singing.

This time, it was lung cancer. This was not good at all. Another operation was needed. And of course, Mary said, "I will be okay." Her faith told her so.

The operation was a success.

Was it a miracle to catch the lung cancer this early? Were the angels looking after her? Five cancers in one's life certainly is a big test of one's faith, that's for sure.

The story does not end here. Yes, there's still more. Good grief!

In November, almost seventeen years later, Doctor B. called. "Mary, you need to get up here as soon as possible. Your exam last week shows cancer in the works."

This time, it was breast cancer.

Another operation.

More uncertainty.

But the *Mary Notes* shows must go on. There were four performances scheduled in December, and here it was November. She told Dr. B., who was now our friend, to schedule her surgery quickly so she could keep the scheduled performance dates. Commitments are also a very big thing with Mary.

He did.

She did.

But it was a tough time for Mary. Again she responded with her familiar faith declaration: "I will be okay."

The *Dallas Morning News* heard about Mary's story, thought it was a good human-interest piece, and put together a nice spread. They played up her grit, determination, and the support of the *Mary Notes* group. They didn't mention faith. The media generally has a way of eliminating God from news stories, but I knew it was faith that had given her that spirit and kept her going, and so did the *Mary Notes* choral members. They had seen it and felt it along the way. Faith and spirit have a way of radiating. You can ask any of the *Notes,* as they call themselves. By now they are part of the partnership. They help on the praying and support that gives Mary her "inner strength."

That brings us to current day with the story not over. Dr. B. called again. "We need to run more tests." We are going back to Mayo the week after next, with a possibility of number seven coming up. That would not be a lucky number. But if our previous experience is any indication, Mary will be okay.

We have learned a lot about cancer during all these bouts. What is more important is we have learned about faith and that working on these crises with God, combined with prayers from family and friends, produces wonderful results. This, I think, is what Dr. B. told me about "miracles."

Mary's story is one of faith prevailing over difficult odds. Without her inner spirit, blessed by the Holy Spirit, her story could have been a lot different. Mary knows that God wants acknowledgement for His wondrous work. Every day, she counts her blessings and praises God. I have seen her amplify her beliefs by letting others know about faith.

Over the years, she has talked with many, maybe dozens of people, who have received the bad news that they have cancer. Comforting them is a big deal for her. I think she is "called" to do that. She calls them, or sits down and talks with them. She tells them the battle can be won with the help of God and good physicians, but it is faith that will make everything turn out "okay."

One thing we have learned, as Dr. B. said: "Even miracles need help." We are pretty sure God wants to help, but He needs to be reassured that He has a partner who believes in Him. If not, the Holy Spirit just may be off and away, doing miracles for someone else.

For all this we say, "Thank you, Lord."

*Jack and Mary Bush are Roaring Lambs and proud to amplify their faith. God has been with them during great and difficult times. Jack is now retired. Kind of. He has published seven books and numerous articles. During his business career he has been President, CEO, Chairman, Director, and Founder of several different companies. Mary has had a wonderful career in music and currently is the Director of a 40-woman choral group that performs all over Dallas. **JBush4421@aol.com***

Thoughts to Ponder
from Even Miracles Need Help

1. Nothing is impossible with God.

2. God does His part, but we must do our part as well.

3. We inspire others through our faith and determination.

> **What areas of your life do you need to actively "do your part"?**

And without faith it is impossible to please God, because anyone who comes to him must believe that he exists and that he rewards those who earnestly seek Him. — Mark 10:27

Faith on the Fault Line

by Kim Robinson

The crack was amazing, longer than anything I'd ever seen—running the length of the ceiling in our large living room, straight down the middle, separating sheetrock and painted texture. Its appearance was a complete surprise. There was no obvious reason for its existence. It came from nowhere and appeared overnight.

The crack in our marriage was different, starting as a hairline fracture, a faint line of doubt that creeped in and spread ever so slowly. Not noticeable at first. Easy to ignore when I first suspected it, growing subtly over time, encouraging tiny openings that widened with each argument, each lie, and each disappointment.

When the crack in our house appeared, we had been married ten years. The marriage crack began three weeks after our wedding, when my husband announced he was purchasing the company where he worked. It was an announcement, not a desire brought home for our joint consideration. It meant going deep into debt, something I was not in favor of, yet something he was not afraid of. I wanted to talk it through, but it simply wasn't up for discussion. The decision was already made. My signature on the paperwork was simply a formality required because we were married. I felt shocked, hurt, betrayed. But people-pleasing and avoiding conflict was my specialty. Arguing about it made me feel sick to my stomach and helpless. I stuffed my feelings and kept my mouth shut. It was the first time I realized that our marriage was not a partnership. It wouldn't be the last.

One thing we had agreed on from the beginning was that we wanted children. By our first anniversary, I was pregnant—one of God's miracles. I had been told it would be difficult for me to conceive. I was ecstatic, and so was my husband. Now that we had a baby on the way, I pressured him to travel less. Surely this would be the turning point that would motivate him to be home more than he was gone, to be the wonderful father I knew he could be. Being the new owner of the company required a great deal of travel. Something he loved, but unfortunate for me. He was doing what he was good at, growing the business, making deals, working in a field he enjoyed. He was a good provider, so I felt guilty about my dissatisfaction. When I complained about his being gone so much, I asked questions like "Will it be like this after the baby is born?" or "Will you want to stay home more?" His answer was always the same. He was doing this for us, for our family, for the future. He assured me that his only mistress was the company.

Within three years, we had two precious children, a daughter and a son. I didn't know the phrase "lonely in the marriage," but that's what I was. I threw myself into caring for the children. I also became active in our church. I had been a believer for several years, but my faith had gathered dust, stored tidily away on a top shelf to be pulled out only when needed. Now, instead of just showing up for worship occasionally, I attended regularly, joined a small group and a Bible study. It was fulfilling to steep myself in a community of believers, to be around fellow pilgrims who wanted to study the Bible and learn how to apply its truths. I wanted to be in church with my husband sitting beside me, but he was not interested. He didn't see the need for God in his life. He was adamant—no church for him and certainly no giving or tithing.

How had I ended up with a husband who didn't share my faith and wanted nothing to do with God? By not putting my faith first; by not trusting God to guide me in choosing a mate, by not exercising the privilege of prayer, by not having my priorities in place when I said, "I do"—that's how. But it was too late to do anything about that.

I was a Christian, but my prayer life was weak. I didn't know how to reach out to God for wisdom and strength to fight for my marriage, and I was embarrassed to talk to trusted friends at church or seek help from a professional. Instead, I spent my time taking care of our children and my own busyness. I was involved in the areas I believed God wanted me serving, but I wasn't working on what would honor Him the most—trying to resolve the issues in my marriage. I couldn't yet see His golden thread weaving my failures and weakness into His master plan.

As the crack in our marriage grew, so did the resentment in my heart. The crack was obvious. The resentment was not. It was a poison moving through a heart formerly filled with hope, trust, and love. Our arguments happened more often, and he no longer assured me that the company was his only mistress—because it was no longer true.

The day we noticed the crack in our house, my husband hired an engineer to investigate. The engineer's report revealed that the cast iron pipes under the house had corroded, resulting in major water leaks underneath the foundation. So much water had leaked into the foundation that it had cracked in two, causing the gaping seam in the living room and the plumbing in the wall to dislodge and leak. The damage would get much worse if it wasn't repaired. An insurance adjuster confirmed the engineer's findings and assured us that our homeowner's policy would cover everything. He would send in his report and get back to us soon.

Except he didn't.

Weeks went by. Our phone calls went unreturned. Finally, we reached a live person at the insurance company, only to learn that our adjuster had been transferred to another city. Our case had been reassigned.

While we waited for movement on repairing our home, I got up the nerve to ask my husband to go to counseling with me, to see whether we could save our marriage. He went to one session. He said the process was not worth his time if he couldn't guarantee the outcome he wanted. When asked what that was, he said he wasn't sure. Honestly, I wasn't sure what outcome I wanted either. I only knew that I'd discovered a lot about myself that needed serious work, but I couldn't make him work on himself. I finally had a handle on how to live the Christian life, but my husband seemed uninterested in a godly wife.

Not long after that counseling session, we heard from our new insurance adjuster. He told us there would be no coverage. We were on our own to fund the repairs.

Sixteen months after we first saw the crack in the ceiling, my marriage cracked for good. My husband moved out. He said I could stay in the house with the children and wished me luck with getting the house fixed. With the closing of the front door, I had become something I never wanted, never dreamed I'd be—a single mother of two children with a broken marriage and a broken house.

At first, I hoped things would be civil between us. But on the advice of his attorney, my husband refined his original suggestions about how to divide our property. Divorce negotiations deteriorated so much that we communicated mainly through our attorneys. Through a former employer, God connected me with a caring, Christian attorney. He guided me through the legal waters and even let me pay him in installments. At one point, my husband's attorney proposed splitting everything in half: the business, proceeds from sale of the house, the kids. My husband would not pay cash for my half of the company, but he would draw up a note and guarantee payments. I didn't know what to do. I didn't care for the business, but I cared deeply about my children. Being without either of them was not an option for me. I spent all my available time at my prayer bench, seeking God's comfort, guidance, and wisdom. Jesus became my best friend, my comforter, an always available shoulder upon which I frequently wept.

One morning, I woke up, agitated as always but feeling unusually compelled to get to my prayer bench. I sat looking out the window, tears ready to spill over. A pair of cardinals were at the birdbath, the male sharing with the female some of the birdseed he had secured for them both. I still didn't know what to do. I didn't have the stomach or the money for a court battle, but I didn't see any other option. I opened my Bible and started to read.

Then God spoke to me. Not in a humanly audible voice, but a voice, just the same. A voice audible to my spirit, which is difficult to describe. It was so clear I'll never forget it. God said, "Give him the business."

Excuse me? I thought. *Is Almighty God speaking to me about my divorce terms?*

I heard the voice again: "Give him the business. In exchange, I want you to ask for the children and your home free and clear, but nothing else—not any part of the business. And when you ask, you must tell him you are doing it because I told you to."

I sat completely still for a minute. Was this really God? Did He really want me to do this? Could He possibly care for me so much that He would help me with the details of a process I knew He couldn't be in favor of? And as for telling my husband why I was doing it, the only thing I could dread more than a divorce was talking to him about God. The times I had tried to talk to him about my faith and relationship with Jesus had been so humiliating. I could not imagine proposing divorce terms, and saying, "God told me to tell you."

But I had learned I needed to look at things through the eyes of faith. Proverbs 3:5–6 says to trust in the Lord with all your heart, leaning not to your own understanding. As believers, we are to walk by faith, not by sight, in obedience to God every day. We are to live out of gratitude for all God has given us, even if it means giving up something we want or think we need. I knew the hand of God was on my life, so I decided to do what God said and let the dollars fall where they may.

I told my attorney what had happened and what I wanted to do.

He said, "As your attorney, I should probably advise against this. As your friend, I don't want to see you lose an asset. But as a Christian, I have to counsel you that if God has said this to you, who are we to disobey God?"

I prayed and waited another day, giving God a chance to show me if I was wrong about His voice. But the certainty only grew. I called my husband. I was nervous, but asked if we could meet. He didn't see much use in our rehashing everything, but agreed to meet one last time. He brought the latest draft of his divorce terms and the draft note receivable for my portion of the business. I asked him to sit down. Then I gave him God's terms, telling him I wanted no part of his business.

He looked at me as if I had lost my mind. "Are you serious?" he asked. "Why are you doing this?"

I took a deep breath. "Because I believe this is what God wants me to do. And He wants you to know it was His idea." The look on his face showed that he completely discounted the "God" explanation, but he was eager to get this in writing before I came to my senses.

Two months later, the divorce was final. The marriage crack was now a permanent fault line. The crack in the ceiling was still there, getting wider.

I took a new approach regarding the crack. Bathing the situation in prayer, I reviewed our insurance policy plus the engineer and adjuster reports. I concluded that the damage should be covered. We had paid insurance premiums for years—premiums I was still paying—and the policy was clear. I decided to find an attorney to help me. Once again, God put the right person directly in my path, this time through a plumber I had hired to assess repairs.

The attorney was young, on his own after leaving a firm specializing in insurance defense practice, because he could no longer stomach their coverage denial on large claims, forcing the insured to either pay for legal help or pay out-of-pocket for the repairs. Most of them did the latter. But I knew I was right. The injustice of it all fueled my desire to fight. He reviewed my case and believed in it so strongly that he took it on a full contingency basis.

God had provided my attorney, but it was still up to me to pray and trust the Lord rather than focus on my fear. The fight lasted seven years. I endured depositions, endless discovery, mediations, and waited while they sent their case to the state Supreme Court, which refused to hear it on grounds that the case had no merit. It seemed, the more I fought, the less progress I made.

One day, my attorney called and asked me to meet him at his office. "This case has gone on longer than I expected," he said. "I have never seen an insurance company fight like this. My practice has grown so much that I no longer take contingency cases. I don't need them."

I swallowed hard. Was he terminating me as a client?

He smiled. "They know that after this long, you are going to fight to the finish. So they approached me about settlement. I have obtained a settlement agreement that will provide enough to fully repair your house from foundation to roof, remove the mold that has grown inside the walls, and allow a modest interior remodel if I take less than the fee we originally agreed on. So that we can both get on with our lives, I've decided to reduce my fee. Are you agreeable?"

An attorney who suggested a lower fee for himself? I was stunned. Only God could have done this. Through tears I said, "Yes!" and thanked him with all my heart.

Eight months later the children and I moved out of our temporary rental house and back into our home. A new house without cracks in the ceiling or plumbing leaks or mold in the walls. A house with a solid new foundation.

Oh, and my former husband's business? Two years after the divorce, the company went under and closed its doors. I hung up the phone after hearing the news, immediately realizing that if I had insisted on half of his company in the divorce, I would have ended up with a worthless asset and no way to pay for the mortgage. Instead, God had provided a home for me and the children.

The strength of our foundation was in the one true God. The

same God had woven that golden thread through my mistakes and my pain to bring me back to a place with the same address, but a new faith foundation, solid and without cracks.

__Kim Robinson__ is a native Texan. She and her husband have six children and fourteen grandchildren. Passionate about blogging and parenting, Kim writes and speaks about challenges facing women and parents. She is the author of the novel Chased by Grace *and speaks at Christian retreats, worship events, and book groups. Kim is active in music and children's ministries at her church and was a Parent Representative on the National Council of Juvenile Justice and Family Court Judges.* __KimRobinson.com__

Thoughts to Ponder
from Faith on the Fault Line

1. God is in the details.

2. Obedience delights our heavenly Father.

3. Press into God no matter what others think.

> **What do you do when God leads you to do something that does not make sense?**

Trust in the Lord with all your heart and lean not on your own understanding; in all your ways submit to him, and he will make your paths straight. — Mark 10:27

The Alien
by Denisa Klein

When I was young, I was punched by a schoolyard bully. His blow was so hard, I did not remember anyone's name. I knew them, but I could not tell them who they were. I couldn't recall my phone number or my address. However, I knew where I lived and could take them there, if they would only let me. I also knew my mother worked at the school, so the school could provide my phone number and address. If they would only tell me, then I would remember.

This was my childhood. I knew what I knew, but I couldn't remember why. At family gatherings, everyone laughed and joked about events, but I had no memory of the event occurring. So it was like I was an alien dropped off on one dark night. At least that would explain a lot of my blank spots. It's funny that I only forgot events and names, but I didn't forget my name, how to write, how to read, or things like that. Was it because I was programmed to know these things from outer space? Oh, my brother wanted me to believe that one.

Because I was raised in a loving home, the memory loss became a "normal" thing. If someone mentioned something I could not remember, my sister quickly told me the story to get me back in the loop. Mother pulled out pictures and pointed out the people, telling me over and over who they were. I was never made fun of, never ridiculed. I never felt inferior—not at home anyway. School was a different story. I was picked on, teased, and always felt inferior.

As time progressed, so did my frustration.

I knew how to read, but I couldn't remember any grammar rules. I knew how to count, but I could only do simple math. Teachers looked at me and said things like "Why don't you know these things? You were taught this in third grade." It was humiliating. If only they understood that I didn't remember my third-grade school work. I became very quiet and a good little wall flower. I didn't want anyone to know that I couldn't remember the past. Don't ask me the title of the book that contains the quote I just said. Don't ask for the name of a song I am singing, or why you never end a sentence with a preposition. I can't tell you.

My frustration also began with my parents at the time of my injury. What none of us knew until ten years later was that I had absolutely no memory of the week after I was hit. I grew up thinking my loving parents, who I had no doubt truly loved me, had completely ignored my injury. You see, I didn't remember going to the hospital, taking cognitive tests, going to school, wearing makeup to cover my black-and-blue face. I didn't remember being watched like a hawk by my concerned family. I only remember getting punched, going to my classroom, having my head explode in pain. Awakened by my good friend, I walked home.

I thought, *How could my mother do this to me? Doesn't she care? Isn't she going to fight for me?*

Have you ever let anger affect your relationship? My anger made me feel alone and dejected.

As a family, we went to church every Sunday morning, Sunday night, and Wednesday night. One would think I would remember many Sunday school classes, but I only have memories of a few lessons. Somehow, the knowledge that God should be in charge of my life, that He loved me, that I was to please Him with my actions, was planted in my head, but I didn't know where in the Bible that this truth was taught.

I may not remember much about my childhood, but there is one event I remember clearly. It happened many Sundays in a row. I was sitting in church, listening to the preacher speak. At the end of every sermon, he asked if anyone wanted to accept Jesus as their Savior. The tug I felt was so strong, it was like a rope pulling me down to him. I thought I had already accepted Jesus, so I assumed I was supposed to rededicate my life to Him or give my life to the mission field. So I rededicated my life again and again. This went on for weeks. Every Sunday morning, I was pulled down to the front. I even started sitting in the very last row, hoping I would be far enough away from that silly rope. Finally, the Holy Spirit got through to the preacher, and he asked my mother about my salvation. He was thinking I didn't really understand what it meant and that I was trying to get right with God.

That afternoon, Mom sat me down on her bed and asked what I knew about Jesus and what He did for me. She explained that I was sinful and could never stand before God with sin in my life. I was shocked. Just how did one get sinless? Because trust me, my cookie stealing wasn't going to stop. She said Jesus died for me, and through His death He took all my sins, past, current, and future to the grave with Him. If I asked to be forgiven, I would be, and then I could stand before God, blameless. All I had to do was accept the gift of life that Jesus had for me. I prayed for Jesus to be Lord over my life and to forgive me of all my sins. The weight that I felt lifting off my chest was wonderful, an amazing feeling.

After the accident, I always knew I was saved, even during the days of wondering if God was really around anymore. Do you ever wonder if God is really around? Is he some entity in the distance, sitting around, waiting for the world to end so he could get even with us? That is how I felt—hopeless—and that the Bible was pointless. Luckily, God never gives up on us. In Hebrews 13:5, God says, "I will never leave you or forsake you."

I always believed Jesus was God's Son, that He died for me, that God was in charge of everything, and that I was to trust and obey God's Word. The problem was, I couldn't remember where anything was in the Bible. I mixed up (and still do to this day) the characters in the Bible. Was it Joseph and Mary or Jacob and Mary? Did Joshua go into the Lion's den or was it Daniel? This makes for some very interesting conversations, but it also caused a lot of confusion in my mind. I knew what I knew, but I could not explain it to anyone. As time passed, I gave up trying to learn anything about the Bible. It was just too confusing, trying to keep all those stories and facts straight. God loved me, and I knew I was going to heaven. The in-between part just didn't make any sense. Have you ever wondered what all the Bible stuff means?

My bitterness toward my parents grew as well. I harbored those feelings that they didn't really care about me, and Satan used those feelings to affect the rest of my life. I left home at seventeen and struck out on my own. I was determined to prove I didn't need anyone, except for my sister. She had been my constant lifeline through everything I had put myself through. She was my best friend—someone I could talk to about anything, without any fear of rejection or ridicule. However, she did try to convince me that I was dropped off by aliens when I was a kid.

I quit thinking about God so much, even though I wanted Him to help me quit feeling awkward and out of place all the time.

I never rejected God, but I didn't see any relevance to the Bible written thousands of years ago. To be happy, I thought I needed to work hard and earn enough money to buy more things to fill the void I was feeling. Because I wasn't filling my mind with the truth of God's Word, I allowed Satan to fill my thoughts with negativity and worldly views that conflicted with God's Word. I looked for worldly solutions to my problems. I never thought about asking God.

As I got older, I wondered if God was real. Was this all made up to make me behave? Were the rules made up by my parents but blamed on God? I was a pretty good child—not a bad kid at all. I just had that darn chip on my shoulder. I didn't respect my parents, and for the life of me, I don't know how my father kept from knocking me flat on my butt a few times. He never laid a hand on me, but he did yell—a lot. So this God thing . . . why did I care? Why did I have such a strong urge to know Him? Why did I care what God thought about me? This really bugged me when I was between seventeen and twenty-five.

At one point during the time I was engaged, I couldn't get past the God thing. Why did it bother me so much that my fiancé had no interest in going to church? Really? Why on earth did I want to go to church? Somewhere in my soul, I knew that if my marriage was going to work, we both had to be on the same page when it came to God. My fiancé didn't have any need to put God in our lives, and I didn't want to put God out of my life. I didn't know why. I could not remember where all this was coming from. Why did this matter to me so much?

We eventually broke up, and I moved to Dallas. My sister also moved to Dallas, and we shared an apartment. Once again, we talked about the God thing. I wanted to know, once and for all, if this was true or just fictitious old-time religious platitudes that our parents had used to keep us in line during my "rebellious" days. I never prayed. I didn't know I was supposed to, so I had no clue how to find the truth. It only made sense that the truth could be found in church, but with so many religions out there, where should we go? I solved the problem by closing my eyes, opening the Yellow Pages to the religion section, and jabbing my finger down on the page. That was the church we would attend this time.

I was amazed how often I got an uneasy feeling during the

sermons at various churches. I felt the message was wrong, not teaching the truth about God's Word, but I didn't know how I knew that. I just knew the preaching wasn't quite right. So we went to a different church every weekend until we were about to give up. One church in downtown Dallas had beautiful stained-glass windows. I really wanted to see inside. The building had so much character. I convinced my sister to go the next weekend. It was there I found God again.

The first class we attended was so interesting. The two guys teaching and leading the singles department were wonderful. They were funny, real, and actually talked to God. Did you know you could talk to God? I didn't. Nor did I know we were allowed to speak to God like He was our friend. These two guys brought the Bible alive and quickly filled in the blanks I had about the old Bible stories. They made everything in the Bible relevant to my life. It was amazing to see how God worked throughout the ages to bring us salvation. The depth at which they taught was infectious.

Now, I can't imagine living my life without God at the very center of everything. The peace I feel is wonderful. Don't think, just because I try to put God first, that my life is peachy keen. We all experience trouble, disappointments, and overwhelming situations, but now I depend on God to help me through the tough times, and he rejoices with me during the good times.

When I look back at my life, I see how God protected me again and again. I put myself into some dangerous situations, yet I always walked away unscathed. I now know that the "feelings" I had were from the Holy Spirit guiding me away from people who wanted to hurt me. The Holy Spirit kept drawing me back to God. The Holy Spirit had brought me to Dallas. The Holy Spirit had been keeping me alive, for my entire life giving me that desire to know God.

I may be like an alien from outer space, but I believe God wants to be part of my life, just like He wants to be part of yours. Romans 3:23 says, "For all have sinned and fall short of the glory of God." He sent us Jesus to take the punishment for our sins.

God's Holy Spirit is always willing to listen, give us guidance, and show us God's love, no matter what. Jesus was sent to die so we can be forgiven for all our sins.

Jesus said, "I am the way and the truth and the life. No one comes to the Father except through me." Are you ready to accept

Jesus as your Savior?

Denisa Klein *was raised in Oklahoma, but a career opportunity moved her to Texas in 1983. She has been the IT Manager of an independent oil and gas company for the past thirty years. After renewing her relationship with God, she became active in Messianic Ministries. She helped establish Messianic congregations in the Dallas/Plano areas. She worked in the children's ministries for twenty years at one congregation before joining Beth Sar Shalom in Plano, where she volunteers in the technology ministry.*

Thoughts to Ponder
from The Alien

1. God has made each one of us unique.

2. We don't have to be a Bible scholar to accept Jesus as Lord and Savior.

3. God leads us to answers when we have questions about Him.

When have you felt alienated from God?

For I will forgive their wickedness and will remember their sins no more — Hebrews 8:12

The Professor's Empty Car
by Nancy Holdeman

When I was eight, my father decided family life wasn't for him. He moved out of our coffee-colored clapboard house at 2925 North Hackett Avenue without saying goodbye. I never saw him load up his station wagon, but his cleared-out closet, bare dusty dresser, and the constant ache in my gut supplied enough evidence. I wish I could say he took a job across the country, and that's why I never saw him. But he lived only a couple miles from us, worked two blocks away, and still parked his car in front of our house.

Until that bewildering exit, I adored my father. I loved how his eyes sparkled when he was happy. I loved the confident sound of his voice and his strong hand holding mine. Around supper time, I often perched on the front concrete steps of our house, counting down the minutes before his arrival. Antsy, I hopped down to the chalk-lined sidewalk, eager to catch a glimpse of him in the distance. I instantly recognized his familiar stride as he turned the corner to walk the two short blocks home from the university campus. My little spirit ignited, launching my legs directly toward my daddy until I slammed, breathless, into his chest. He scooped me up with one arm, briefcase in the other. His hug was worth all the dimes, nickels, and pennies in my piggy bank. Looking up, I caught a glimmer of joy in his eye and deposited it in my heart as we walked the final block toward home.

My father was a professor, and during the more carefree summer months, I was his protégé. Six years old, the youngest of four daughters, I couldn't keep up with my sisters and their friends. I followed dad around the yard, pestering him with questions. I liked "helping" him and learning the ways of the world from the master teacher—the joys of mowing the lawn and talking to neighbors, the importance of cutting a sharp, straight edge to the grass along the sidewalk, and best of all—tying up stacks of old newspapers with twine. We loaded them into the back of our cavernous Ford station wagon and hauled them to the recycler. I loved the adventure. And Dad let me keep the seventy-five cents we got in return. I was rich. In every way.

Dad's abrupt departure from my world was hard to

comprehend. All I knew for sure was that he was gone—at least the father part. The professor still parked his car in front of our house. He wanted full advantage of the free permit that came with our address, since parking was hard to come by near the crowded university. I soon learned that he was never going to come in to see me or check if I was okay. I never understood why. And since he never explained it, I had to reach my own conclusion: the parking place was valuable, and *I was not.* The painful message pierced my heart every day when I got off the yellow school bus and glanced at his empty car. I cut across the neighbor's lawn so I wouldn't have to see his beige driving cap and sunglasses on the seat.

That was as close as I got to him. An empty car.

On rare occasions, he'd slip in the side door to grab a tool from the basement and disappear like a vapor. Those brief, detached appearances stung just as much. More often, darkness veiled his departures, and he chose the easier option to bypass the house at Hackett Avenue. He'd slide into the front seat of his 1970 Ford Country Squire, pull away from our front curb, and drive toward his better life just over the bridge. Did he ever wonder how his four daughters were coping? He should have.

Inside the house, his wife was disintegrating. His children had to take care of her when they did not even know how to take care of themselves. With her mind tormented by his rejection, she became addicted to tranquilizers, passing out for hours. With kids in the car, she swerved off the road. When the drug effects wore off, my mother's raw emotions took aim and fired directly at my sisters and me. She needed to accuse someone for the misery she couldn't escape. From elementary school through college, the neglect and verbal assaults continued. Mom's mental health fractured even further, descending into paranoid, psychotic breaks and terrifying tirades.

As the same pathetic scene replayed outside our home for a decade, the car models changed but the man who drove and parked them did not. I hardened myself, the scar tissue building up over time.

My father wanted a life without me. It wasn't long before I wanted a life without him.

Anger created a scab that covered my open wound much better than the daily confusion and pain. Stronger, defiant thoughts rose to numb the internal ache: *I don't need him. I don't need her. I don't need anyone.* Eventually, those thoughts shifted into a vow: *I will take care of myself.*

For years, that single, subconscious oath fueled every action and achievement. At the very least, it ensured my survival, but it also delivered some benefits. God used my bold determination to accomplish His purposes. When I stumbled across a magazine insert detailing a ten-week overseas mission trip for teens, I knew I had the perfect opportunity to escape my volatile home environment for the summer. I signed up immediately and raised the funds. Soon I was on my way to Florida for boot-camp training.

While teaching construction skills my team would need for our work in France, the leaders shared some wonderful truths. I learned that Jesus came to earth to sacrifice His life, bear the penalty for my sinful choices, and restore my broken connection with God. I had always believed in God, but I never knew He desired a personal relationship with me and went to incredible lengths to secure my salvation. At the age of seventeen, once I understood the amazing gift of grace He offered, I gave my heart to Christ.

I identified so readily with the love of Jesus and His gift of eternal life, but a close relationship with God the Father eluded me. For years, God had seemed aloof and removed from the details of my life. It wasn't true, but my warped perspective obscured His presence. I pursued more palpable rewards—friends, fun, a college degree, and a profession. Soon, it paid off.

Supporting myself, independent and free, I opened a new world. I liked the freedom and ability to shape my own life. Empowered, I viewed my intense drive and soaring ambition as laser determination, and I welcomed the rewards and status I earned along the way.

I landed in a career that furnished everything I wanted. Excitement. Advancement. Eighty-hour work weeks seemed normal—even noble. Six promotions in seven years supplied the recognition I had always craved. It seemed the universe had rewarded my efforts with success, and more importantly, with money—the currency of independence. And security.

While friends dated and planned their dream weddings, I silently scoffed. They wanted a man, a family—which were weak and fragile desires. My goal was to own a house by the age of thirty. That was something solid to bank on. So I bought mine at twenty-nine. With acreage. I saw all that I had made, and behold: it was very good.

I will stop at nothing to ensure my success. It wasn't an overt proclamation, but more like a compulsion, driving me to pursue my goals at any cost, even if it meant driving my health into the ground. As it turned out, not even I could work fifty consecutive sixteen-hour days without a day off—while swallowing six Advils a day for the tension headaches, caffeinating all day, and calming down with alcohol at night. It was a lethal combination.

Apparently, I had been bleeding internally for several days. Precious pints of blood seeped into my intestines through an ibuprofen-induced ulcer. When I passed out, I had already lost half my blood. I survived, but the doctors informed me that I would have died if my blood hadn't clotted at just the right moment. Raw sores lined the inside of my mouth, a sign of blood poisoning and a circulatory system struggling to keep up.

It took six months to build back my blood volume and my strength. During that time, I learned what it felt like to be weak, and I didn't like it. For the first time in my life, my body failed me. It continued to let me down. With a severely weakened immune system, I was no match for an onslaught of viral infections that ravaged what was left of my health—one virus after another. Weeks became months as I withered away inside my home. Bound to my bed, I felt like a prisoner of my body and circumstances beyond my control. Despite a barrage of doctors, diagnoses, and treatments, I was not recovering.

Like the towering walnut tree outside my home, which was shedding its leaves for winter, my body gradually lost every trace of strength. I received a devastating new diagnosis: post-viral cardiomyopathy—heart failure. There would be no going back to work, no reclaiming the life I knew. All the savings I had accumulated quickly disappeared, swallowed up by a sinkhole of medical expenses.

Even the man brave enough to date me chose to extricate himself from this unwelcome situation, citing the I-didn't-sign-up-for-this clause. I'd be fine, though, since I'd decided long before that men were unreliable and unnecessary. I'd be fine, if I could just keep my house—my sanctuary. But without an income, that too fell out of my grasp. A cheerful realtor named Jack posted his glossy red sign on the front lawn.

I was a shadow of my former self. A strong will could not rescue me from a body that had already given up. I could no longer care for myself. *I could not keep my vow.* I couldn't even climb the stairs. While I waited for the house to sell, nice people from the neighborhood church mowed my lawn, washed my dirty clothes, and cleaned my house. I felt like an invalid. I was nothing without my career, my identity. I was losing everything I valued and worked so hard to gain. Without physical strength and confidence to shore me up, serious cracks appeared in my mental foundation.

On September 11, 2001, I woke up to the worst terrorist attack in United States history. As it unfolded live on television, I watched in horror as the second plane full of passengers flew directly into New York's World Trade Center, exploding in a massive fireball. In disbelief, I witnessed each majestic tower collapse, entombing thousands of innocent lives in a toxic heap of crushed concrete and twisted metal. My mind could not absorb the enormous tragedy and loss of life. It was too much. Something within me broke.

I collapsed into my overstuffed chair by the window and sobbed. I cried for hours—paralyzed—as if the weight of all that grief had landed on me. *I'm falling apart.* I couldn't seem to pull myself out of it. I called four people before Suzie answered the phone, and like a good friend, she arrived at my door within minutes. Unsure how to help her crumbling friend, Suzie gave me a quick hug, then stepped inside to tackle something more tangible. She cleared a layer of clutter from my kitchen, humming as she wiped the counters clean. She changed my bed linens, hoping that a fresh set of yellow, floral-print sheets might lift me out of my pit. It was a sweet gesture, and I tried to smile. But the flood of tears continued, impossible to quell.

I needed help, so I called a counselor in Madison I'd read about. Steve was a pastor who counseled people using methods that went beyond traditional talk therapy and invited God into the process. "Transformational prayer," he called it. Steve had experienced so much healing himself that he became a certified full-time practitioner. He invited me to try a session. Since he didn't charge a fee, I had nothing to lose. I booked an appointment for the following week.

Monday morning, my friend Brenda pulled up to my house with a travel mug full of hot coffee and a prayer for God's blessing. She drove the hour-long trip to Steve's office while I stared out the window, wondering what had happened to me. As the mile markers ticked by along Interstate 94, I noticed a dead deer and other unfortunate animals that had been hit by speeding cars, cast to the side of road to rot. Some had been run over so many times, they were flattened. That was how I felt.

Steve's office was located in an old Catholic monastery in the hills outside Madison, overlooking Lake Mendota. The aging campus housed a Buddhist retreat center and a few other random tenants. I thought it was odd—not the usual place I'd expect to find a Christian counselor—but Steve loved to break with convention. Clad in a bright red collegiate sweatshirt, blue jeans, and athletic shoes, he looked more like a coach than a clinician.

Steve greeted me with unexpected warmth, inviting me into his small, minimally equipped office. He was anything but serious, and his face beamed with joy—quite the contrast to my melancholy demeanor.

"How ya doin'?"

He didn't seem at all rattled by my road kill analogy. Then I launched into my family and health history.

Steve interrupted and grinned. "Oh, I don't need to know that. God already knows, and He can't wait to help. He'll lead the way if you let Him. Just listen, look inside, and be honest. I'll be here to facilitate your conversation with Him."

A conversation with God. That was a new concept.

With Steve's kind coaching, I closed my eyes, and we entered God's presence to start an honest dialog, which began with an extended stretch of silence. Unphased, Steve explained that there was obviously something blocking my connection. He asked me to look around for any painful or angry places. My mind leapt to the searing image of my father's parked car in front of our house and the cumulative impact of his daily choices to neglect his children. As an adult, my spirit rose up with indignation, appalled that any parent could be so calloused.

Steve acknowledged my genuine emotion, yet gently redirected my focus. "Can you look at me, Nancy?"

I looked up into his compassionate eyes.

"In order to heal," he said, "the strong, angry woman needs to step aside so that little girl can face the reality of what happened."

It took some time and prodding, but I laid down my armor of self-protection. And when I did, the tears of a thousand days found their first honest expression, and an unspeakably sad child whispered her answer to the question that had plagued her all her life. *She must be so worthless, that her father would not walk twenty steps up from the curb to see her.*

My little soul had internalized that distorted belief. It had become my unspoken, internal landscape, enmeshed with dozens of other lies. Articulating this realization in Steve's presence helped me understand the depths of damage that God wanted to expose and heal. It was both painful and precious.

Every Monday for the next six months, and regularly over the next two years, Steve prayed and probed while God worked on my heart like a skillful locksmith. A lot more was locked inside, emotional debris from too many traumatic experiences at the hands of a mentally unstable mother. Memory by memory, we revisited the painful and scary places. It wasn't an easy process as we unearthed buried pain and entrenched patterns. But God artfully exposed the lies and removed them one by one. He filled the raw places with beautiful truths, carrying the sadness away. It felt like a miracle every time.

The most meaningful breakthrough was recognizing the truth that God wasn't at all like my earthly father. God loved to show up, come inside, and check how I was doing. I came to know and love this Abba Father and cherish my relationship as His beloved daughter. I couldn't wait to visit with Him. I relished our intimate connection since He had always seemed so distant before.

As my heart healed and began to look more like His, God delivered an unexpected revelation—an image of my father: sad, lost, broken, sorely in need of forgiveness and a loving touch from Jesus. Would I offer that gift? Dad was about to turn eighty, and who knew how long he'd be on this earth?

After a few months of wrestling with the idea, I got on a plane to Fort Lauderdale and drove north to Pompano Beach. Just as the sun started to set, I steered my polished rental car onto the gravel bank in front of Dad's worn-out, shell-pink stucco house. I sat in the car for a few minutes, contemplating the irony and difficulty of the choice God was leading me to make. God's love was compelling me toward my father's door, something I could not have done on my own.

When Professor Smith opened the door, he was arched over and shirtless, wearing stained khaki shorts and slippers, a shadow of the strong and confident man I remembered from my childhood. The years and memories had left their mark on his soul, but he welcomed me in. With a glass of orange juice, he beckoned me to his back yard to bask in the sunshine. Sitting on bleached-out plastic chairs under the palm trees, kicking the mix of sand and weeds that used to be his manicured lawn, we began the awkward conversation. It took hours, over several days, to arrive at a meaningful exchange—a challenging quest as I shouted over his hearing loss and the growl of single-engine planes taking off from the nearby airstrip—but we got there. I shared my story, the impact of his choices, and what really went on inside the brown house on Hackett Avenue.

He wept with remorse, explaining the little he could. I offered him the gifts of grace and love that I had received from my Savior. I watched his eyes tear up again, but this time his shoulders let go of a lifetime of unexpressed grief. They were poignant, unforgettable moments. I will always treasure the impact of that conversation and the connection that followed. In a sacred exchange, straight from the hand of God, I had found my father and gave him the gift of grace. It was as easy as getting out of my parked car, walking up the steps, and knocking on his heart.

Nancy Holdeman *established her professional career by creating innovative marketing campaigns for Fortune 500 companies. After fifteen years of agency work, she now devotes her efforts to nonprofits. Her communications company, "Shine Media," advances the reach of vital organizations around the world. Nancy lives in Dallas, Texas, with her husband Mark. They enjoy scenic mountain getaways, wandering rustic nature trails, and bike riding with their dog Elsie, who relishes the scents and views from her custom carrier. Contact Nancy at* ***ShineMediaCreative@gmail.com.***

Thoughts to Ponder
from The Professor's Empty Car

1. God is a good Father, even if your earthly father wasn't.

2. Freedom from broken dreams and hurts often takes time and effort.

3. Show grace to others as God showed grace to you.

> **For what do you need to forgive your earthly father?**

See what great love the Father has lavished on us, that we should be called children of God! And that is what we are! — 1 John 3:1

Out of Darkness into Light
by Shirley Gomez

Growing up, I should have been the happiest girl around. I had a father who never ceased to express that I was the apple of his eye and a mother who devoted her life to caring for our home. But I wasn't happy.

Born of Indian descent, I grew up in the Philippines. At different times, my parents migrated to the Philippines from India, settling in Bacolod, the city where I was born. My father came to join his older brother who worked in Bacolod. He met my mother there, who was already living in Bacolod with her family. My father got a job working for my grandfather (my mother's father) at one of his stores. After some time, my father and mother married. When I was six months old, we moved to Manila. With four older siblings, three brothers, and one sister, our house was full. I shared a room with my sister, who was nine years my senior.

Sadly, the main cause of my unhappiness was my oldest brother. He was very abusive—not just to me but to our entire family. It was obvious from his actions that he was an angry and deeply wounded soul. He often demonstrated his anger through irrational and physically hurtful behavior.

To avoid going home after school, I often took long walks alone, wallowing in loneliness and despair. When my father, an exporter, went on occasional business trips, I spent countless hours cooped up in my room, trying to avoid my brother. Without my father's presence, my brother found greater opportunity to torment me and the rest of the family.

Being Hindu, our family traditionally went to the Hindu temple on Sunday to pay our respect to so-called "gods." During my early teens, I began to wonder and developed philosophical questions about who the Christian God was. I was curious about what He looked like. Was he Indian like me? Or perhaps American or Chinese? I also wondered if he was aware of my misery. I turned to the "religious" teachers—the Catholic nuns who taught my religion classes—for the answers I was looking for. But even they could not offer answers that satisfied.

God, however, knew of my quest. He sent my cousin to me—

who not too long ago had left the Hindu faith to follow the living God. During the two weeks of her visit, in a gentle and non-judgmental manner, she told me how she had come to believe in Jesus Christ and that she had accepted Him as her Lord and Savior. With the senseless wisdom I had gained from being a believer in a false Hindu prophet, I debated everything she said. But my cousin had planted a grain of truth in my mind. God promised that "His Word that goes out from His mouth will not return to Him empty, but will accomplish what He desires and achieve the purpose for which He sent it" (Isaiah 55:11 NLT).

And that it did.

After my cousin left, I couldn't help but think about all she had said. I was sitting in a chair one afternoon, gazing out a window in the living room, when her words echoed in my mind. Suddenly, for reasons I can't explain, it started to make sense—like a light bulb had been turned on within me. My cousin's words led me closer to the answers I had been looking for. It dawned on me that what I was seeking was exactly what my cousin had found—a relationship with a living God.

I approached my mom and asked if we could start attending church. Being a Hindu her entire life, it was inevitable that my mom would think I had gone insane. Even though the idea of attending church was rejected by my mom, a still, small voice within me kept insisting that I approach my father with the same idea. This really didn't make sense, because my mom—not my dad—was the "religious" one in my family.

Years later, I heard my pastor say that if something can be explained, then it most likely isn't from God. And though I could not understand why the voice was prompting me to go to my dad, I did it anyway. I went into his room and sat beside him on his bed. After suggesting the idea of going to church, I learned an amazing thing. My father had been watching *The 700 Club* on television and had prayed the prayer of salvation with the host of show.

The following Sunday, my dad and I, and even my mother, went to church. It was on this very day that my father and I accepted Jesus Christ into our hearts as our personal Lord and Savior. And though it may have seemed that my mom too had made the same choice, I later discovered that she never really did. She just did what every good Indian wife would do: follow what her husband did, even if she didn't agree or understand. We attended a Pentecostal church regularly. I later joined a Baptist home church whose members consisted of Indians—Sindhis like ourselves. The church was pastored by a missionary couple whose hearts' desire was to lead Indians to a true knowledge of the Lord.

After becoming a Christian, I can't say that everything was smooth sailing from there on out. In many ways, my life turned upside down. Jesus warned us that "in this world we would have trouble" (John 16:33). My father passed away about a year later, and the only comfort I had was to know that he died a believer. But our family had suffered a great loss. He was the provider of food, shelter, and all the material possessions we needed. And now, in the blink of an eye, he was gone. We rushed him to the hospital on a Sunday afternoon, and he died the following morning. We never knew exactly what caused the internal bleeding that led to his death. I was right there with him when he said goodbye to this world.

I immediately felt like a lost sheep without a shepherd. I no longer had an earthly father who would provide and protect me. I now had to trust and rely on my heavenly Father—a Father I could not see, but who promised to never leave or forsake me.

The situation with my brother worsened after my father died. The two younger of my three older brothers left for the United States, and my mother and I were left to deal with the emotional and physical abuse of my oldest brother, which got more severe by the day. Finally, we had no choice but to leave. Early one morning, my mother and I escaped like fugitives, without any clear destination in mind. We relied on the kindness of missionaries to provide temporary shelter and food. By this time, my mother had returned to the Hindu faith. When we could no longer rely on the missionaries, my mom and I left for Bacolod and stayed with relatives for six months, moving from one home to another like Gypsies. Leaving Manila didn't keep us safe from my brother, who followed us all the way to my uncle's house in Bacolod. His tormenting continued, leaving us hopeless and in great despair. Then, when all seemed lost, God provided the way for my mom and me to come to the U. S.

Although living a great distance away from my brother brought tremendous relief, we had to face a new set of challenges. We didn't have our own home like we did back in the Philippines. We

98

relied on my aunt for a room in her house. Since neither my mom nor I had a car, or knew how to drive, we were dependent on my aunt for transportation. This predicament made it difficult for me to work or go to school. I was stuck at home. Since I had no college education, the only job I could qualify for was that of a telemarketer. And though I was fortunate to have my mom and my uncle, my dad's brother, both of whom provided financial support, I struggled psychologically and emotionally. I struggled because I carried with me the brokenness and scars from my past. What made it worse was I had no direction or purpose in life.

During my loneliness, I took walks and poured out my heart to God. I would wonder and query what His purpose was for my life. Exactly what was He trying to accomplish, and how much pain must I go through before His work in my life was complete?

In 2001, ten years after coming to the U.S., God finally revealed His will for my life: I was to be a teacher. How God revealed His plan still amazes me. I began attending a small Indian church, where the pastor gave me the opportunity as a volunteer to teach English to Indian and Pakistani people from nearby communities. Later, I volunteered as an "English as a Second Language" (ESL) teacher at a mega-church. Three years after that, God paved the way for me to go back to school.

During my last year of college, I met my husband to be, Joseph, an Indian who had come to the States from Singapore. He was a Christian. It had been almost twenty years since I felt a desire to be married, and I was beginning to give up on meeting someone who would be the mate I needed. Then in the spring of 2006, the Lord answered my heart's desire. He sent Joseph just when I was beginning to believe I was destined to live a life of solitude.

After three years of writing research papers, cramming for exams, and completing projects, I finally graduated in the spring of 2006 with a Bachelor's degree in Interdisciplinary Studies. I immediately started working for a prominent school district in Dallas. Challenges I faced at work as a middle school teacher led me to question whether I was indeed meant to teach. It then dawned on me that although I was fulfilling my calling to be a teacher, I wasn't working with the students I was intended to teach. My experience in teaching began as a volunteer ESL instructor to adults, not to grade school or high school students. I soon realized that if I were to ever teach at a college level, I would need a master's degree. With Joseph's encouragement and God's prompting, I went back to school once more, this time for my graduate degree, which I completed three and a half years ago. Praise God!

Not only did the Lord help me attain a graduate degree in Reading and ESL, but He even opened the door for me to teach at Dallas Baptist University (DBU), the very school from which I graduated. I remember driving on campus to go to my classes, thinking how nice it would be to teach at this university. Then I quickly reminded myself how farfetched that dream was. But in January 2014, a month after graduating, I was offered a job as an ESL instructor at DBU's Intensive English Department, where I currently work. I go to work each day thanking God for such an awesome opportunity, which I don't take lightly, for I know it is only by God's grace and mercy that I am where I am today. I am in awe of what He has accomplished in my life.

Joseph and I are approaching our ninth wedding anniversary. I wish I could say that getting married solved all my problems, particularly the loneliness I used to feel as a young girl. The truth is, life has been everything but perfect. It's been more of a rollercoaster ride, filled with lots of ups and downs. Joseph and I continue to seek God's will for our lives, at times feeling confused as to what that will is. It is then that I must remind myself that I am no longer the lost little girl I once was. I am His child. I trust that in due time He will reveal His desire for our lives. Until then, just like the apostle Paul, I press on and continue to run the race that is set before me.

The Christian life is not an easy path, which is why the Lord said, "narrow is the way that leads to eternal life, and few are those who walk in it." One thing I am sure of: there is no other way and no other God who can love me enough to die for my sins. There is no other God who can forgive me of every evil thought and deed I have committed. And no other God can provide me with the hope of eternal life. Therefore, amidst all the struggles and challenges I continue to face in this life, I press on toward the One who loves me with a love that cannot be comprehended. And though I cannot see Him, I know He is with me, and will be to the end of my days.

Shirley Gomez is a former teacher at Dallas Baptist University and taught a course on English as a second language for fifteen years at a Dallas/Fort Worth mega church. After growing up in the Philippines, and living in Dallas for many years, Shirley has recently relocated to Nashville, Tennessee. You can reach Shirley by email at:

SanamSurtani@yahoo.com.

Thoughts to Ponder
from Out of Darkness into Light

1. False religions can never satisfy.

2. Through prayer, God can provide escape from oppression.

3. We all have a God-given purpose.

What has God called you to do?

In their hearts humans plan their course, but the LORD *establishes their steps. — Proverbs 16:9*

Liberated in Grace and Mercy
by Jessica Lusk

"Jesus . . . Jesus . . . Jesus!"

I woke myself up with my own muffled screams of help for what seemed like the millionth time. Sitting up in bed, I shuddered at the recurring night terrors. I was reliving a real-life nightmare, which occurred eight years earlier, when I was sixteen. I was robbed and almost raped and kidnapped.

I closed my eyes as scenes from the event flashed in my mind as if it had just happened. But it wasn't just the event that haunted me—it was eight years of bondage from the hate and unforgiveness I still harbored.

At 6:30 a.m. on February 4, 2006, I was working at a barbecue restaurant and convenience store. Two male employees manned the morning shift with me. Both were behind the restaurant, preparing the briskets on the smoker. I was alone in the store, which was not uncommon or anything I feared.

When the door dinged with the entry of a customer, I was focused on preparing the breakfast sandwiches for our deli section. I turned to my left to acknowledge the customer. When my eyes met his, I froze. My spirit knew something was wrong. Having become a Christian at age twelve and filled with the Holy Spirit, I had an overwhelming visceral sense to be on guard. I knew this was a prompting of the Spirit. If there had been a panic button to call employees in the back to come to the front, I would have immediately pushed it.

A still, small voice whispered, "Do not turn your back to him." Facing the customer, I stood, body clenched, with my back pressed against the counter. He walked confidently, like he had a plan. He moved over to the ATM machine and fumbled with the keypad. Seconds later, he walked down the first two aisles, then made his way to the counter and asked what town we were in.

I answered his question.

The way his eyes burned into mine made me want to disappear, but I had nowhere to go.

He walked to the deli section and watched the pecan cobbler warming under the heat lamp. "Is that cobbler any good?"

"It is, but it's still frozen."

He walked aimlessly down the fourth aisle while continuing to make small talk.

I began to loosen my guard.

He walked to the end of the deli section, where an ice cream bin stood at the wall. The space between the ice cream and deli section was a walkway to behind the counter—my territory. He stared at the ice cream, then walked to the last aisle. "Say, do you have any ice cream or something? I'm just so hungry."

A red flag waved violently in my spirit. I had watched him stare at the ice cream. Why would he ask if we had any? Before I could answer, the ding of the microwave announced that my breakfast sandwiches were cooked. I walked to the microwaves, two feet from the ice cream bin.

He followed my walk.

"Yes," I said, "we have ice cream. It's down here." The microwave dinged with a second alert. I turned my back to him for just a moment, to open the microwave. With it dark outside, when I looked up, the large window in front of me acted as a mirror. I watched this man walk from the nearby ice cream bin into the small space that didn't belong to him or any other customer.

He entered my territory.

He kept coming.

I stood frozen. I watched as he grabbed my long blonde ponytail from behind and yanked me closer to him. His lips were on my ear. threatening me, whispering profanity.

I could smell him. I felt his breath and lips on my neck. And I laughed. I thought it was a joke, a cruel joke.

Within seconds, I realized it wasn't a laughing matter. The man, or the demon in this man, was serious. He ordered me to get him the money as he dragged me to the cash register.

I emptied it for him.

He ordered me to lock the door, but I didn't have keys to lock the door. He didn't believe me, becoming angry as he dragged me around the counter near the front door. I repeatedly cried I didn't have keys. My state of terror became even more intense when we reached the door. A car parked in front of the store had its back-door open.

He dragged me to the door. He was going to take me.

I screamed for the other employees.

The man stopped, still holding me tightly, and asked if someone else was at the store.

I said yes, they could get him keys, more money, whatever he wanted.

His demeanor changed. He seemed to like the idea. He violently turned me around and with his arm around my neck, dragged me to the door to the back of the store.

I was scared for my life.

His eyes were crazy, flooded with rage.

I stopped fighting for a moment and turned to look into his lost eyes. "Please. Please! I want my mommy. I just want to see my mommy again." Tears were streaming down my face. I became a sixteen-year-old again. My knowing everything, and my I-didn't-need-my-parents attitude dissipated as I begged to be in my mom's arms one more time.

It's strange how, in times of crisis, we tend to cry out to the ones we think we don't *need* anymore, including God.

This man couldn't have cared less about my deep cries to let me go. It actually made him angrier. We went through the door that led to the back of the store. The office door was to the right. To the left, the entrance to the kitchen. The two male employees were nowhere in sight.

I screamed for them, trying to break free.

He yanked me to him and wrapped his left hand around my throat, choking me. He jabbed something in my side with his right hand. "Calm down, or I will shoot you," he screamed.

I froze. It never occurred to me that he had a gun. Tears streamed down my face. With a shaking voice, I "calmly" called for the employees.

They appeared at the back door of the kitchen, while we were standing at the other entrance. I was relieved to see them. They were going to help me. They froze in shock for a few seconds. Slowly they walked through the door. The man yelled for them to stop. They put their arms in the air in surrender, and he ordered them to the floor.

This was a pivotal moment in this scene of terror. I watched as these two men, the ones I thought were going to save me, slowly—almost as if time had stopped—lower their bodies to the kitchen floor. Their hands gripped the concrete, their noses and cheeks touching the floor.

It hit me. They could not save me. Evidently they were not supposed to.

As anyone would be in this scenario, I was fearful. Afraid for my life.

God met me in my fear. I felt His power beckoning to me. "Jesus," I screamed. "Jesus! I need You." I learned from an early age that calling upon the name of Jesus is like calling on the nation's armed forces, but more powerful.

As I continued my calls to God, one of the employees on the floor said there was a safe in the office behind us, and he had keys. Obviously, he thought more money would convince the guy to let me go.

The idea of going into the office intrigued the intruder. He ordered the men up from the floor, commanding them to unlock the door to the office.

The men obliged. Once the door was unlocked, one of the employees grabbed my arm to pull me into the office.

The intruder did not like this. He pulled me to him even tighter as he spewed profanity at the men. He ordered them to go into the office, lock the door, and not come out.

My heart sank. I was alone with this stranger again.

His body pressed against mine, his lips on my neck.

I was so confused. Why didn't he demand the money out of the safe? Why didn't he just let me go? Wasn't he scared someone else would come in? It would appear as if my concerns were not his. He pulled the hat on my baby blue hoodie yanking me up to him. He violently turned me around.

"Jesus," I whispered. "Please help me."

I knew in my spirit what was going to happen next.

"Take off your clothes," he said in a demonic tone.

I just stared at this man, a lost soul. "No!" I said boldly.

He looked at me as if I were the crazy one, his eyes filled with rage once more. His following words were profane and too crass for me to repeat.

I shook my head uncontrollably. "No! Jesus, Jesus. Jesus!" I cried. Jesus was the only power I had. The men I thought were going to save me couldn't. Only God could.

106

I then remembered every tactic my daddy taught me as a child, preparing me for a situation like this. "Act crazier than them," he said. My inner survival mode kicked into high gear. I hadn't seen a gun yet. In my mind, I would have rather have been shot than raped. So I took my daddy's advice. I acted crazier than the senseless man in front of me. I began kicking the stack of boxes in front of us.

He grabbed hold of me from behind.

I thrashed my body loose from his grasp and prayed out loud.

The look on this man's face was one of shock. He looked scared.

There is power in the name of Jesus. There is power in that name.

He fled.

I could easily say it was something *I did* that saved my life that day. But I know better. It was the power of the Holy Spirit in the atmosphere. It was calling on my heavenly Daddy to intervene in this dark and demonic situation. My God is real.

I don't remember a time of not believing in God. From a young girl, I talked to God, knowing He was there, listening. But this day changed my relationship with the Lord forever. I tapped into the power of God and the fact that He dwells in us. With Him, we are powerful beyond comprehension.

However, this episode opened the door for the enemy to attack me on many levels. Never in my sixteen years had I been scared of anyone or anything. I was described as "fearless" by family. No longer was I fearless. I feared nighttime. I had night terrors, reliving the events of that morning. I hadn't noticed skin colors before. Now I was leery of any African American male. These fears opened the door for years of bondage and hate that spread in my heart.

I slowly sunk into a dark place. I wasn't me without my "fearless" attitude. So I put on an armor of hard exterior instead of the armor of God. I became harsh and uncompassionate. Many of my friends and family didn't enjoy being around me anymore. We lived in a small town, and news spread like wildfire, even to surrounding counties. When the intruder fled, he headed north and was caught in the next county by the Department of Public Safety when they laid spikes on the highway.

His trial began in November 2007, more than a year after his assault in February 2006. By this time, I had graduated high school and was in my first semester of college. I continued to battle my demons alone. I pushed everyone away, including my parents. My mom encouraged me to talk to her. When I wouldn't open up, she asked me to speak to a therapist. I refused. I insisted I was fine. I was not fine. I just didn't know it yet.

Life went on. After spending days in the trial, recounting this dark day, watching actual footage of the man wrestling me, caught on surveillance cameras. Seeing this man in person, not just in my nightmares, triggered something in me, something dark. I was angry at God and at the world. I didn't know how to cope with these emotions. During my testimony, the defense attorney painted a picture of the white girl being racist, trying to send the African-American man to prison. It enraged and humiliated me. It was obvious from the evidence, seeing the footage of him assaulting me, that no part of my testimony had anything to do with race. But it's funny how the mind works. It seemed, after the experience of the trial, Satan slithered his way into my mind even more. The seed of racism was planted and blossomed before I could recognize it.

My attacker was sentenced to prison—ten years for Aggravated Robbery. The District Attorney tried to add Attempted Sexual Assault and Attempted Kidnapping to the charge but wasn't successful. The judge considered the fact that the man had served in Iraq and was dealing with Post Traumatic Stress Disorder (PTSD). I didn't care. Soldiers who came home with PTSD didn't rob stores or assault females, ruining their lives and giving *them* PTSD. That sounds dramatic, but it was the truth. My life was never the same after this incident. A simple trip to the grocery store could turn into an emotional meltdown. Fear was sucking the life out of me. I was so jumpy. I had a cart full of groceries when an African-American man looked at me oddly and triggered paralyzing fear. I deserted my full cart and fled the store.

To this day, I have to sit in certain seats and directions in restaurants. I cannot have my back to people. I refuse Brookshire's cart hopping service in my town. No way do I want an unknown male following me to my car.

When the trial ended, I felt like I could breathe. Or so I thought. If you know the legal system, a sentence of ten years or less allows you to apply for Community Supervision, or parole, after so much time served. So there I was, still healing from the first trial, only to find out we had to go back to trial in April 2008 for a motion to get Community Supervision.

I was working as a secretary at the District Attorney's office. I had become close with the DA and his staff during the preparation of the first trial. When I found out they had an opening, I applied and was hired on the spot. This made the second trial less stressful. However, I was still a mess inside. But no one knew it. The judge denied the motion. The man remained in prison.

I was sitting on the first row behind the defendant when he rose and turned toward me. Guards flooded the area, restraining him. He turned to the judge and begged her to speak with me, then turned to face me with a look of pure hatred. "I want to speak to you and apologize." His demeanor showed otherwise.

I was speechless. There were guards around my mom and me. All I could do was shake my head no. I couldn't talk to him. I was fearful of him. The guards ushered me out of the courtroom, and I was trembling as we walked into the hallway. I felt so bound with fear and hatred. Again, the trial hearings hit the media. I couldn't seem to escape from this nightmare, either in real life or in my nightmares.

I was young and didn't know how to deal with the attention and pity. It was an impressionable time in my life. The world said I should hate him, that I should want him to go to prison for a long time. The world said I should be racist. The world said I was a victim. The world never mentioned the word "forgiveness." My fleshly mind could not fathom "forgiveness." It never even crossed my mind.

Sadly, I clothed myself in *What the World Said*.

Four years later, I moved to a new city where I met a man who forever changed my life. I knew he would be my husband. Early in our courtship, I felt it necessary to tell him about this event. His eyes were wide as he listened intently to my testimony.

I retold the events with fear and hatred.

He grabbed my hands. "Let's pray. Lord, thank you for this beautiful woman sitting next to me. Thank you for being with her in this situation. Lord, I ask that You meet her attacker in prison. Show Yourself to him. May he come to salvation. May Your face shine upon him. May you continue to heal Jess and show her Your grace and mercy."

Wow!

Honestly, I was taken aback by his prayer. My flesh was hurt that in this moment, he prayed for the criminal more than he prayed for me. That was complete *victim mentality*. In the six years since that terrifying day, it had never dawned on me to pray for my attacker. A huge seed was planted that night. I had a choice to be a victim, living in fear, or I could admit to my psychological issues rooted from this tragedy and seek God for true healing.

In the years that followed, it was a slow journey wrapping my mind around forgiving. The Lord was continuously revealing His grace and mercy. One day, it hit me. How can I expect God to forgive me if I am withholding forgiveness for this man? We are called to a higher purpose than *What the World Says*. I wrote the man letters but never sent them. It was healing for me. I released my anger and slowly began speaking forgiveness. The Lord was wooing me to Him through this dark season in life.

But the night terrors never let up.

In August 2013, my husband and I were sitting in church when our pastor announced that they would be hosting "Wednesday Night Testimonies" for the next two weeks. I immediately felt an undeniable prompting by the Holy Spirit to give my testimony.

I fought the Holy Spirit. I did not want to speak about this. But I gave my testimony anyway, and my recurring nightmares stopped.

Two years later, I received a phone call from the DA who had tried this case. He was at a restaurant when a man walked up to him and asked if he remembered him. The DA called to tell me that my attacker was out of prison and worked in the same town where I now lived. This was my test. Did I truly give this harbored hate to God?

After several weeks of prayer, I had a strong urge to see him and face my fears. I went to the restaurant where he worked and sat at a back table. I looked at him from a distance, because I wasn't ready to speak to him. It was between God and me as I fearlessly whispered, "I forgive you."

I experienced a release like I had never known in my twenty-six years. I chose to clothe myself in God's grace and mercy, rise up, and not be a victim anymore. I chose to forgive the unforgivable.

I was liberated. Liberated in "grace and mercy," and it's a

beautiful place to be.

Jessica Lusk *earned a degree in journalism and communications and has been a published writer for ten years. The Lord is guiding Jessica through a season of healing since the tragic loss of her husband in January. He is also guiding Jessica to share about her season of grief, widowhood, as well as about His grace and goodness through her blog page. Jessica is currently writing a non-fiction book. Only twenty-eight years old, Jessica has a one-year-old daughter, Abigail.* **JessLaneLusk.blogspot.com.**

Thoughts to Ponder
from Liberated in Grace and Mercy

1. Call on the name of Jesus when you are in trouble.

2. Unforgiveness keeps us in bondage.

3. Pray for those who have wronged you.

Whom do you need to forgive?

Forgive us our sins, for we also forgive everyone who sins against us. — Luke 11:4

The Dance of Autumn Leaves
by Sydney Hewitt

As I headed out the airport terminal toward home, my cell phone rang. My brother's deep voice on the line said, "Dad has quit swallowing again, and I just needed you to know. I can't go to the nursing home today because of work."

As I held the cell phone to my ear, my heart sank. I told him I was just pulling out of the airport terminal from a weekend trip to Tampa with my husband. I would drive home to dump my luggage, pick up our dog from the boarder, and head directly to the nursing home.

I called my husband in Tampa and left a message. At least he would know that Dad was in further decline. The years of watching our father's decline with Alzheimer's had taken a toll on our family. Now, in the late stages of the disease, we could only give Dad our love through small kindnesses. Medically, nothing we could arrange for him would ease the progressive disease. I had become a prayer warrior during this sad time, and so as I drove home, I prayed for my father to bypass as much suffering as God would allow, and just fall asleep into His arms.

I was moving in slow motion. No matter how fast I tried to navigate from one small task to another so I could make the hour drive to the nursing home, I seemed to be in a time warp. After what felt like hours, I was back in the car driving to see my father. I prayed that God would wrap Dad in His arms at that very moment. *Please Lord, don't let him be afraid or suffer. Help me get there fast and safely. Help me know what to do.*

Upon entering the nursing home, I was greeted by the nurses at the control counter. Dad had been at this facility for only a week prior to my trip to Tampa. As I entered the private room, Dad was asleep on his twin mattress that lay on the floor. At 83, he was still a big man of 6' 3", and looked as if he would fall off the tiny bed if he moved at all. His breathing was strained, and with each exhale came a deep groan. His hands were clenched at his chest, not relaxed as someone in a deep sleep. I tried to wake him by stroking his stiffened arms, but he did not open his blue eyes. I already knew how much I would miss his happy grin and that wink he had given me my entire life whenever I bounced into his view. The tears I had been holding back for several days pooled in my eyes until they fell hotly down my cheeks. I was sad that I was alone at my father's side.

As I sat on the floor next to him, I wished that my husband could suddenly materialize and put his arms around me. I was startled when one of the nurses walked in and offered me a chair. I declined. It was easier to sit next to Dad on the floor. The room felt so still and uncomfortably warm.

It was November in Texas, and we were having a warm and humid fall. I went to Dad's window to open it for some fresh air. His room was situated on a lovely courtyard with a large red oak in the center. At the moment I raised the window, the wind picked up and a cool breeze engulfed me. Leaves began to fall from the tree. They swirled in a beautiful, circular "last dance" to the dry ground. I thought of that old song, "The Autumn Leaves," and I whispered the words to myself, realizing that I too would find the days long after Dad's passing.

I thanked God for my father's life and all that he had meant to me. I became aware that in God's gentle timing, I was witnessing a beautiful and poetic natural progression of Dad's life and passing—through the swirling red and gold leaves that were falling. It was *his* time, the last dance for Dad and me. It was humbling to be so fully alive and fully aware, as my father lay in his final day on this earth, still with me.

Blurry visions of my childhood filled my mind. I was in the living room with my bare feet on top of Dad's wingtips, moving with him to the sounds of Sinatra and Benny Goodman. I smiled with the thought of how Dad and Mom loved to dance with each other and with us. Another watercolor memory came to mind—the daddy-daughter dance when I was in high school. He and I waltzed elegantly on the dance floor of the downtown hotel. Mom had dressed me in a red satin gown, and Dad wore a red rose on his lapel. Next came the vision of Dad at my son's wedding reception, now without my mother but dancing with my sister and me that night. I was enjoying an unforgettable memory of Dad having such fun with all of us.

With eyes closed, I bowed my head and prayed that Dad would be comforted and at his passing be greeted by loved ones he had missed so much, like my mother. "Please God," I prayed, "Allow Mom to be there waiting as Dad takes his last breath—so he won't be afraid."

As Dad's disease progressed, he became like a child, easily confused and terrified. I prayed for Dad's eternal life. Memories of him in a suit and tie, driving us all to Mass each Sunday; and after church the fantastic breakfasts of pecan pancakes, which were his hallmark in our family—these were welcome and blessed memories in that moment. I realized that this is all one could ask for in the final day of our life, that our children would call us blessed and would have felt blessed by our life as their parent.

Standing in the breeze of the open window, I prayed. I noticed movement in the direction of Dad's bed. Dad's arms were outstretched to heaven, and he was smiling. He had been comatose for the entire time I had been in his room, with arms and legs contracted and stiffened. But now, with an angelic smile on his face and his arms reaching fully to heaven, I knew God was answering my prayer. My mother was welcoming Dad. After several moments of reaching, Dad's arms slowly formed a circle as if he were holding someone. How could my prayers have been answered so completely? Who was I to deserve such a gift for the one I loved? I was struck by the awesome power of my connection to God and His constant reaching toward me throughout my life.

At that moment, I knew God was leading my father home with the gentleness of a father with his child. It was all I could do to see through my tears, but Dad had begun to use his hands as if patting the invisible back of the comforting angel who had come to take him home.

Hours passed slowly that day, and finally night overtook his small room in the nursing home. Dad was having difficulty breathing, and he seemed to be burning up with fever. Both my sons had come by to see their grandfather and to visit with me for a while, but now the room was dark and I was fearful about what was to come. I spoke assertively to the head nurse to expedite a hospice team to assist Dad immediately. However, I waited for hours as Dad continued to struggle. I used cool cloths on Dad's face, neck, and arms. Since his swallowing reflex was lost now, I swabbed his mouth and lips with moist lemon-flavored swabs to ease his thirst. I wanted to do so much more for him, but it was all I knew how to do—other than to pray. I felt so helpless. I wanted to do so much more to comfort him.

Suddenly his door opened, and my sweet niece entered the room like an angel. She was in her nursing residency at Baylor hospital, and so I knew when she entered the room, she would help my father.

She made an important phone call to her Nurse Supervisor and before we knew it, the hospice team arrived to bring Dad the comfort pack he so needed. Within a short time in their work with Dad, he became restful and was breathing much easier. They felt he would rest peacefully through the night.

After a few hours of seeing Dad's labored breathing subside, the team convinced my niece, her mother who had come with her, and me to go home for some sleep. We could come back early in the morning. They were confident from past experiences that Dad would rally for a day, maybe even more.

Soon after, we left Dad in their care to return to our own beds. I set my alarm for six o'clock, but the phone rang before the alarm. I knew the moment I heard the hospice nurse's voice that Dad had passed away. He had passed just moments before she called. She said he was peaceful and at rest when he simply stopped breathing.

I was so upset that I had not stayed all night with him. She told me she felt that Dad would not have wanted me there at his moment of death, because that was the kind of father I had described him to be. He was our protector, our tall tower, the one we could always count on—and always my hero.

In writing about the memories of being with Dad during his final day, the most important thing to share is that Dad's life was one that produced much good fruit—one that provided life and love and strong values, many friends, and much joy. Most important, God loved my father and was faithful to him, in his life and in his death, and now in his eternal life in paradise.

I am so grateful and humbled that I was with Dad to pray for him during the transition that each one of us must enter one day at God's bidding. I pray for all his children to be greeted at the moment we take our last breath, by Mom and Dad in this same mysterious way.

And now, as the autumn leaves are starting to fall once again this year, my mind will ever drift back to these memories. As the wind picks them up and they dance, swirl, and shimmer in the air, I will remember that for all things there is a season in God's perfect plan for His creation. And I will be glad that our prayers can move the hands of God, and that we are held safely in them, forever.

Sydney Hewitt writes educational training materials for adults as well as children's curriculum materials for Early Childhood schools. Her writing has evolved over the years since the birth of her grandchildren, about whom she writes stories. Her prayer is that God will be honored and glorified by her tender recordings of how He has shown up boldly throughout her life. One day she hopes the many stories written about the miraculous will fall into place and be bound together in a book.
JSHewitt1@gmail.com

Thoughts to Ponder
from The Dance of Autumn Leaves

1. When Christians are absent from the body, they are present with the Lord.

2. With the hope of eternal life, we do not grieve like the rest of mankind.

3. God comforts those who mourn.

> **What fond memories do you have of loved ones who passed away?**

There is a time for everything and a season for every activity under the heavens: a time to be born and a time to die, a time to plant and a time to uproot — Ecclesiastes 3:1-2

The Venetian Blind Syndrome
by Barbie Cordier

God is wooing each one of us out of spiritual blindness, but are we open to His calling?

I was blind for over forty years of my life—but now I see (like the words to that famous song). I call it the "Venetian blind" syndrome. When Venetian blinds are closed, you can't see out, and there's very little light coming through. However, with one small tweak of the Venetian blind wand, the light comes streaming in, and it's a whole new world that's always been out there. Now you can see it.

Here's my story of finding the Light.

I'm Barbie—married to Ken—seriously. It's a match made at Mattel. I met the Ken doll in Germany when I was a military club manager. He worked on a nearby base as an Air Force officer. Ken Cordier has served our country honorably, not the least of which was being a POW in Vietnam for over six years. Yes, freedom isn't free. He frequently gives talks on "Faith, Family & Freedom" and is now writing his book: *Guardian Eagle*.

I'm an Air Force brat. That simply means that my dad was an Air Force officer, and our family moved frequently. Just to put that in context, I attended nineteen different schools. Sure, one can learn a lot in nineteen schools, but not necessarily the important knowledge. True wisdom begins and ends with God. Plus, I had no roots but One, which we'll cover in a moment.

When I started working, I got into a cycle of working, getting bored with work, going back to school to gain a better job, then getting bored with the next job and going back to school. All in all, I ended up working for big companies, small companies, private industry, government, and for myself. I earned three college degrees to prove that I was smart. Ha! However, something was always missing, and in the end, I knew *nothing*. I should say, nothing of *real* importance back then. But now I know to "seek ye first the Kingdom of God" (Matthew 6:33), "to fear the Lord—that is wisdom, and to shun evil is understanding" (Job 28:28).

In my last corporate position, I had the dream job, wining and dining corporate clients around the world for an airline. Wow, what

119

a life, right? Oh, yeah. I thought I was having a blast, but I was empty. There wasn't a lot of meaning in anything I did, and I knew I could be replaced in the corporate world in a nanosecond. Have you ever had feelings like that, times when you wonder if anyone cares? Then remember this verse: "Cast all your cares upon God, for He cares for you" (1 Peter 5:7).

Even worse than feeling empty and a mere "cog in the corporate wheel," I didn't like who I was becoming. I was playing the corporate game in a male-dominated industry and heading down the wrong path. Do you know that a driving ambition does you no good if you're on the wrong road? It's like climbing the ladder of success and realizing that it's leaning against the wrong wall. But we're always headed in the right direction when we walk with God.

Ken and I had just moved to Dallas from Washington, DC. We had lived on Capitol Hill for eight years and declared that we needed to "upgrade our friends." You may know that Washington tends to be bureaucratic, transient, and not reflective of reality outside the DC beltway. It has been said, "Show me your friends, and I'll show you your future." The Bible says, "Bad company corrupts good character" (1 Corinthians 15:33). Another saying on The Hill is, "If you want a friend in Washington, get a dog." Little did we realize that the first friend we would meet upon moving to Dallas was Jesus. And let me tell you, your friends are automatically *upgraded* when they all flow from Him.

I started a business venture on the side. My new CEO said to "put God first, family second, and career third." I was willing to align my priorities along those lines, but I didn't know who God was. I had to find out. So I asked myself, *Who is God and where can He be found?* In fact, long ago in my youth, I asked my mom, "What is faith? If you don't have it, how do you get it?" Although she was a wonderful Christian influence in my life, her teaching never really took root until years later. Isn't it interesting how God plants those seeds, or puts out those breadcrumbs, just like the story of "Hansel and Gretel," to lead us back to Him?

I now know that when you seek Him, He will find you (Jeremiah 29:13). So where does one seek and find God? First, there is the Bible, God's Holy Word. I like to think of the word BIBLE as an acronym standing for "Basic Instruction Before Leaving Earth." But the Bible often seemed too complicated for me. Has it ever

120

been for you? It wasn't until I got a version I could easily understand, like the Contemporary English Version, that it really started to come together for me. Of course, now I realize there are all kinds of versions available—one for every day of the week. There's even a Bible app you can download on your smart phone and carry it with you everywhere you go.

The lessons in the Bible are for us to:

Know it in our heads.

Stow it in our hearts.

Show it in our lives.

Sow it in the world.

How else could one find out about who God is? How about in churches? I had always wondered why there were so many churches. What did *all* those people in *all* those churches know that I didn't know? Have you ever thought about that? Hmmm. They knew something I didn't know, and I was certainly going to find out what.

Even though my husband was a Christian, we never went to church except to get married in one. While we were in the States, we had gone through a period of watching Robert Schuller on television, but moving overseas and living there for eight years, we never got connected to a faith-based community. Ken called himself a "Christian backslider," attending church under coercion of his family in his youth. The only reasons I went to church in my youth were either to please my mom, to see my friends, or because they had air conditioning when we didn't have it at home—and in Texas, we went anywhere for air conditioning.

When Ken and I moved to Dallas, we started attending church and a Sunday school class. I went through five years of Disciple Bible Study there too. Still, after all that, the knowledge was getting into my head, but that's a long way from getting into my heart. I now know that many people warm pews but have yet to establish a personal relationship with the Lord Jesus. I was one of them for many years.

It wasn't until I attended a nondenominational spiritual retreat called The Walk to Emmaus that Jesus became very real to me. This retreat is named for the passage in Luke 24:13–35 where Jesus appears to His disciples after He was crucified. I confessed my sins and put my trust in Him as my personal Lord and Savior that night in July 2000. It was then that my spiritual eyes were opened.

Scripture tells us that "all have sinned and fallen short of the glory of God" (Romans 3:23). As our Bible teacher says, "all" means *all.* Christians aren't some sanctimonious elitists who thumb their collective noses at others. Rather, we recognize that we are all sinners and have been saved by grace through faith in Jesus Christ our Lord (Ephesians 2:8). "Sin" is choosing to go our own way and do our own thing instead of being obedient to God. It's a separation from God.

People often think that if they're good enough, they can erase this sin barrier between them and God. But the reality is that we can't be good enough, and there is nothing we can do to restore the broken relationship with God. We simply can't earn God's salvation (Titus 3:5).

"God demonstrated His love toward us, in that while we were still sinners, Christ died for us" (Romans 5:6). The Cross (+) has turned a negative (-) into a positive (+). Think of it. Once you come to the reality that you are loved and that it has nothing to do with what you do, that it's all about what *God* has done through His Son Jesus that gives us everlasting life, it becomes crystal clear. I now see God's hand on my entire life, just as it has been and is now on yours. We must keep following the bread crumbs, God's bread crumbs, leading us back to Him and to our everlasting Home.

It's been said, "It's better to be a billboard for Jesus than a mere sign of the times." God tells us in the Bible, "Do not be conformed to this world, but be transformed by the renewing of your mind" (Romans 12:2). We must be open to receive what God has in store for us. This is where faith comes in. "Faith is the assurance of things hoped for, the evidence of things not seen" (Hebrews 11:1). Faith helps us accept what we cannot understand. We try to get our four-pound brains around the Master of the Universe. I don't think we can reason or even fathom the workings of God, and He cautions us that His ways are not our ways (Isaiah 55:8), as Fitzhugh said in the quarterly booklet, *Our Daily Bread*:

"We need God's guidance from above,

His daily leading and His love,

As we trust Him for direction,

To our course He'll give correction."

Think about what it's like to listen to a radio station. First, we must have the radio, the physical equipment. That represents us, our eyes and ears and mind to receive the message. Then we must have the equipment in the *on* position. That means we're receptive and ready to receive the message. Then we must be *"tuned in"* to the right channel. Otherwise, all we'll get is static.

Knowing the Lord Jesus Christ brings an amazing total transformation that begins in our heart and spirit. Even in a prison camp, being starved and tortured with his comrades, my husband Ken knew the words of Mother Theresa were true: "When Jesus is all you have, you realize Jesus is all you need."

My prayer for you is that you too will see the Light. That you will allow the love of the Lord to shine into your life—tweak that Venetian blind wand—and have your radio equipment positioned to hear the message. Once this happens, you will never be the same. I pray Philippians 1:9–10 over you: "That your love may abound still more and more in real knowledge and all discernment, so that you may approve the things that are excellent in order to be sincere and blameless until the day of Christ."

Fishermen use hooks, cowboys use lassos, and God uses *love* to woo us into a relationship with Him forevermore. God's love is personified in His Son Jesus Christ. By His death on the cross and His resurrection, Jesus has removed the sin barrier between us and God. "For God so loved the world that He gave His only begotten Son, that whosoever believed in Him shall not perish but have everlasting life. For God did not send His Son into the world to condemn the world, but that the world through Him might be saved" (John 3:16–17).

With my airline background, I sometimes refer to the safety briefings the flight attendants give onboard. You know how they say: "In the unlikely event that the cabin loses pressure, the oxygen masks come down. Put on your oxygen mask first. Then help those around you." I have simply put on my oxygen mask, Jesus Christ, and I am helping you to breathe Him in—to survive and to thrive.

Once you accept Christ, *you* are under new management. Your mind, soul, heart, and spirit are renewed. You no longer have to *be* it all, *do* it all, or *know* it all. It doesn't matter where you've been or what you've done. What matters is where you're going. He is in control. Isn't that freeing? "Ye shall know the truth and the truth shall make you free" (John 8:32).

Earlier, I said I had no roots growing up. I was searching for *who* I was, but when the spiritual blinds were removed, I realized *whose* I am—a daughter of the King. Christ gave me spiritual roots and a firm foundation. He can do this for you too.

There are only two things that the Bible tells us will last forever: (1) God's Truth, as revealed in His written Word and the living Word, Jesus Christ and (2) all of us are going to live forever, either *with* God in heaven or *without* Him in that other place.

"The way of life is above to the wise, that he may depart from hell beneath" (Proverbs 15:24).

Leadership guru, John Maxwell, states: "There's a choice you have to make in everything you do. So keep in mind that in the end, the choice you make makes you."

The Mattel doll story of "Barbie & Ken" is a fantasy. Even the seemingly dream job of wining and dining corporate clients disappoints. But there really is a "happily ever after" forever and ever and ever after, if you choose to open your spiritual blinds by putting your faith in Jesus Christ. I have, and I am eternally grateful for Him and to Him.

***Barbie Cordier** and her husband Ken live in Dallas. They've attended Roaring Lambs Bible Study for about thirteen years. She thanks God for Mary Kay and thanks Mary Kay for God. As an Independent Mary Kay Sales Director for over twenty years, she and her Believer Achiever Unit have earned the use of twelve free Mary Kay cars. Her interests include Bible studies, book clubs, Bichons, Toastmasters, P.E.O., politics, and travel.*
MaryKay.com/BCordier1
BAchiever@sbcglobal.net

Thoughts to Ponder
from The Venetian Blind Syndrome

1. We must open our minds to the possibility of a Savior, before we can accept Him.

2. A career will not satisfy like a relationship with Jesus.

3. God will place like-minded friends around you when you seek Him.

> ### In what ways do you need to open your spiritual blinds so God's light can shine?

Do not be conformed to this world, but be transformed by the renewing of your mind. —Romans 12:2

Shattered, but Not Swept Away
by Ophelia R. Greene

Have you ever been beaten down by a life storm? In 1971, God rescued me from a raging storm that scattered debris throughout my childhood. I sought cover from family violence for nineteen years, but God provided a way out of the devastation by providing the funds needed to attend college. Without the Lord's intervention, I don't think an advanced education would have been possible.

The government awarded financial aid for three-and-a-half years. In 1974, I graduated with a Bachelor of Science degree with an emphasis in accounting. When I applied for financial aid, we were dirt poor. But God—who always had my back—used our poverty to qualify me for a full grant. I graduated college debt-free.

I learned that when you are in a storm, it doesn't matter how great or high the waters seem. God always provides a way to escape. He can keep you from being swept away. After graduation, He gave me a tremendous opportunity to work in corporate America. In my senior year, I interviewed with two companies in Dallas, Texas. I was offered a full-time position with Atlantic Richfield Company, where I worked for twelve years.

In Dallas, my life transformed as I matured. I grew as a business professional and became an independent, single woman with a desire to marry. Three years into my career, I met someone, and we were married in 1978. Not a match made in heaven, the marriage ended after a year and a half. For the record, and without visiting all the details, it was a biblical divorce and another rescue. I had always attended church, but I did not follow the Good Book until after the marriage failed. God provided a way for me to know Him deeper when He led me to a powerful church congregation and gave me an opportunity to attend Dallas Theological Seminary. As a result, I surrendered to God, who had present and future control over my life. I became content in my singleness, applied God's Word to my life daily, wanted to serve the Lord more, and desired to marry a "knight in shining armor"—someone who loved the Lord and wanted to do life and ministry together.

In 1988, my church hired me to direct the Administration

Department, and in June 1989, God brought my "knight" into my life. He was a seminary student. We received marriage counseling and married six months later. We were covenant keepers, to God first and then to each other, a match made in heaven. At least that is what I thought—until September 13, 2011.

My happily-ever-after was shattered by another storm.

It was a day at home like any other day. My husband, a seminary professor, was due home from a ministry trip to Houston. His employer had given him a sabbatical for the summer and fall, hoping he would be refreshed and back on campus in January. I arrived home around 6:00 p.m. I was really looking forward to spending time alone with my husband, because he had been out of town for three days. I was glad he was home. We were best friends, even though the relationship had been strained lately—due to illnesses, stress, his uncertainty about what he wanted to do in ministry, and our financial situation. Things were not progressing the way he or I desired. However, I loved him, and he loved me. Like most marriages, it was not perfect, but it had worked for twenty-one years, or at least I thought it had. I also thought our commitment to Christ Jesus was greater than our circumstances, and if we remained properly aligned with the One who created marriage, we could fight and win against the enemy's attacks— because we were wearing our spiritual armor.

I pulled into the garage after a busy day at work. As I entered the house, my husband was talking on his cell phone. I wanted to give him a big hug, but I did not want to disturb his conversation. I just said, "Hi, honey." He waved and continued his conversation. I walked through the kitchen to the utility room to put something on the shelf. When I saw folded clothes, I decided to take them upstairs. As I was putting away the clothes, he came upstairs.

"Ophelia, we need to talk."

I said, "Okay." I thought he wanted to talk about how distant he had become over the past few weeks. Maybe he would offer an apology or discuss his ministry plans, since he did not want to return to the seminary. I was looking forward to a long conversation, since he had been out of town. Back in 2010, my husband had started a new church in DeSoto, Texas, and resigned after ten months. I understood that resigning from the church would help him physically by removing stress.

He could not continue to function with severe migraine headaches and insomnia, so his doctor started him on a regimen of meds. I was not sure what he was taking, but it did not appear to help. I really did not want him to take pills for sleep deprivation, mixed with pills for migraines, because there are dangerous side effects such as sleepwalking and dizziness. I was not sure what was really happening, but I knew that God put us together. We would get through this storm if we stayed anchored in Him. I prayed constantly for my husband's physical and emotional wellbeing. I was committed for life.

We walked downstairs, I got a glass of water, and then we sat at the kitchen table to talk. Never in my wildest imagination did I think the next words I would hear would be: "I want a divorce."

My heart sank. I couldn't believe what I was hearing. I felt like I'd been struck by lightning, and many thoughts swirled through my mind. *My beloved is asking me for a divorce. What is wrong with him? He is breaking his promises to the Lord and me. He knows that divorce breaks God's heart. He must be out of his mind.*

I thought my spouse was totally committed to Jesus Christ and me. I thought he was a real promise keeper, one who kept his oath even when it hurt. I looked at him and said, "Divorce? Who is she?"

He looked at me and said, "There isn't another woman. When I am at home, I feel suicidal. I cannot sleep in the bed anymore. You can have everything. All I want are my books."

"I don't want stuff," I said. "I want us." The revelation that he did not want his marriage was shocking.

The Lord brought to my memory all the wonderful poems, cards, and notes he had shared with me over the years, filled with loving words I truly believed. I knew the Lord was aware of my husband's plans to disobey Him and renege on his covenant of marriage. I was blindsided, but the Almighty was not. In addition, I knew I had been a loving and supportive helpmate for over two decades. I believed the Lord would vindicate me in *His* timing. Nevertheless, the experience was painful and disheartening.

The Holy Spirit sustained me and sheltered me in this unexpected storm that threw me into shock. The shock waves went through me during the wee hours of the night as I lay in bed alone, unable to sleep because of the heaviness of my heart and the utter confusion. All kinds of emotions were pelting me like hail during a North Texas spring storm. There was anger, disbelief, pain, disappointment, rejection, embarrassment, betrayal, loss—and concern for our sons.

My husband had provided marriage counseling and performed many weddings over the course of his thirty years in ministry. I had witnessed at least twenty weddings. His leaving made no sense. I hoped this would end like the story of the prodigal son. The Bible says, "When he came to his senses, he went home" (Luke 15:17–18). I heard a pastor say that if the prodigal son came to his senses, then at some point he must have lost his mind, if just for a moment. I was not sure if my husband had lost his mind, but he had lost something. He told me he had a deep void within. He operated with a quiet arrogance.

What happened to the spiritual man I married?

Did he convince himself that to get better physically and emotionally, he needed to leave his ministry and marriage and start over? Was his decision self-centered instead of others-centered?

With the help of the Holy Spirit, I determined that my husband and I were in a mammoth storm, a spiritual battle. The enemy loves to destroy marriages, and he does not care about collateral damage. Our marriage was the target. Therefore, I developed a plan of attack. I tried to reason with my beloved the next day.

"Dear," I said, "are you sure you want a divorce? Do you not want to go to counseling?"

He shook his head. "No."

I told him that divorce would lead to adverse consequences for our family and friends. I do not believe he had thought about his integrity or testimony. But his mind was made up. The enemy had corralled him.

He spoke to me in a subdued voice with little emotion. He was seeking an unbiblical divorce, and it did not seem to matter to him. He just wanted to leave. How do you walk away from twenty-one years of marriage? I kept trying to win him back, but to no avail. His inner struggle and discontentment had taken over. In one hasty decision, his integrity became a myth. He did not have a biblical basis for his action, but he convinced himself that he did. He had quenched the Holy Spirit, and that made it easy for him to disobey God.

A couple of days passed, and I approached him again about counseling. Again, he just wanted a divorce. When I asked him why he wanted a divorce, he said, "I have already told you." Later that day I asked him if I could read something to him that he had written to me, and he said no.

As I looked at him in disbelief, I was thinking, *What can I do to win him back?* In less than two months, he had made a 180-degree change. The person that I heard was not the man I had known all these years. My best friend was gone, as if the mild-mannered Clark Kent had turned into someone else. In this case, it wasn't Superman.

I began to pray silently as I prepared for work. I had started working again to help financially, since our money was running short, and it was putting more pressure on him as he struggled with his physical pain.

August 30, 2011 is a key date for me, because it is the day that my husband filed for divorce.

A week later, while I was at work, my husband called to tell me that he had dropped a fluorescent bulb on the kitchen floor. It shattered and he swept the floor. He warned me to be careful when I came home. At 6:30 p.m. when I came into the house, one of our sons was in the kitchen talking to him. As I was about to walk toward the bedroom, my husband said he had something he wanted to show me. He ended his conversation with our son, and we walked to the bedroom.

He pointed to the nightstand, where a letter covered with plastic and sealed with duct tape rested. I read the heading, which said, "Petition for Divorce."

I looked at my beloved and asked, "What is this?"

He said, "I don't want to talk about it right now."

I said, "Okay, when can we talk about it?"

"Tomorrow."

He left the bedroom, and I went to my closet where I often prayed. It was a closet, not a war room.

I read the document and discovered that my husband had hired a lawyer and filed for divorce on August 30, the same day I started the part-time job. The county court had attempted to deliver the document on three occasions, but was not successful because no one was home to open the gate of our gated community. My husband had returned to DeSoto from his trip to Houston, just in time to receive the document that was delivered for me. He had me served me with divorce papers while we were living under the same roof, and I was still cooking for him.

With the petition for divorce, I came to grips with the fact that my husband no longer wanted our marriage. My happily-ever-after was no more, so I prepared to move from our home. He prepared to relocate to Houston.

On November 22, I officially moved from the home that we had lived in for ten years. The lovely smaller place was only three miles away. God smiled on me again in the midst of the heavy rain of tears.

What do you do when your happily-ever-after has been shattered? Well, because of the difference God had made in my life over the years, I chose to cultivate good emotions. I climbed out from under the heartbreak with arms stretched up to the Father. He is all-powerful and can heal any wounds. Therefore, instead of staying injured and angry, I listened to the Holy Spirit and allowed the healing balm of the Word of God to wash over me. When I felt grieved and alone, the Holy Spirit reminded me that I was not alone. Instead of feeling unloved, I felt the love of the Lord. Scripture tells me that His love never fails. Instead of being worried about things I could not control, I chose to trust and rest expectantly in Him, knowing that I would see the goodness of the Lord in the land of the living. The Lord gave me courage, and I became better as the He helped me forgive my husband.

During this journey, I began to journal. As I wrote and expressed my thoughts, God allowed His healing and recovery process to begin in my heart and life. When we are able to forgive, we become a better witness for God. Through this process, He gave me the words for my book entitled, *Love Notes from a Clergyman: Encouragement for the Brokenhearted*. God used the storm of betrayal, rejection, and abandonment that He had allowed in my life to encourage and empower others and remind them that no storm is too big for Him to handle. It does not matter if the storm is the loss of finances, a violent attack by a stranger, an unwanted divorce, or sudden death of a loved one. He is able. He has taken my pain and given me praise and a platform. I am a witness that He can take the pieces of our lives and do amazing things. I never imagined I would write a book that would help those who hurt. Not only have I written one book, by God's grace I have written two.

The journey that led to my being single after twenty-one years of marriage was not one I would have chosen.

Question: What do you do when your happily-ever-after is shattered?

Answer: Trust God and rejoice, albeit healing is a process.

Long before I knew, God knew my "knight" would not honor his commitment. God gave me a peace that helped carry me through the storm. I trusted Him with my pain, and He turned the pain into praises. He gave me opportunities to share my story to encourage others. I am standing firm today because of the love that I have for the Word of God and the belief that for those who love God, all things work together "for good" for those who are called according to His purpose—even when we do not always see the good. Why? Because God is faithful. Trust Him in your circumstances and in the storms that threaten to sweep you away.

Ophelia R. Greene, originally from Louisiana, has resided in the Dallas area since 1975. She is a mother, author, accountant, organizer, and founder of Annie's Gifts of Love Charitable Foundation, Inc., a nonprofit organization that encourages survivors of domestic violence. She has been a member of Oak Cliff Bible Fellowship for eighteen years. She holds a B.S. degree in accounting from Grambling State University, and a MABS from Dallas Theological Seminary. She currently serves as an Office Manager with Grissett Enterprises, LLC.
AnniesGiftsofLove.org
OpheliaGreene.org

Thoughts to Ponder

from Shattered, but Not Swept Away

1. God is the glue that can restore our shattered lives.

2. Other people's choices may cause us pain, but God can heal the wound.

3. When difficulties come, we need to anchor ourselves to God.

How has God made a mosaic from your shattered pieces?

When you pass through the waters, I will be with you; and when you pass through the rivers, they will not sweep over you. When you walk through the fire, you will not be burned; the flames will not set you ablaze. — Isaiah 43:2

Return to the Palace

by Laverne Stanley

Once upon a time, long, long ago, a little girl was born into a family with three sons. She was loved very much, and they even called her Princess Ann. She knew she wasn't a real princess. After all, they weren't rich. Her father worked very hard, and they didn't have many luxuries—but they always had enough.

A wonderful and benevolent King ruled their kingdom. Everyone was encouraged to visit Him in His palace as often as they wished. So the little girl accompanied her family to the palace at least once a week to hear the King share His wisdom and ask everyone to love and forgive one another, just as He forgave them.

One day when Princess Ann was almost ten years old, the Royal Prince, the King's only Son, spoke to her and asked if she wanted to be a *real* princess and become a child of the King.

She said she would like to think about it.

He said that was fine and continued to tell her how much He loved her.

One day, she told the Prince, "Yes, I do want to be a child of the King." Her parents already called her Princess, and now she was a real one. There was a wonderful celebration, and everyone in the palace rejoiced.

Princess Ann visited with the King in the palace every week and listened to His Words carefully. She learned that she had been adopted by the King and would always be a member of His family. She was a true Princess.

She grew up to be a fine young lady, following the guidance of her loving parents and living a life she knew would please the King.

Then she became acquainted with two sisters, Vanity and Pride. They were popular and wanted her to join their group. Being popular had become very important, so of course she agreed. Oh, what adventures they had.

It wasn't long before the Princess wanted to spend all her time with her new friends. She stopped visiting the King and the Royal Prince in the palace and became disobedient to her parents. She broke their rules and disrespected them. Eventually she abandoned her parents and the King, who loved her more than life itself, and

134

moved to a far country with her new friends.

Her parents asked the Royal Prince to intercede with the King on their behalf. They knew He was their only hope that their daughter would return. The King was happy to help. He sent her letters through a special Messenger, telling her how much He loved and missed her. He begged her to return home. But the Princess rarely opened or read the letters. She was having too much fun with Vanity and Pride. They really knew how to live. She was a Princess, after all, and entitled to have fun—to enjoy everything the world had to offer.

Sometimes the Princess missed her family and the King, but those yearnings were pushed aside by her friends. They didn't want to talk about Him. They were loyal to their father. He took them places and introduced them to fun people and activities, but she didn't really like him. She'd caught him stealing and telling lies, and she wasn't always comfortable with the places where he took them or the things he had them do. But she was having fun.

Time passed, and the Princess grew up and married Prince Charming. However, Vanity and Pride moved in with them too. They were joined by a couple of Charming's buddies as well, so their marriage wasn't happy. She and her friends eventually moved out and moved on.

Princess Ann did visit her family through the years and even visited the King's palace occasionally, although she wasn't interested in what He said. His Words made her feel guilty for some reason. Why wasn't she happy? She had everything she wanted. When she tried to talk to her friends about her feelings, they encouraged her to cheer up and offered a new source of fun.

More time passed, and Vanity and Pride came around less often. She didn't feel like going out and having fun very often. The things that had been fun, well . . . now they weren't. She guessed she was just tired and getting old. Her parents were gone now, as well as two of her brothers. She had casual friends she'd made through the years, but no one she was close to. Everyone seemed to have forgotten she was a princess. She wasn't sure herself.

One day while she was feeling particularly alone and depressed, a special Messenger delivered a note to her from the Royal Prince. It was an invitation to attend a party at the palace. The note said the King Himself expressed His great desire to see her and even said it would give Him great joy if she would attend. It also said He missed His Princess.

She read and re-read the note. She was surprised He remembered her or cared enough to want to see her again. She was still His Princess. She then remembered the letters He had sent to her over the years. She searched until she found them and read each one—hope and excitement building with each of His love notes.

With joy in her heart, Princess Ann journeyed to the kingdom and palace as quickly as possible. She hoped she was not too late. When she arrived, the palace had bright lights shining in every window, and a river of beautiful music flowed through the open doors. She knew there were many people in the palace and on the grounds, but she only saw the Royal Prince standing at the entrance, smiling at her with welcoming arms open wide. She remembered that one of His love notes said He would forgive her if she would confess her wrongs and return to Him. She ran to Him and fell at His feet, begging Him to forgive her. He lifted her up and said she'd already been forgiven. With joy in her heart, Princess Ann knew she would live happily ever after.

~~~~

Is this story a fairy tale? I guess it could be, but it's my story . . . how God forgave me and brought me back into fellowship with Him. It's the story of how He would not let me go. His Messenger, the Holy Spirit, continued to speak to my heart while I was in the far country and drew me back to the King, God our Father, and His Son, Jesus, the Royal Prince. No matter how far I wandered or turned my back on Him, He never turned His back on me. He continued to pursue me, His Princess.

If you have wandered away from God and have replaced Him with things, people, a career, or activities, He's waiting for your return with open arms. As in the story of the loving father of the prodigal son (Luke 15:11–24), God loves you and watches for your return. You'll always be His Princess.

Dear Father God, we love You and worship You for who You are, the Great I Am and Creator of all things. We thank you for all You have done for us through Your Beloved Son, Jesus Christ. His life, death, and resurrection have made it possible for us to become Your children and inherit eternal life in Your Presence. David said in Psalm 32:5, he confessed his transgressions and was forgiven. In 1 John 1:9, John tells us that if we confess our sins (wrongdoings), You are faithful and will forgive us. Thank you, Father God, for your endless love, mercy, grace, and forgiveness. Thank you for never letting us go.

In Jesus' name, amen.

Laverne Stanley *was born in Maryland to Christian parents and has been active in church all her life, striving to learn how God wants to use the gifts and talents He has given to her. She enjoys writing and painting and has served as church clerk, library volunteer, pianist, Bible teacher, and crafter for missions' fundraisers. She recently retired from the government and looks forward to the next adventures God has planned for her and to spending time with her grandchildren.*

StillStory@gmail.com

Thoughts to Ponder
from Return to the Palace

1. Vanity and pride hinder our relationship with God.

2. You, too, can be adopted by God.

3. When we turn our back on God, He anxiously awaits our return.

How have you forgotten the King of kings?

Here my cry for help, my King and my God, for to you I pray. — Psalm 5:2

Curveballs

by Sonny Gann

I love all aspects of the game of baseball. My earliest memories of the sport take me back to Lubbock, Texas, when I played on a little league team coached by my dad and sponsored by Varsity Bookstore. Baseball became my game. Dad taught me how to pitch and as I grew taller and stronger with each new season, he instructed me on how to throw different pitches.

My favorite two pitches were a two-seam fastball and a curveball. Along with the mechanics of throwing correctly was the ability to throw strategically. Without boring you with all the elements of throwing a certain pitch at a certain time, the sole purpose of the curveball is to disrupt the batter's focus. When the curveball is thrown correctly, the batter sees a fastball coming right at his ribs and then the ball dives. Please don't judge me, but I remember times when I actually laughed when I watched a batter quickly lean back to avoid getting hit, and then realize the fastball was not a fastball at all. The batter swung wildly in an attempt to make contact with the curveball. My aspiration to become a "big-leaguer" ended in Junior College when my coach informed me that my fastball wasn't very fast, and my curveball looked a lot like my fastball. That is a bad combination for a wanna-be big-league pitcher.

The summer of 1970 was our last summer in Lubbock before we moved to Dallas. That summer, I made the highly coveted (at least for a thirteen-year-old) Little League All Star Team. The accolades of stardom filled my head as the paparazzi was relentless. ESPN did not exist at that time, but I am confident there would have been non-stop coverage of the Lubbock Little League All Star game. I was *somebody*. However, reality hit when we realized the opposing team had a lineup consisting of other All Stars, and there was a reason they were selected.

Those guys could hit.

For me, just being selected was the best part of the All-Star process. Having to perform at the All-Star level, living up to All-Star expectations was a whole new dilemma, but it did not detract from the wonderful feeling of being selected.

Earlier that year on a Sunday morning at Flint Avenue Baptist Church, I experienced another "All Star" moment. I didn't perceive that this Sunday morning was any different from any of our previous Sunday mornings. We sang some hymns and passed the gold offering plates with red felt on the bottom to keep the coins from rattling around. Brother Giles delivered the message, and I knew we were nearing the end because he was talking real loud. Then he almost whispered the last words of the message. At that moment, the choir sang the first of many verses of "Just as I Am." This was the same as any other Sunday morning, except for what was going on inside me.

I had this feeling that my heart was going to leap out of my chest, and my mind was clear with this thought: *I know I must go up front to meet Jesus.* I knew God was speaking to me. It is also impossible to properly put into words what was happening in my soul, but I was being transformed. I had seen other people go up front during the final hymn, but I never really understood why. As I reached the altar, Brother Giles leaned over and softly placed his huge hands on my shoulders. He asked if I wanted to accept Jesus Christ as my Lord and Savior. Yes, I did. I felt like an All Star. I was baptized two weeks later. Just before I walked into the baptistery, my dad asked if I understood what I was about to do. Just like he did when he was teaching me to pitch, Dad was right beside me, giving me words of encouragement.

Dad knew something I did not know. He knew I would need to be reminded of what I felt when I responded to Brother Giles affirmation of my faith decision.

Dad knew I would need to relive the moment I was lifted from the cool water of my baptism.

Dad knew that I would need to reclaim the intimate relationship of those Christ-centered moments.

Dad knew that I would face some curveballs, and indeed, he was right.

My life has had some curveball moments. Those moments when I traveled through life with confidence, as if I was standing at home plate, firmly planted in my position in the batter's box, knocking fastballs over the fence. I saw life coming, and with appropriate timing and my eye on the ball, I was making all the right swings. But then, what I saw as a fastball situation, suddenly took a turn. A curveball of life that caused my knees to buckle, my heart to break, my mind to race, my confidence to be shattered, and my purpose to be dismantled, creating chaos in my life. Standing in the batter's box of life, with my bat of purpose, protection, provision, and pride, I found myself at times, unable to move the bat from my shoulder.

One of those curveballs came in 1990. My wife and I were expecting our second child, and this was a normal day. My wife, Pati, had scheduled a routine visit with her doctor that morning, and I was at my office in Las Colinas. I received a call from the doctor's office instructing me to come. A rather shocking request, but my fastball swinging optimism kicked in. I determined that this was a good thing. I even decided they were going to surprise me with an announcement that we were having twins. As I drove to the doctor's office, I went so far as to start picking potential names.

As I entered the waiting area, I was quickly summoned to a door leading me to an office. This was not an examination room but the doctor's office, with a large wooden desk and big leather chairs. Pati was standing with her back to me at the opposite end of the office, near a window. As I moved toward her, she turned and put her hand up for me to stop. Her face was swollen from apparent sobbing, and she angrily told me to stop.

A curveball moment.

I was expecting excitement, not hate, disgust, and anger. The doctor came in and instructed Pati and me to sit across from him at his desk. Pati would not even look at me.

The doctor laid out the scenario for me. As part of the normal pregnancy tests, they drew blood from Pati and sent it to a lab, which they do for everyone. The next bit of news was devastating. He said Pati had tested positive for HIV. I suddenly understood the hate and disgust that had been directed at me. I do not recall the entire conversation, for a tsunami of emotional chaos overwhelmed me. The moments of silence were interrupted by outbursts of pain from Pati and then by the doctor's voice: "I am so sorry."

I was lost. I had no words. All I could think to do was beg for God to help me. And then it happened. As if my dad was standing beside me, giving me words of encouragement, I remembered an instruction that Dad gave me as I went off to college. An instruction that had purpose at that very moment in the doctor's office. I began to think through the ways a person can contract HIV. Neither Pati nor I had ever been with anyone else. If Pati was HIV positive, then I should be too. However, I had been giving blood every six months to Carter blood bank and had recently received my "gallon" pin. I did not have HIV.

Clarity of thought came upon me that this HIV result was wrong. There was no scientific, medical, logical, or physical possibility that it could be correct. So I confidently took my position in the batter's box and blasted that curveball out of the park. I told the doctor that we were not leaving his office until Pati and I were both tested. She and I provided blood samples and the results were returned as *all clear*.

Jeremiah 17:7 says, "But blessed are those who trust in the Lord and have made the Lord their hope and confidence."

In 1993, I attended a weekend event called the Walk to Emmaus. Several people in my church had attended the four-day retreat, and it seemed to always come up as a topic of conversation. Because I had heard about it so often, I was open to the idea when a friend asked if I would like to go. So in October 1993, I attended the Walk to Emmaus, #29 in Dallas and sat at the table of Matthew. I have heard many people say their Walk to Emmaus weekend changed their life. Others describe their weekend as inspirational, informative, or just a good time spent with some good folks, eating good food. For me, the weekend was a change in thought regarding my priorities. One was how I was allocating my time. I heard a guy talk about Christian action, and it struck me that I didn't participate in Christian action but was glad others did.

I decided to rearrange my priorities and find a place to serve. Before I knew what was happening, I was being introduced to the sixth-grade Sunday school class as a helper. What? I didn't know anything about these creatures. I vaguely remembered sixth grade. That was when I learned to throw a pretty good curveball. So I plugged in to the sixth-grade Sunday school class and ended up teaching it for several years.

And then it happened.

My daughter Melissa was in the sixth grade, and I was her teacher. Along with Melissa were Laura, James, Adam, Michael, Kimberly, Jacqui, Tricia, Amanda, and Rhonda. A fantastic group of kids. But one kid drove me crazy. She was annoying, always asking questions. Rhonda. That year initiated a series of curveballs, none of which I saw coming.

Rhonda was a good athlete, but she was a *great* softball player. She and I talked baseball and played catch at youth events. I went to most of her games. Many of her church friends watched her play and chanted, "Roo Roo Roo," when she came to bat. It was just fun and games until some truth began to surface. We heard that her family life was a mess. For reasons that only God knew, Rhonda saw me different from the other teachers. There was a deeper level of need as she continued to cope with her life at home.

She did an amazing job of not letting her home issues interfere with her performance. However, all that effort was taking a toll on her soul, and she began to cope with that struggle in a negative way, which frightened all of us, taking us to places we were not prepared for. It was a curveball I did not see coming. Several months of the proverbial rollercoaster ride consumed our prayer life and many of our evenings as we walked beside Rhonda. Many evenings were spent visiting with her and praying that I could bestow upon her a great wisdom or truth that would somehow free her from her struggle. Bypassing several months of details, let's fast forward to a November evening in 2006.

After my prayer-filled thirty-minute drive, I was sitting in my car in a dimly lit parking lot, preparing for my visit with Rhonda. My prayer time was rudely interrupted as my phone rang, and it was a friend from church who wanted to chat. He asked where I was, and then he asked if he could pray specifically for my visit with Rhonda. I had reached the point with Rhonda that I did not know what to say or do to "fix" her life. Many hours of talking and praying had seemed to fall on deaf ears—hers and God's. My mind and my body reached that point of exasperation where applicable thought and logical next steps were vague. I distinctly remember telling God that I was frustrated. This role I was playing for Rhonda wasn't working, and I was finished. It was probably time for me to step away. This was now a curveball I could not handle.

Just as if God was sitting in the car with me, His words were clear: "Well, it's about time."

Say what? I am not God. Therefore, the miracle Rhonda needed was probably not my expertise. Perhaps it was time for me to simply *share* God and stop trying to *be* God. As I walked in to visit with her, I knew this was going to be a significantly different visit. I was through trying to fix her.

We sat at a small table facing each other and chatted for a few minutes. At some point, I took her hands in mine and said, "Rhonda, as of this moment, I am through. I will continue to love you, walk with you, and support you, but from this moment forward I am through trying to fix your life. I am getting out of God's way, and my prayer is that you will too. I am asking that we give up this battle and just let God do what He wants to do in your life." I have paraphrased some of the dialog, but there was a transition taking place. At that very moment, seriously, Rhonda's life changed, and so did mine.

The sequence of events over the next three days was as miraculous as the parting of the Red Sea and walking on water. Several years later, she completed her studies and became a Licensed Nurse Practitioner, happily married, with two children, which means I have two grandchildren.

So what happened? There are moments in my life when my pride has delayed God's blessing. The enemy knows very well that I pride myself in being able to fix things. I am talking about a wide variety of things like relational, emotional, job related, and household projects. I don't need any help. However, the enemy knows I won't give up, so he just keeps throwing curveball after curveball. I just get frustrated and more determined. I dig in harder, maybe change a stance or alter my swing, but pride keeps me in the batter's box desperately trying to fix it. But God . . .

I love that truth, "But God." In Rhonda's case, as soon as I called out, it was as if He was pacing in the dugout, eagerly waiting for me to call on Him so He could take my place in the batter's box.

I receive amazing assurance when I read in Psalm 50:15: "Then call on me when you are in trouble, and I will rescue you, and you will give me glory."

I cannot share my story about Rhonda without sharing a similar story about my daughter Melissa. She graduated with honors with degrees in English, Latin, and a Master's in Education. She is very bright and an amazing woman and educator. We have a fantastic relationship, but it would be a lie to tell you it has always been perfect. She has thrown me her share of curveballs over the past thirty years. Ironically, she never had any interest in actually throwing anything. I believe she is very thankful that Rhonda came into our lives, just so I would have somebody to play catch with.

Our relationship in 2011 was a rollercoaster ride. Melissa was going through a very difficult time, and I found it important—my duty—to fix things in her life. That's what a daddy does, right? After several months of relational curveballs and several heart-wrenching, tearful discussions, our relationship was a mess. I was a mess. I was daddy, and I fix things, especially in the family. Even more when it impacted my daughter. I pleaded with God to fix her and probably shared with Him exactly what I was sure He needed to do. After all, I do have my Master's Degree in Professional Counseling.

After many sleepless, prayer-filled nights, I decided to confront her one more time. I was confident my words of wisdom were exactly what she needed. I picked up some Chinese food for our dinner and arrived at her house. As I sat out front, I prayed for divine intervention. I remember very little about that evening, but what I do remember are these words from her: "Daddy, the one time in my life I have needed you the most, you have not been here for me."

That was a curveball I did not see coming.

In other words, "Daddy, I need to be embraced. I need a hug. I don't need your worldly counsel, psychobabble, or theological insight. I just need you to love me."

But then God said, "Here's the divine intervention you requested, but it ain't for her." Stand up, open your arms, and embrace your child with the same embrace the father offered to the prodigal son. The story is told in Luke, chapter 15. A specific verse offers an example of a daddy's embrace. "And while he was still a long way off, his father saw him coming. Filled with love and compassion, he ran to his son, embraced him, and kissed him" (Luke 15:20).

My life has been, is, and always will be filled with curveballs. Those moments in life that I do not see coming as I go through each day, digging in, expecting a fastball that I can crush, only to receive a curveball I cannot handle. Now, I can choose to be prideful and dig in harder, or I can accept the fact that there will be moments when I need to accept God's grace, mercy, and unfailing love, understanding that those difficult moments have a purpose.

I need to remember that moment at Flint Avenue Baptist Church when I knew God was speaking to me, to remember when I came up from the water drenched in blessed assurance of new life, to remember God whispered, "Son, don't you remember my instruction?" I need to remember to embrace the truth that He is God, I am not.

Dad knew I would need to relive the moment I was lifted from the cool water of my baptism.

Dad knew that I would need to reclaim the intimate relationship of those Christ-centered moments.

Dad knew that I would face some curveballs, and indeed, he was right.

I do not like life's curveballs, but I do not fear them. I know they will come, and I pray that I will see them for what they are, drop my bat, and call on God to step up to the plate in my place. And I know He will.

Jeremiah 29:11–13 says, "'For I know the plans I have for you,' declares the Lord. plans to prosper you and not to harm you, plans to give you hope and a future. Then you will call on me and come and pray to me, and I will listen to you. You will seek me and find me when you seek me with all your heart."

When life's curveball stares you down, and you don't know what to do, call on God. He's the Master at throwing a change-up.

Sonny Gann was born in Lubbock, Texas and moved to Dallas in 1973. He is married to Pati, and they have two daughters, Melissa and Rhonda, one son-in-law, Bill, and two grandchildren, Rylee and Reed. Sonny received his Bachelor's degree in Business Administration from Dallas Baptist University and his Master's Degree in Professional Counseling. Sonny serves at Gateway Church as a Deacon. His book, Him Changes Everything, *was published in 2016 by Burkhart Books.*

HimChangesEverything.org
Sonny.Gann@gmail.com

Thoughts to Ponder
from Curveballs

1. Life with always throw us curveballs.

2. God wants us to be someone else's cheerleader.

3. When trials come, remember the God of your salvation.

What curveballs has life thrown you?

This is what the Lord says: "Cursed is the one who trusts in man, who draws strength from mere flesh and whose heart turns away from the Lord." — Jeremiah 17:5

Kill'n Snakes

by Sue Arrington

What comes to your mind when I say the word "snake"? You may have grimaced at the mere mention of the word. "Snake" or "serpent" is referred to in the Bible eighty times, mostly in reference to Satan. I have used the phrase "Kill'n Snakes" for most of my adult life. The women on my father's side of the family, especially my grandmother "Ma," frequently used that expression. One day, I asked Ma where the phrase originated. This prompted one of her famous stories (She was the storyteller of our family, a lost art that I gladly inherited). She asked me to sit down by her feet. I eagerly obeyed, because I knew I would soon become privy to an informative, as well as an enlightening, bit of information.

As she unraveled this particular account, her eyes drifted off with a misty twinkle. Her story took me back to the family farm in a rural, mostly German, community in Indiana called Haubstadt. She called to mind the dark-brown brick farmhouse in the country, which I visited many times as a child. Her simple words painted a picture in my mind of a time long ago. Through Ma's perspective, I peered through the window of the farm home and saw my great-great-great aunt methodically guiding a rustic plow, hooked up to a huge work horse. Ma went on to explain that from a distance it looked as if this ancestor was whipping the horse. She smiled as she told me that was not the case. You see, as my aunt's calloused hands guided the crude wooden plow, churning up the rich Indiana soil, a snake sometimes appeared unexpectedly. She neither stopped to grimace nor ran away, skirt tail a blowing in the wind. No, this strong German woman would not let this untimely nuisance detract her from her appointed task. She unceremoniously bent down, grabbed the creature by the tail and cracked it midair, like a whip, never breaking stride with the plow and killing the snake. Thus, the phrase "kill'n snakes," and our legacy was born.

Whenever and wherever any of the women in our family were engaged in hard laborious tasks, whether it be house cleaning, child rearing, or working in a World War II military vehicle production plant, whenever they were overworked, underappreciated, or just plain getting after it, you could often hear the phrase, "Oh, I'm just kill'n snakes."

Another snake—Satan—has been turning up as my nemesis since I was a very young girl. The purpose of my story is to show that there is no darkness so empty, no physical affliction so paralyzing, no heartbreak so shattering, no abomination of the body, mind, or soul so severe that it cannot be conquered by the power of the Holy Spirit and faith in Jesus Christ. I know this to be true because I have experienced all these events and more in my sixty-five years on this earth. It's a lot packed into one lifetime, but I consider it all a gift from God.

My blessings have come through teardrops too numerous to count along a painful journey. I have no way to describe my story in any terms other than a bondage of my body, mind, and soul. Satan, the snake, is an equal opportunity destroyer. The prince of this world attempted to drag me down into a pit of hell so vile that a good Christian woman would be too ashamed to verbalize it. This is my story of a life governed by the heavy hand of a spiritual, physical, and mental bondage that nearly claimed my physical body, but more importantly my eternal soul.

For six years, I suffered a physical illness so paralyzing that my life was almost extinguished. For a lifetime, I was plagued by mental and emotional oppression. Only through God's grace was I set free. After traveling to the valley of the brink of death, I emerged, restored.

To the world, it looked as if I had achieved great success. This little girl from Evansville, Indiana, at the eleventh hour, was given an opportunity to attend college. Through a course of God-orchestrated events, I rose to an executive corporate level with one of the largest department store chains in America. I knew every major airport, dined at four-star restaurants, and lodged in exclusive hotels. I was a Cosmopolitan lifestyle woman. I had made it, or so I had convinced myself.

However, one day as I looked out over the wing of a corporate jet, a voice spoke to my spirit in distinct terms. "What do you think you are doing? Here you are, flying around in My sky with your life in the gutter."

Through tear-filled eyes, as I stared at the billowing clouds, my mind rewound back to a moment almost six years earlier, a point in time shortly after the final papers were signed on my second divorce. I closed my eyes as I returned to that sorrowful place beside a pool of water in the moonlight. My clenched fists rose to heaven in defiance. My mind replayed my life as if it were some sort of tragic movie where I could not push the stop button. As scene after painful scene unfolded in front of me, I couldn't take it any longer. I journeyed back to a particular moment in time where, in complete defeat, I cried out to God, "I'm tired of doing things Your way. From now on, I'm going to do things my way." What had decades of trying to abide by "the rules" of being a good little Christian girl gotten me? There I stood, divorced for the second time, in West Texas of all places, with two small daughters whose whole world depended on my ability to survive yet another life-altering event. I had been willing to take life as it was dealt.

Not this time.

I was going to take control of my life and take charge of my destiny.

How did that work out for me? While my professional life was right on target, the brass ring almost within reach, my personal life and the lives of my daughters were in shambles. I bounced from relationship to relationship, searching for something to make me complete and fill the emptiness inside. The emptiness had been my constant companion for as long as I could remember. This constant searching led me on a journey spanning several states and major cities, each one providing a meaningless stop along the path to nowhere.

I dried my tears, straightened my designer suit, and filed this epiphany away in the recesses of my troubled soul. I couldn't do anything about it anyway. It was out of my control. Out of my control, yes, but not out of God's flight plan for my life. A corporate downsizing forever changed the trajectory of my life. Following a path I mistakenly labeled as "fate," I returned to the scene of my defiance: West Texas. It was the very ground where I took over the controls of my life, or so I thought. As I look back upon this fateful moment, I realize it was at this point in time (my return to the desert) when I released the controls of my life and handed them over to the ultimate Auto Pilot, God.

Through His intervention and divine appointment, I found myself sitting on a pew in the back of a tiny church, where after a lifetime of searching, I met the man God chose to not only be my husband but also my partner in ministry, my dear Kent. I had no inkling he would also be the man who would become my caregiver, lifeline, and soul mate through the darkest time of my life.

Eight years ago, I entered a room appropriately labeled "Recovery Room" in a hospital, following a brief same-day surgical procedure to repair a pain pump implanted in my abdomen. My physical condition was abysmal. I weighed two-hundred pounds, required the use of braces to walk, was attached to an oxygen machine twenty-four hour a day, was taking fourteen medications, and had my funeral planned. I had a DNR (Do Not Resuscitate) order in place at my local hospital, where I had been an almost monthly patient for six years. But now I was in a different hospital in a city, fifteen miles from my home.

An accidental overdose of morphine in the recovery room that day became the catalyst for the most amazing, defining moment of my life. I coded twice, was placed on life support, and lay in a coma. During those two times that I was "away," I encountered God not once but twice.

During my first encounter, God asked me to look at my life, particularly the twenty years I had lived away from Him. As I watched scene after scene unfold, I saw in living color just how far I had fallen away from Him. I was ashamed. My physical being was restored through an injection of a strong medicine designed for severe overdoses.

I coded the second time.

This time I heard God distinctly say, "Get back down there. We are not done cleaning up this earth." As I lay for fifty hours in a coma, attached to life support, He showed me I would travel to Africa for Him and that I would develop yet another women's ministry. I saw myself doing these things. Each of these revelations have happened. When I emerged from the coma, my body was completely healed, and the "spiritual me" was also restored. I no longer required any of the many medications or medical contraptions to stay alive.

My year of recovery was difficult. I endured the near dissolution of my marriage and survived a stay in a mental hospital after being diagnosed with a total breakdown. The myriad of doctors didn't know what else to call it. God had a plan for even that challenging time. God placed me in a particular hospital for a particular reason.

He prepared me to minister to a few specific women in their darkest hour while I was living one of my darkest hours.

Prior to my illness, I thought I knew who God was. I thought I had a relationship with Him, because I had attended church most of my life. I had even done some good things that I thought He wanted me to do. I was sure He directed me to champion the cause of Victims of Domestic Violence by establishing a shelter and a women's center. And it was His design, but I thought that *I* had to accomplish those assignments in my own strength.

If we had time to recount all the events of my life, you might be prompted to exclaim that the incidents you read about could not possibly have happened to one person. My story may even sound like a spoof of one of the worst soap operas ever written. Divorce, serious physical and mental illnesses. Abandonment and abuse. Unfortunately and fortunately, all of it is true. I have learned how to "count it all joy." I have lived it, all of it, and I have emerged with one purpose: to give hope to those who feel that their circumstances are too shattering to survive.

In that moment, when time hovered between two worlds, I saw below me just how lost I had been. I had been constantly running. I ran from rejection, abuse, fear, and disappointment. I ran to find answers and comfort in a world where I became a part of all its sordid hopelessness.

From the moment of restoration in the recovery room in a dusty West Texas desert town, I have never felt alone. The soul wrenching, bottomless pit of emptiness vanished. From that point forward, I have never been afraid. There have been occasions since that time when the old me would have crumbled into a mound of hopelessness. But now I know I am not alone. I have nothing to fear ever again.

In the middle of a jungle in Africa, I was not afraid.

When I underwent a biopsy, I was not afraid.

When God called my husband, my awesome husband, the man who fed me through a feeding tube, the man who loved me through the tough times, when God called us to serve in a volunteer ministry at Dallas Christian College, my husband resigned from his job of thirty-six years. We sold our home, got rid of nearly all our possessions, and took a great big leap of faith. I was not afraid, because I knew God was right beside me, directing my steps.

He will never abandon me. He will never reject me. He will never abuse me. He loves me just as I am. He loves *who* I am. No more running to find myself. I know who I am. I am His. My life is His, and He wants to use my life, my history, my right now, and my future for His purpose.

I may have been a victim of "snakebite" in the past. And I know for a fact, the old serpent will continue to pop up now and again as I am plowing the fertile fields of ministry for God's purpose, but a future filled with "kill'n snakes" is nothing to fear when you know you have access to the strongest anti-venom known to man—the power of Jesus Christ.

Sue Arrington *is serving with her husband Kent as full-time volunteers on the campus of Dallas Christian College, where they are lovingly referred to as "Mama Sue" and "Phat Daddy." Her extensive business background includes both nonprofit and corporate leadership. She's been featured as the guest speaker at numerous women's retreats in Texas and New Mexico. Her diverse mission ministry has touched the lives of people in the Bush Country of Uganda, Africa as well as Jerusalem, Israel.*
    SueArrington88@gmail.com

Thoughts to Ponder
from Kill'n Snakes

1. Without the Holy Spirit, problems are magnified.

2. Satan seeks to steal, kill, and destroy.

3. We have authority in Christ to thwart Satan's attacks.

> ### How has the enemy
> ### of your soul attacked you?

Behold, I have given you authority to tread on serpents and scorpions, and over all the power of the enemy, and nothing will injure you. — Luke 10:19

The Box on the Shelf
by Rachelle Alspaugh

Her closet door slowly opened while my fingers gripped the handle tightly, physically expressing my fear of what might spill out of me. When I peered inside, a perfect little white princess dress screamed at me in the silence. Then the beaded jacket just her size mocked me, while the sight of her pink nightgown made my eyes fill with tears.

"No. I can't do this right now. It doesn't make any sense. I can't even process this reality, no less deal with it or even grieve over it." I stuffed all the emotions threatening to pour out of me into a box, taped it up as tightly as I could, and set it high upon the shelf inside her small closet. Maybe someday I could bring it back down and face the contents, but not today. Not now.

My thoughts spun in absolute confusion, grappling with this unexpected turn of events.

"What do I do now?" The closet door creaked as I carefully closed it and walked out of her room. The adoption had failed. They denied our request to adopt both her and her older brother from Colombia. That little girl I'd grown to love and adore more than I ever imagined would not be coming home to me, after all. I'd never hear that precious seven-year-old voice over my phone. She'd never see the beautiful clothes in her closet or the toys that already filled her room.

I walked into my son David's room and felt the same overwhelming grief. Half of his closet held clothes that Juan David would never wear, the top bunkbed constantly reminding us of his absence. David was sleeping soundly on the bottom bunk, while the bed above him, prepared for a brother, remained empty.

Why did God ever let us meet them in the first place? Not just meet them, but immediately fall in love with them, pursue their adoption for fourteen long months, and develop a close relationship over the phone throughout the whole process? Our entire life revolved around bringing Viviana and Juan David home to make them a part of our family. But now what?

"It's not right for kids to not have families." The hosting program motto repeated itself in my ear. We wanted more than anything to embrace them as our children. We bravely answered the call. We attended all the trainings, made all the right preparations, but no one prepared us for a loss like this.

In addition to our grief, a weight of guilt hung heavily over my shoulders. Viviana expected us to visit her someday and bring her gifts, but Juan David knew we planned to adopt them. His twelve-year-old mind already assumed we were his forever family. What did this outcome now mean for him? What would it do to him?

"Will I ever know what happened on their side, when their government closed our case?" I tried to pray, but only questions came out.

So many questions. No answers.

I guessed I'd never know the answers on this side of heaven.

The natural introvert inside me took over. I pulled away from those closest to me. I built up walls—huge, thick walls. I withdrew into myself more every day. I stopped answering the phone. I spent more and more time alone. I screamed at God every morning on my way to work. But as soon as I arrived at school, I wiped away my tears, washed my face, and focused my attention on my job and my second-grade students.

Thank God for those students. They kept me busy, focused, and sane. Most of all, they helped me keep moving. If not, I would have completely fallen apart.

I thank God for a simple, short strand of emails I received from Colombia during those hard months between November and March, unexpected emails from Juan David and Viviana's older brother, Julian. His sweet messages let me know how they were doing, assuring me that they still thought of us and would always love us.

After six months, the emails turned into daily messages and long, virtual conversations. The more I "talked" to Julian, the more my tears fell. God gave me someone to talk to about my grief, someone who could give me answers from the other side. He gave me the chance to process my emotions and finally grieve.

A full eight months after the adoption failed, I bravely gripped the handle on Viviana's closet door. As the door slowly opened, I reached for the box up on the shelf. Opening that box of grief caused a flood of tears, but I knew it was time. You can only postpone grief for so long, and God gave me just the right person to help me through it. Who knew?

At the same time, God placed me in Julian's life to become the loving mother figure that he needed as he finished high school without the support of a family. During that year, another family began a legal process to care for and support Juan David, and a single mother from Spain adopted Viviana. Now, he also grieved losing them.

A full year later, my husband, son, and I boarded a plane for Bogotá, Colombia, to meet Julian face-to-face, now eighteen and considered an adult. We spent two full weeks with Julian, a young man that God gave us the privilege to know and love as the son we could never adopt. He filled a huge void in our lives, and we filled the void in his.

We thought Colombia would always hold memories of hurt and bitterness, but we instead found a beautiful country, a rich culture, and a precious young man on the brink of starting life alone.

Our pain held purpose, after all.

Eight months after returning home from Colombia with a new song in my heart, one morning conversation with Julian replayed in my mind.

"If you had another chance to adopt my brother, would you do it?" he said.

I said, "Of course, we would. But he's with another family now, and I just want him to be happy. Besides, according to Colombia's rules, we can never try again. The door is closed to us."

Julian tried to hint at the fact that things didn't seem to be working out well with Juan David's new family, but I wouldn't let my mind go there. I had given Juan David back to God months ago, and I trusted that God must have chosen this other family for him.

Now I stood confused all over again, wondering if God allowed Julian to ask me that question for a reason. The legal process with Juan David and the other family eventually came to an end, just as Julian suspected.

"But, God, I let him go. I gave him back to You. I trusted You to join him with the family You'd chosen for him. What's going on? What are you doing?"

Julian now pleaded with us.

"Please. Try again."

"Julian, we can't. The door is closed. Your country is very firm on this. Once denied, always denied." Besides, I couldn't even fathom going through the international adoption process again.

"No, God," I said. "Please don't ask us to do this again." While I begged God to close the door, Julian begged us to open it and dare to walk through.

God knew we wouldn't act, mostly out of fear. So He placed certain people in our path to connect us with a Colombian attorney who could open the door they said could never be reopened.

While spending a second summer in Colombia with Julian, God gave us the privilege of meeting the attorney, pleading our case once again with the men who originally denied us, and actually reuniting us with Juan David for a few days.

"You know no one has ever done this before, right?" they said. "We don't even know if it can legally be done. We're going to have to present your case to the head of adoptions to see what she says."

After staying in Colombia for four weeks, we returned home, not knowing what would happen. A month later, we received official word that they had reopened our adoption case. Thus began another long year of tedious paperwork, raising unimaginable funds again, and enduring constant stress and panic.

"God, who does this? Who gets knocked to the ground but still comes back for more? Will this process end different from the last one? What if they come to the same conclusion, that we are not capable of being adoptive parents?"

I thought I'd dealt with all the contents within that box of grief, but apparently I hadn't. I dealt with the emotions over losing the kids, but now I had to get that box down and dig deeper. I had to process all the rejection and the ongoing effects. I had to face my anger toward God, toward the men who had denied us, and toward myself for letting the kids down.

Like a mother facing intense anxiety through a pregnancy after previously giving birth to a stillborn child, panic threatened to suffocate me.

"What if we empty our wallets and our savings all over again—for nothing? What if we put ourselves through this and still can't bring Juan David home? I can't handle losing him again, and I can't imagine what it might do to him."

I'm so grateful for all the prayers of family and friends who carried us, mainly me, through that whole process. Today, when I open that closet door, I don't see a box of grief on the shelf. I see shelves and hangers full of clothes that Juan David, my adoptive son, proudly wears to school each day. When I look around the bedroom that once held dolls and toys for Viviana, I see a shelf that holds pictures of all three siblings—Juan David, Viviana, and Julian. When I look at the walls, I see artwork that Julian gave me and paint colors that express Juan David's personality.

I see a large wall poster of Bogotá, Colombia, a place where miracles do happen.

Rachelle D. Alspaugh *is a mom to both a biological and an adoptive son. She spends her time teaching Bilingual Education, leading Bible studies at her local church, hanging out with family, writing poetry, and traveling the world whenever possible. She has written a two-book series called* Surviving the Valley, *including the books,* Unexpected Tears *and* Painful Waiting. *She also blogs about how she sees God working in her life.*
FromTheHeartOfRachelleD.blogspot.com.
Contact her at RAlspaug@verizon.net.

Thoughts to Ponder
from The Box on the Shelf

1. A "closed door" doesn't always mean no.

2. Memories of hurt and pain can be transformed into peace.

3. Our answers to prayer may look different than we expect.

How has God reopened a door you thought was shut?

And we know that in all things God works for the good of those who love him, who have been called according to his purpose. — *Romans 8:28*

Finding a Safe Harbor
by Elizabeth Dyer

Thank God, I was alone as my car made its way down the Oklahoma country road. The ugly tears, the shouting at God—I wouldn't want anyone to see this. But it was happening so often that my car had become a place of refuge, away from anyone hearing me beg God to change what was happening to my life.

"You said it, God," I shouted. For my whole life, I had believed what He said in the Bible about having plans for me—plans for good and not disaster. But lately my life had become a disaster. "Is this how You show love to me—after all I've done for You?"

Oh, yes, I was one of *those* people. I could give the checklist of all the things I had done, thinking God owed me something in return. So here I was, screaming my list at God. "I went to Bible college, served on the mission field, and saved myself for marriage. Was all this not enough?"

Growing up, I often talked to God like a small child would talk to her imaginary magic genie in a bottle. I was saved from sin and knew my future was secure in heaven. But I held on to an incomplete belief regarding prayer. Oh, I wasn't obvious about it. I didn't ask for cool bikes or fancy clothes. I felt comfortable believing God would always keep me "safe" when I traveled, because I asked Him to. I trusted Him, so He would certainly not allow "storms" to hit my life. I was a "good" person.

As a young mother, I was unaware of the pride seeping into my prayers. My vulnerability with God progressed to a self-righteous tone. "God, I thank You that You have given me a great man, *unlike her* deadbeat husband. You have given us great kids and a comfortable life. Thanks for the wonderful but time-consuming job my great husband has. And Lord, we have such a great church where my husband is an elder, Sunday school teacher, and head of committees."

As much as I studied and taught the Bible to others, how could I miss the parable that Jesus taught about the Pharisee in the temple? He strutted around with verses strapped to his clothing, tassels hanging from his robe to flaunt his holiness, and doing all the right things in order to be accepted by God. Looking back, *I was* that

Pharisee. I thought I could earn something from God—His love, His satisfaction, His pat on the back.

When my husband began to have some unexplained health issues, however, my conversations with God became more frustrated and confused. I continued attending church and even teaching children's church, but secretly I was having trouble reconciling my faith and my circumstances. I used my car rides to sort through the differences between what I was teaching in children's church and what I was experiencing at home. I just knew my husband was dying of some sort of cancer, but he wouldn't get help. I begged God to get him to the doctor, because then God would "fix" everything.

Late one night, I was finally able to drag my husband to the hospital emergency room. I waited anxiously in the ER as they hooked him up to all sorts of monitors. What a relief that we would finally have an answer to his peculiar episodes and behavior. When the doctor walked into our tiny room to discuss the diagnosis, the world stopped spinning for a moment as I only heard one unimaginable word: alcoholic. I *knew* it was a mistake. "Tell him you don't even drink," I shouted. He just lay there as a man whose closet full of skeletons had been revealed.

My marriage suffered dramatically from that day forward. The mental health of my spouse and my desire to control him seemed to collide at every turn. *Father God, You will fix it, right?* I *knew* He would work miracles, and all the addiction and everything that went along with it would go away. I knew the stories of deliverance from enemies in the Old Testament. I knew the prison-release stories in the New Testament. I believed God would smooth all the rough patches in our marriage.

After many promises of "I'll change" and "we can get through this together" from my husband, I committed to making the marriage work. *How hard can it be, right?* I began to monitor every water bottle, the large leather work bag, the car, the garage, under the bed. You get the idea. I became a law enforcement officer to my husband's addiction. I was going to "fix" this. And the harder I worked, the farther we drifted apart, and the more I shouted at God. "You cannot be serious. Is this what I get for all those years of following You?"

After nearly twenty years of marriage, the bottom fell out.

Because my husband lost his job, I had to give up homeschooling my kids so I could work. Making only minimum wage, my job wasn't even close to closing the great chasm between our needs and our income. *What's the point of working?* I asked myself. *It seems so pointless. This isn't the same godly, disciplined man I married. He is a shell of a man, defeated by addiction. And the weight of his choices isn't just crushing him—it's crushing me.*

How was I supposed to pick up the pieces of this chaos and make something beautiful again? Which brings me back to the shouting match with God on that Oklahoma country road. It brings me to that moment when I shouted something at God and felt Him shout a loving rebuke back.

"You said it, God." I continued to press my case. "What is the point with faith, God? I did all the right things and still it's turning out worse than I imagined. I said "for better or worse," and You gave me worse. Where is the blessed life I was supposed to get? Do You really love *me*?"

I drove in silence for a moment, meditating on the verses about God's love. But this time, those verses didn't help. My emotions were telling me something contrary to scripture. *God, do I even believe anymore?*

Sometimes you must get to a desperate place in life to ask that question—do you really believe—before you can understand that you really do. At this moment, I was truly desperate. Nothing was the way I wished. And even as I cried out, "Do I really believe anymore, God?" I noticed that I had added the name of God in the question. Deep down, I knew the answer—yes, I did. And when the answer hit me, I felt what can be described as a holy tap on the shoulder.

My dear precious Elizabeth, I felt Him saying. *You are praying for healing, for health, and all good things. But I want you to pray, not for your will but for Mine. You think, dear daughter, that your will is good and right. But when it's specifically your will you ask for, you are trying to control Me, your Creator.*

I drove in silence, wiping the tears away, letting His words hit me like the rebuke I needed to hear. I thought about the miniscule amount I was being paid at my job and how insufficient it was. Looking back, I believe God put me in that job at that time to show me I couldn't control the situation. God was at work, but I couldn't see it. He was preparing me for a future of trusting fully in Him.

Changing my prayer to say, "His will, not mine," released me from the job of controller to the position of submission. But changing my prayer didn't "fix" everything. My husband's health deteriorated dramatically. The bills piled up. God showed me I needed to release the control I thought I had on my spouse, my kids, their education, our finances, and my time. Brick by brick, the foundation I had built crumbled. I had made a shipwreck of my faith. For my faith to grow, the truth of the matter was that my husband *did not* have to be fixed. Our finances might be in the gutter, but I could still trust God. I *could* be joyful, even when storms were hitting us from every direction. I was ready, finally, to trust God completely.

To pull this family together, held by a loosening thread, I decided we needed to keep a family tradition of attending the state fair. It was the first activity my husband and I had done together as young adults. Oh, that wonderful booth with cinnamon rolls. I could almost taste the buttery sweetness. We had dragged the kids there for years, telling them the story of the cinnamon rolls. My husband had purchased cinnamon rolls in September, froze them, and brought them out for breakfast when I came to visit after living abroad.

The state fair was not going to bypass us, not this year. My husband could barely shuffle along the aisles of the buildings. We settled him in the folding chairs to watch the cooking demonstrations while I wandered off with the kids. We were going to have fun, with or without him. In rallying the troops, I had the joy of the Lord manifesting itself. At first, the kids seemed a little perplexed that we could just leave their father there. As they saw their mom as a strong and capable role model, the thread that was barely holding us together as a family wrapped around their hearts. I wanted them to tuck that character trait away in their hearts for some day in the future. Our joy in the Lord was not contingent on someone else. I wanted them to always know that when life leaves you bloody and beat up, God is the safe place you can run to.

My husband continued to spiral lower and lower. *Surely this is as bad as it can get, right?* These conversations I had with God continued each time I got in the car. Most of the day, my mind was spinning in silent conversation with God, a constant tug-of-war in my heart. Do I trust? Do I not? But I was growing stronger with each prayer. Every day brought renewed joy. My faith had to be all I needed. My God was not a genie in a bottle. He had a purpose—and it wasn't my comfort and my happiness. His purpose was to mold me into His character and make my life reflect Him.

Could I continue living life like this?

Could I remain married to this stranger in my home?

Could my children ever succeed in life after this?

My children needed me to remain strong, leading them until the leader was able. They knew life was crumbling. But I desired to model a life submitted to God. Someday they would encounter a crisis of their own. Someday they would need to depend completely on God. I just didn't know how soon they would get to experience this on their own.

A few months after my car-drive epiphany, we were sitting in the Christmas Eve service at church. Ahhh, we had made it through the hardest part. My husband was getting counseling and medical help. We were sitting in a pew, all together, my husband's arm wrapped snugly around my shoulders. My eldest son had received a full-ride academic scholarship to my husband's alma mater. We still had our home, and my husband was setting up a home business.

God, You are pulling us out of the storm. We are going to make it.

But five days later . . . we were in another ER, this time in a different state and town. After the most challenging two years, we had taken a short family trip to pull ourselves together. We needed a good ending to the year. But it became clear that my husband was not feeling well. What started as a cold progressed to an ER visit. Upon our arrival at the hospital, it also became clear that my husband, while in many ways better than he had been in months, was also very ill.

As I sat alone in the ICU, my prayers came out in sobs. My children came and stood by the bed of their father, unsure what the future held. My friend drove the six hours to us to take my kids home until we could bring their dad back to the city. Once again, I was alone with God. I returned to my previous beliefs—I expected God to "deliver" since I had finally submitted completely to His will. The machines beeped in perfect rhythm, keeping my husband alive. *This wasn't how I expected Your will to work out. I was looking forward to the emotional and physical healing I was sure You would send. How does one say goodbye forever? How do I let go of him?*

Following advice from my husband's family, I allowed the doctors and nurses to cease their efforts and allow my husband to leave my arms and fall into the arms of his heavenly Father. I released such a guttural cry from my lips, never before or since heard.

God became more real at this moment than ever before. The storms of life revealed that my faith could become a safe harbor. The only thing I had left was my faith, so I had to understand what it was made of. I drove home, alone in my car once again. This wasn't how I expected to return to the city. Being isolated for hours gave me ample time to rest in God's arms for comfort and peace. Song after song on the radio spoke to me, bringing sweet memories of my husband—the longest continuous prayer meeting I have ever experienced.

On the day before the funeral, I sat with my Bible in my lap. *God, I don't know what to say.* The only thought I could come up with was to look for someone in scripture who had lost a loved one too early. I flipped my Bible to 2 Samuel 12 and found the passage where King David, a man after God's own heart, had made one bad decision after another. Here he was, with his newborn baby dying because of *his* sin and failed attempts to control the situation. God seemed to whisper in my ear to switch the word *baby* or *child* to my husband's name. The passage was like a neon light brightening my heart. *You mean, I did all I could to help, and I release him into Your peace?* David prayed and fasted while the baby was alive, hoping God would save the child. But after the child passed away, David washed up and went to worship. He couldn't bring the child back. But he knew he would see the child in heaven. I smiled: *This is my hope as well. My husband is finally healed and healthy. He is in heaven with You, worshiping at the throne.* And he is missed every single day.

I don't have the answers to all my questions, especially the ones about why God didn't heal my husband or how our marriage could have come to this point. But at the end of the day, I have to trust that God has my best in mind. His ways are not my ways. I wanted to share a different testimony. I wanted the healing of a marriage and a husband. But God has chosen my testimony to be this one. My husband understood grace and mercy more than I ever will.

And now I understand trust in God like I never have before. When faith is all you have, you find out it is all you need.

This life isn't what I ever dreamed it would be, but because of my faith in God's love and because I have submitted to His guidance, I find joy in living. It isn't found in my circumstances, that's for sure. It isn't found in a full bank account either. My safe harbor in Christ has not been without storms. But that's the beauty of the harbor. It is a place where I can anchor my faith during those rough times that come all too often. It is a place of protection for my soul.

Yesterday I was driving in the car, the Oklahoma sun shining brightly. "Father God," I said. "You truly love me." I rolled the window down and opened the sun roof. "My future is bright too, isn't it? We are in this ride together, God. Through the ups and downs, curves and dips, and even when I run off the rails."

Elizabeth Kay Dyer writes with *"A Widow's Might,"* a ministry to widows by widows. She lives in the Oklahoma City area with her six children named after Bible characters, plus a dog named after a grandpa, and a cat named after a German racecar driver. You can follow her ministry and her page on Facebook or on the web at **AWidowsMight.org.**

Thoughts to Ponder

from Finding a Safe Harbor

1. God is willing to listen to our rants.

2. Our "whys" may not be answered on this side of heaven.

3. Joy is not always found in our circumstances, but can always be found in God.

When have you been angry with God?

For my thoughts are not your thoughts, neither are your ways my ways," declares the Lord. "As the heavens are higher than the earth, so are my ways higher than your ways. — Isaiah 55:8-9

Fairy Tales Unraveled
by Debby Efurd

When I was little girl, I couldn't wait to get to my grandmother's house so I could crawl into her lap as she read my favorite bedtime stories until I fell asleep. My imagination would run wild. If you like animals, perhaps *The Three Bears* was your favorite. If you listened intently to *Pinocchio,* you learned never to tell a lie. Little girls dreamed of their Prince Charming when *Cinderella* was read. If you didn't get what you wanted for Christmas, then maybe *How the Grinch Stole Christmas* was your story. But the tale I was always drawn to was *Snow White and the Seven Dwarfs.* Funny, it's a story that has the same themes as my personal story—those of control, choices, and consequences.

Have any of you wanted to star in your own fairy tale where you lived happily ever after? I did.

My parents loved and doted on me, because I was the baby of the family. They saw to it that I went to church every week, I took every kind of lesson imaginable, and I practiced the piano daily. But as much as I was loved, the discord of dysfunction and conflict clanged loud and clear within the confines of our home. With multiple marriages and half-brothers/sisters, we were a blended family before the term became popular.

I thought all families were like ours: keeping secrets, manipulative, never hugging, never expressing our feelings—and avoiding conflict until someone exploded. I was always walking on eggshells. When my parents fought, my mother scooped me up and drove to my grandmother's house for refuge. By the time I graduated from high school, I was eager to leave home. I could do better on my own. Like the fairy tales, I wanted my "knight in shining armor" to rescue me. Surely my family wasn't the way families were supposed to be.

When I was twenty-one, I met a guy who said he loved me and wanted to spend the rest of his life with me. He said I was his perfect match, and I thought my Prince had come. When I told Mr. Charming I was pregnant, he told me he was still married.

I found myself at a crossroad. I couldn't have a baby and not be married. I couldn't tell my parents or friends, because I was too embarrassed about what they would think of me. I was alone, scared, and naïve. How could I have gotten myself into this situation? I would go to any length to find a way out of my "inconvenient problem."

I can never forget the drive to the abortion clinic that Saturday morning. I drove myself. No one spoke to me. No one held my hand. I remember the sterile smell, the whir of the vacuum.

"Good news, you don't have a baby anymore," the abortionist said.

I couldn't breathe. I wanted to throw up. Tears streamed down my cheeks. After I left the clinic, I sat in my car and cried for a long time. I kept telling myself, *No one has to know. You can go on with your life. You can forget about this.* But that was the furthest thing from the truth.

There were two deaths that day—my baby's and mine. Little by little, bottling up every emotion, not crying or laughing for years, I shut myself off from friends and family. For fear they would see me for who I was, I didn't look people in the eye. I was more concerned about myself than an innocent baby, and my self-esteem hit rock bottom.

I turned to every external comfort I could find to soothe my inner turmoil, building up walls to hide shame and guilt. For the longest time, I was uncontrollable—excessive drinking, prescription drugs, and overeating, which led to an eating disorder. I made bad choices in dating relationships—filled with physical and emotional abuse, bouts of depression, and thoughts of suicide. I was angry and bitter, lashing out at anyone who crossed my path. But I continued to keep my secret. I didn't want to be judged.

Because I thought I was in control, I married a man against my parents' advice. After all, it was my life. I knew best, and love *could* change all, right? As the physical and verbal abuse occurred more and more frequently, I kept telling myself that. Even though I knew deep down, my parents were right. I was filled with too much pride to admit I was wrong.

In the years that followed, there were continued conflicts and losses. My half-brother was killed in an accident. My parents divorced. My marriage was failing. But a blessing in the midst of chaos was the birth of my son. Becoming a mother sparked a desire to be a better person. I wanted to do everything "right" for my baby. I had someone to take care of, to watch out for, to be accountable for.

With my marriage now ended, I turned my attention to my son and being a super mom.

For over a decade, I was a single parent and devoted all my time to my boy. I also took care of parents with declining health and worked more hours than I could count. Despite the heavy schedule, we started going to church. I guess something there must have rubbed off, because I began to pray over my situation.

After she lost her eyesight, my mother moved in with us. My dad moved into a retirement home nearby. But I still longed for a family. I wanted a man I could respect, a marriage that would last, and a good role model for my son. I often wondered what was going to happen to us after my parents were gone. I even prayed. "God, if You're up there, what's going to happen to us? Can You make us into a family? Is there someone who could love my son as much as I do, even though he's spoiled? Could that man be okay with a blind mother-in-law living with us?" Not long after that prayer, Cary showed up. We married a year later. And then I had a *big* family—his, mine, and ours.

Cary and I faced a lot of struggles. We started our lives together with a blended family, financial problems, and job losses. Both my parents faced terminal illnesses and passed away within nine weeks of each other. Our family pulled together to comfort one another. But I realized I no longer had a home to run to or anyone to seek advice from. With both my parents gone, I was the matriarch of the family. I had no clue how to be a matriarch.

A pivotal moment came in 1997. On October 1, I arrived home from work. As soon as I walked in the door I knew something wasn't right. I received the call later that night from Parkland Hospital. There had been an accident involving my husband.

Because of a severe manic episode, Cary had been speeding. He rear-ended a Jeep stopped at a red light, locking bumpers and flipping both cars into the air. The Jeep that Cary hit burst into flames, trapping the driver in the front seat.

Cary ran to help the driver. Despite the flames, he pulled the man out and carried him to a grassy area, staying by his side until paramedics arrived. The victim, an eighteen-year-old man, asked Cary to tell his wife and child that he loved them. That may have been the last words this young man spoke. Both the victim and Cary were transported to Parkland with second- and third-degree burns.

The next day, we learned that the young man had passed away, leaving a seventeen-year-old wife and an eight-month-old baby boy. Reporters and attorneys started calling. We were sued in both a personal injury lawsuit and a civil lawsuit. Cary was charged with criminal negligent homicide and assault.

For his mania, Cary was transported from Parkland to Terrell State Hospital for thirty days of treatment. I was working fifty hours a week, had a business with no hope of keeping it afloat, employees we were responsible for, kids in school, and no money. Debts were piling up. And I was overwhelmed.

We filed bankruptcy and had three sets of lawyers to pay. I was holding down my day job, an evening job, and looking for a weekend job. To say I was angry would be putting it mildly. I was mad, bitter, and resentful. It was all Cary's fault. Sadly, I didn't think about the young family who lost their father. I wasn't thinking about Cary, who grieved over his role in the accident. I was too busy whining about me. It was all about me.

You may remember another fairy tale where the fleeing character cries out, "Run, run, run, as fast as you can. You'll never catch me. I'm the Gingerbread Man." Every fiber in my being told me to run away. My flesh desired to leave Cary and do what I'd always done. But I didn't. We had children, family, and friends. People were watching our every move. Friends and even some of my family thought I'd be justified in leaving Cary. Although this wasn't the fairy tale I had signed up for, it was the story I chose, one of honoring a commitment made years before, when I said to Cary, "In sickness and in health." With that commitment, I was setting an example for our children and many others.

Healing came gradually. It started with the trial, letters to the victim's family, restitution, setting up a trust for the victim's son, paying back debts, working hard, starting over, and a big dose of humility. I can't say exactly when the turnaround in me happened, but at some point, my "prison" evolved into a "sanctuary" where I was meeting Jesus up close and personal. I was less concerned with possessions and what people thought about me—and more concerned with others. Feelings didn't govern my decision to stick with Cary. I still wasn't sure how I felt about Cary. I didn't like him at that moment. I wasn't even sure I loved him, but I didn't leave him. I made a decision, acted on that decision, and the feelings eventually followed. "He who began a good work in you will carry it on to completion until the day of Christ Jesus" (Philippians 1:6).

As I look back over the months during that tumultuous drama in our lives, I see many unexplained miracles. The only item untouched in the blaze was the Bible in the front seat of the victim's Jeep. Apparently, he had been a believer. Equally amazing was the evidence left on Cary's forearms from helping that young man. To this day handprints of that young man are still visible on Cary's forearms. It's a constant reminder of the imprint tragedies have on our lives and the One who brought healing.

But I was still holding on to one part of my life I thought was impossible for even God to heal—my "secret." By now, science was revealing the truth about life before birth through sonogram technology. Memories I thought had been buried came back to haunt me. Feelings of hopelessness, guilt, and regret consumed me. I couldn't forgive myself and couldn't imagine how God could forgive what I'd done.

But God *was* at work. Sitting in choir week after week, I witnessed peace on the faces of other choir members. I heard joy in their voices. I heard transforming testimonies of how God acted in their lives. Whatever they had, I wanted it too.

One Sunday, the pastor spoke on forgiveness.

The choir sang:

All to Jesus I surrender;
All to Him I freely give;
I will ever love and trust Him,
In His presence daily live.

Refrain:

I surrender all, I surrender all,
All to Thee, my blessed Savior,
I surrender all.

I heard Jesus whisper, "Debby, are you sure? Have you *really* surrendered everything to me?"

I had reached a breaking point. I said, "Jesus, I can't carry this burden anymore. Please help me." At that point, the dam holding back thirty-eight years of tears broke. I was holding on to Jesus for dear life.

Soon after that Sunday, I volunteered at a crisis pregnancy center. Other than to my husband, I had never admitted my abortion to anyone. But for some reason, I didn't hesitate to tell the pregnancy center coordinator. To volunteer, anyone who has had an abortion must go through post-abortion recovery. I had no clue what I was signing up for, but I said, "Yes, sign me up." I really didn't think I needed a recovery group, but if that's what it took, okay.

I walked into that gathering as a rebellious, helpless, hopeless, and angry person. I walked out peaceful, hopeful, forgiven, and free. For the first time, I was able to accept God's gift of forgiveness. I was finally able to breathe. I was washed squeaky clean. At last I realized I would one day see and hold my son Aden.

Jesus said, "You will know the truth and the truth will set you free."

Over the years, God revealed Himself to me, chipping away at walls I had constructed, and then He uncovered a secret so well hidden I thought I'd take it to my grave. But secrets and isolation kill. And God didn't want that. The Dutch Christian, Corrie Ten Boom, once said, "There is no pit so deep that God's love is not deeper still." I had dug a deep pit for myself, but Jesus was more than able to pull me out and fill my void with love.

My story did have a happy ending, just like my beloved fairy tales. Once an angry, empty, fearful, hopeless, rebellious, young girl, I am now a secure, hopeful, peaceful, and joy-filled woman of God. What is impossible for us to accomplish is possible for Jesus. Scripture says, " 'For I know the plans I have for you,' declares the LORD, 'plans to prosper you and not to harm you, plans to give you hope and a future' " (Jeremiah 29:11).

Will there be other disappointing tales in our lives? Most certainly. Today though, my story is rewritten, not because of "Who *I* am" but because of "*Whose* I am." Looking back now, I see God's hand weaving a beautiful tapestry in my life. God was at work in the details as I reconciled with my parents, teaching me how to have a relationship by bringing Cary into my life, helping me to make amends with people I had hurt, and seeking honesty with myself and others. God was at work in the details as Cary led my ex-husband to faith in Christ and gave the eulogy at his funeral.

God provided an earthly father for my son. And God is at work in me each time I share what He's done in my life.

I want to tell you about one other book. It's not a book of fairy tales, but one filled with stories of ordinary people who were used in extraordinary ways by an awesome God. One miraculous story describes Jesus' birth in a stable in Bethlehem. That same Jesus walked this earth and willingly sacrificed Himself on the cross for all mankind.

The miracles of change that happened in my life can happen in yours too. Whatever your circumstance, whatever you've done or didn't do, it doesn't matter. What does matter is having the desire to know God through faith in Jesus Christ, not in our heads but in our hearts.

The Bible says in Romans 3:23: "For all have sinned and fall short of the glory of God."

"Sinned" means we have missed the mark. When we lie, hate, lust, or gossip, we have missed the standard God has set. In thoughts, words, and deeds, we have not met God's standard of perfection.

Romans 6:23 says: "The wages of sin is death."

By sinning, we have earned death and should be separated from God forever. You may think, what's so good about that? Well, here comes the good part.

There was no way we could come to God, but the Bible says God came to us instead. Jesus Christ died for you and me.

Romans 5:8 says: "But God demonstrates his own love toward us, in that while we were still sinners, Christ died for us."

Christ took the penalty that we deserved for sin, placed it upon Himself, and died in our place. Three days later, Christ came back to life to prove that sin and death had been conquered and His claims to be God were true.

The good news gets better. You can be saved through faith in Christ.

Ephesians 2:8–9 says: "For by grace you have been saved through faith, and that not of yourselves; it is the gift of God, not of works, lest anyone should boast."

Friends, this same peace, joy, and assurance of salvation can be yours. All you need is a humble heart and an honest desire to put Him first. If you've never made the decision to accept God's gift of salvation, pray this prayer.

Dear Jesus, thank you for making me and loving me. I realize I need You in my life, and I'm sorry for living my life on my own terms apart from You. I ask You to forgive me. Thank You for willingly sacrificing Yourself on the cross for me. Please help me understand it more. As much as I know how, I want to follow You from now on. Please come into my life and make me a new person. I accept your free gift of salvation. Please help me grow as a Christian. Amen.

Debby Efurd *is a speaker, author, and pro-life advocate. As a former Founder and President of the collective ministries of "Initiative 180" and its program of abortion recovery, "Peace After the Storm," she provides education, counseling, and support to those suffering the emotional pain of abortion. Debby graduated cum laude from Dallas Baptist University with a B.A. in Counseling. She is the author of* Go Tell It! *and is an active blogger,* **DebbyEfurd.com.**

*She can be reached at **Debby.Efurd@gmail.com.***

176

Thoughts to Ponder
from Fairy Tales Unraveled

1. There are no secrets from God.

2. Jesus can fill your empty tank with His love.

3. Broken fairy tales can be rewritten by the Lord.

What secrets are you trying to keep from God and others?

He brought me up out of the pit of destruction, out of the miry clay, And He set my feet upon a rock making my footsteps firm. — *Psalm 40:2*

In the Midst of Angels
by Sharon Patterson Payne

Photo proof of heaven . . . could such a thing exist? It is human nature to be ambivalent or skeptical of claims there is physical proof of God's existence.

Many times, I have heard folks say, "Show me some tangible proof God is out there, and I might be a believer." As for myself, I say, "Absolutely and unequivocally, *yes!*" I am confident because I have tangible proof.

God's love guided me toward this epiphany. During my childhood, I always had a sense of a divine being, even though I did not grow up in a religious environment. As I moved into adulthood, my Christian journey made me aware that at some point in my walk with my heavenly Father, chances were I would receive *my call* from Him to serve in a capacity that would both honor and glorify His name.

In late August, when Texas summers are brutal by nature, the blistering sun capped off a sweltering afternoon and began its descent over the horizon. I perched myself on the steps of my front porch and began snapping photos with my digital camera, attempting to capture that "perfect sunset."

With its panoramic view of the rolling countryside, the front porch invited many beautiful sunsets. Each afternoon, as the tired, drenched sun slowly descended toward the horizon, its warm silver rays shot upward through the clouds to the heavens, scattering profound hues of mystical splendor in every color of the rainbow. There, I found the peace and tranquility to unwind at the end of each day.

Yet in the midst of all the peacefulness, nature's beauty was overshadowed by a cold, harsh reality. My life was in shambles. On this particular day, the front porch provided a harbor from one of the biggest storms of my life.

As my marriage of thirty-two years ended in divorce, I sat in quiet solitude and photographed the sunset.

I was in deep thought about what was ahead, post-divorce. Where would I start this "reconstruction" process? I had not been on my own for over thirty years, and there would be no one to lean on for support if something went haywire.

I had to find a place to live. I was the one having to leave the household that I had known and loved for so many years. I had to forge into the frightening unknown territory of managing a new environment, different in every way. My parents passed away. I had no siblings and no children of my own.

Loneliness engulfed me. Fear and uncertainty became new and unwanted intruders, clinging to me like leeches seeking a new host. In an attempt to "shake off" those feelings of despair, it was in my own sacred silence that I sensed God would help me chart the unknown course ahead. I knew deep within my heart I would somehow make it. The only certainty I had was that God was at the wheel of my soul, and He was the one—the *only* one with the roadmap—who would drive me safely to the destination of *His* choice, not mine.

For months, I pondered the age-old saying, "Every dark cloud has a silver lining." I was experiencing that dark cloud in a multitude of ways. Where in the world was the silver lining? The storm clouds in my life were getting darker every day, with no silver lining in view.

Sitting on my porch in awe and wonder, I felt God's presence everywhere. From out of the blue, my emotions burst into a raging river of tears. In grave despair, I sobbed uncontrollably as I cried out to God to hear my plea. "Lord, please reveal what my true purpose in this life is, according to your divine plan for me, and let me live it. Please send your almighty angels to show me the way."

The moment I finished praying and began to stand up, the strangest feeling came over me. The feeling started at my feet and moved upward through my body and out the top of my head, as if a wave of unexplainable energy had momentarily consumed every thread of my being. When I stood upright, the tears were gone, and the feeling of deep despair transformed into peace and utter joy. It all happened in a matter of seconds. I took a long, deep breath. With the exhale came the smile that has remained to this very day. At that moment, my life took a sudden and unexpected turn, setting wheels in motion for one of God's miracles to unfold right before my eyes. Unimaginable, life-changing, soul-altering, and near-unbelievable events were taking place in my life.

One week later, I was photographing another beautiful sunset.

In the tranquil moments just before nightfall, I snapped one last photo of the day. "What just happened?" With my heart racing from a surge of adrenalin, I could scarcely catch my breath. Hands shaking with sheer excitement and anticipation, I reviewed the photograph I had just taken on my small, inexpensive digital camera.

An angel?

Could this be a *real* angel?

Was I dreaming, or was this the real deal? I *thought* I had taken a photo of the countryside between dusk and nightfall. Where did this image come from? I took another shot. This time, many angelic images aligned with bright glowing bodies, all sporting the sweetest little halos.

A camera glitch? It has to be a camera glitch. Those thoughts raced through my mind as I continued to photograph. Yet the images kept on coming. *Another camera? I will try another camera and see what happens.* I bolted from the steps and ran into the house to retrieve a second camera, one with a different megapixel and a different brand. As I snapped away, more and more images appeared. By that time my blood pressure had probably reached stroke level. This was, by far, the most exhilarating and overwhelming moment of my life to that point. Had God *actually* sent His angels to help show me the way?

I know one thing for certain: When God decides to "call" you and sends His angels on a mission, you had better take a seat, strap yourself in tight, and double-check to be sure you are securely fastened. God was about to escort me on a photographic ride of a lifetime—a spiritual journey into a world of astounding beauty and immeasurable wonder.

This was a world I had only read about in the Bible and learned through those who had shared their near-death experiences. As God began to gently lift the invisible veil between heaven and earth, an uncharted dimension emerged that almost knocked me off my feet. A holy dimension waiting to be acknowledged, explored, and photographed by *me*. A holy dimension meant to be revealed to others, compliments of our heavenly Father.

From that day forward, my life forever changed. Since August 2009, I have filled digital memory cards with over 5,000 spiritual images, some angelic and some of an entirely unexplainable nature.

The most interesting aspect of this journey is that the images captured on all my digital photos were *not* visible to the human eye. I would simply hold my camera above my head, pray, and take the picture. When I reviewed the camera's monitor, some of the most beautiful and spectacular images of angels and other spiritual beings were there. I could not believe my eyes.

The most beautiful images were those taken after sunset and into the night. I could barely bring myself to put my camera down. Just the anticipation of what the next image would be on that monitor fueled me into a constant state of overdrive. Obviously, God had presented me with these spectacular photographs for a reason, but what was it? What did He want me to do with them?

My first step was to have an expert examine them. I made an appointment with the Chairman of the Physics department at a local university. The moment he cast his eyes on all the images, he was speechless. He had never seen anything like them in his life and could render no professional opinion as to how any of the images related to the law of physics. He did request permission for his office to review and study one of the photographs once I obtained copyrights on all of them. Off the record, stated from his personal perspective, he thought they were spiritual in nature.

Next, I requested a retired Professor of Religion from the same local university to examine them. Upon completing his review and evaluation, he felt they were all spiritual in nature and thought a vast majority of them were angels. He was astounded by the majestic beauty of the angelic beings and the unbelievable rays of light they emitted through the beautiful blue halos that surrounded them.

Having been employed in the county government's court system for twenty-five years, I was always around news reporters. I shared my images with a reporter friend who worked for a local news station. She wanted an "exclusive" to feature my story on a local morning show. Prior to the airing, the news station took my photos to a professional photo lab to be evaluated for authenticity. All clear. No evidence of Photoshop tampering. For the news clips, they even interviewed on camera the lab professional who evaluated my photos. My story was not only featured on the morning show, but on the Five, Six and Ten O'clock Evening News.

I joined a writers' group at church and published my first e-book about my journey with the angels. In the past two years, two of my true angel stories were published as features in a popular national magazine, and I am working on more books for the near future. In New York City in 2015, I was named one of the VIP Women of the Year from one of the nation's largest women's organizations. I receive requests to speak to groups, churches, and organizations about the power of prayer and where it can take us, sharing my beautiful angel photos on large drop-down screens. Hospitals and nursing schools have invited me to share my story and photos with large audiences of volunteers and students, to help them aid patients who face illness and end-of-life struggles and need the blessings of the presence and comfort of angels.

Shortly before I was to speak to a very large audience about the miracle God had blessed me with, I rounded the corner aisle of a local department store and there, staring at me was a decorative little sign that read, "God Doesn't Always Call on the Qualified, But He Always Qualifies the Called" (author unknown). That was my "sign." I felt unofficially "qualified" by all spiritual standards. From that point on, I knew that as long as I gave it my all, God would qualify me to go forth and spread the Good News to all who would receive it, solidifying how much I loved, honored, and adored Him.

In the past two years, I have taken it one step further. Not only do I have memory cards of still shots, I now have videos to share. Yes, videos of actual interaction from God's beautiful messengers as they appear around us during prayer.

What next? Only God knows. He has shown me that without a doubt, when you *pray* to Him, when you *trust* in Him with all your heart, and when you place your *faith* in His unconditional love and guidance, the sky is the absolute limit to what you can accomplish.

Just for the record, my divorce might have been the dark cloud that surrounded me just before this journey began, but the silver lining that followed was nothing short of a miracle. I found a perfect little house situated on a small lake with a western exposure. Longhorn cattle adorn my backyard fence each evening, as beautiful birds of every species serenade me like a masterful choir. Almost every afternoon, a beautiful sunset over the lake is waiting to be photographed—and then there are those beautiful angels who followed me to my new home.

I remember the day I first saw my new home, just prior to purchase. I had searched everywhere, and nothing seemed to fit the bill. I was about ready to throw my hands up in the air when I saw the ad in the newspaper. I called my realtor, and the next day we went to check it out. On a five-foot easel in the entryway stood a painting of a beautiful angel with outstretched arms, as if ready to embrace and welcome me. At that moment, I knew I was home. An offer to purchase was made that day, and the rest is history.

From that point on, every obstacle that was presented was quickly diminished as God and His angels began to "clear the clutter" in my life, thus enabling me to get on with the divine business at hand—to carry out my purpose in life according to God's will, just as I had prayed for.

And that purpose? To expand the realm of spiritual awareness to others, just as God expanded mine. To give those who need tangible proof that there *is* a God who loves them unconditionally. To show them all the evidence they need through the photographs of heaven, which God entrusted to me. To keep fanning the flames of this miraculous gift that God has given me and scatter the embers as far as I can in order to glorify His name.

God has a predestined roadmap to "somewhere" for all of us. Sometimes the choice we make regarding which road to take turns out not to be the best. Often, the road of life becomes damaged with bumps and pot-holes. It can even be washed out from under us by the storms. Hence, we are forced to take a detour down an unfamiliar road. You never know—a turn, a detour, a fork in the road, or a road less traveled could very well place you on a new super highway leading to the destination you were meant for from the beginning.

I am living proof that miracles can result from the bad, the sad, and the unexpected. I look in the mirror each day with a grateful heart and say, "Thank you, Lord, for the lessons learned, for the miracles witnessed, for the blessings received, and for your unconditional love, grace, mercy, and forgiveness. I made it. I love You with all my heart."

Sharon Patterson Payne is a freelance writer, speaker, and author of Angels In The Sunset, *a true picture book story of her journey with God's angels. Her true stories have been twice published in* Woman's World *magazine, and she is currently writing fiction, nonfiction, and a children's book. Sharon's passion is to help expand the realm of spiritual awareness for others, sharing the power of God's love. YouTube Video: "Photo Proof of Heaven." Contact Sharon at*

SharonPattersonPayne@gmail.com; SharonPattersonPayne.com

Thoughts to Ponder
from In the Midst of Angels

1. Angels are mentioned in the Bible nearly 300 times.

2. The detours in our life may result in new assignments from God.

3. Sometimes God allows us to peek into the spiritual realm.

How has God rerouted your life?

He then added, "Very truly I tell you, you will see heaven open, and the angels of God ascending and descending on the Son of Man." — John 1:51

The Power of Words

by Cecilia Bacon

"You never know when a moment and a few sincere words can have an impact on a life." — Zig Ziglar.

I have loved words since I was a young girl. I enjoy learning and using new words. When I was a child, we got copies of Reader's Digest from one of my mother's friends. My favorite game from that magazine was matching a list of words with definitions. My answers weren't always correct, but I learned a lot and loved playing the game.

Whether we know it or not, words affect all of us. We treasure words of encouragement, and we often repeat favorite words or phrases from a movie.

When my kiddos were growing up, they frequently said things that would either send me into fits of laughter or have me asking if my behavior needed to change.

When my son was five, he quizzed me about marriage. I remembered someone saying that boys want to marry someone like their mother. So I asked him, "What kind of girl do you want to marry? Someone like me?"

"No," he quickly said. "You're too bossy."

Some of the most precious words I ever heard were from my mother when she was in the hospital, near the end of her life. I asked her if we were "square." You see, my childhood was difficult, and as a teenager and young adult, I was rebellious. I needed to know if we were okay, if there was anything I needed to address. She patted her bed and invited me to come lie down with her. We talked for a long time. After our discussion, I knew we were square. Those were sweet words of comfort that day, giving my heart peace at her funeral.

My husband doesn't always speak a lot of words, but when he does, I listen carefully. He is gifted with wisdom, his words are good, and he often delivers them with hysterical humor. On our tenth anniversary, he wrote me the sweetest note, which I cherish to this day.

As I said my daily prayers today,
I started with the normal things.
Lord, thank you for this day.
But then I remembered today was a special day.
The anniversary of my life beginning again with
the most wonderful woman in the world.
Thank you, Lord, for my life and the wife
that you have blessed me with.
Without her, the things in life that you
give me would have little meaning.
I love you with every breath I take.

I felt loved and treasured from these words.

This year, my husband and I will celebrate our thirtieth wedding anniversary. He shared some loving words to me in humor. We were discussing family health issues and what we might face as we age. He simply hugged me and said, "Well, bag, nag, or sag, I still love ya Babe." Those words were much different from what he spoke on our tenth anniversary, but I felt just as treasured and loved.

We all have words we need to share, as well as words we sometimes need to change in our lives, don't we? This is especially true when we say things in anger or frustration. Those words might be devastating to anyone, but certainly to a child.

When I was a child, some words confused me and hardened my heart. Up until I was seven years old, my family members were victims of domestic abuse at the hand of my father. He was an abusive alcoholic —a man who, when intoxicated, was filled with unquenchable rage. My mother took the brunt of his abuse and threw herself in front of him when he attempted to go after one of her children. Unfortunately, this only enraged him further, and he beat her until she was no longer able to fight—or she was unconscious. His *words* were powerful and painful, since most of his words were spoken with his fists. She was married to him for eleven years and had five children before we escaped, but not before I heard a lot of words that did emotional damage to my little heart.

Our escape was on a hot and confusing summer day. Confusing because my mother was doing something out-of-character. She was encouraging my father to drink as much as he wanted. He should have been at work, but he went to his favorite bar at lunch, got drunk, and came home, where he abused my mother terribly. He demanded a meal, so she made him some food and kept serving him whiskey.

Because drinking brought his rage attacks, my older sister and I were terrified. Eventually, he passed out, face down on the sofa, and my mother moved into action—as fast as her battered body would allow. She loaded all of us into the station wagon, with instructions to be quiet and lock the doors if our father came out. After going back into the house, she brought out haphazardly packed bags and suitcases that she and tossed into the back of the car. Taking one final risk, she took his wallet from his back pocket and removed all the money he had, then walked out, never to return.

We lived in Louisiana, but Mother made the long trek to Oklahoma to her mother's home, stopping only long enough for bathroom breaks. When we arrived at my grandmother's home, one might expect she would have been happy to receive her daughter and grandchildren in such dire circumstances. That was far from the case. Her home was tiny, with two bedrooms and one bathroom. With another adult and five children ranging from two months to eight years old, she was overwhelmed. Although we had a place to stay, we knew we were not welcome. The years of training to be silent and invisible while living with our father certainly came in handy while living with our grandmother.

The greater problem was that my maternal grandmother was not only hardhearted, she was a "party girl." While we lived with her, freedom to have her drinking partners over was put on the back burner. We were frequently reminded that no one would be happier than she would be when we left. My mother was aware of her indiscretions, which was the primary reason she stayed with my father for so long. She knew she would be trading one set of problems for another.

That summer, Mother worked multiple part-time jobs while she looked for a full-time job that paid well enough for us to get a place of our own. Because she didn't make a lot, she hired high school students to babysit us, or took advantage of activities at a nearby church that provided free childcare. Because the childcare was free, she quickly enrolled all of us in Vacation Bible School (VBS).

Although it was a long time ago, I recall it was mostly a fun week. However, two things stand out in my memory, both associated with words. First, we memorized John 3:16, which I can still recite in the King James Version. "For God so loved the world, that he gave his only begotten Son, that whosoever believeth in him should not perish, but have everlasting life."

As we memorized that verse, our VBS teacher talked all week about God and Jesus and how God sent Jesus to the world to save us. The more she talked, the more my heart wanted to know this Jesus. He sounded nothing like my father, and I craved a relationship with a nice man. Unfortunately, she ended our week by saying some words that were not in the Bible. She had good intentions, but the words broke my heart. She said Jesus loved us so much he would always protect us from harm.

I don't remember anything else she said that day.

What I remember is the horrible feeling I had when, in my child's mind, I felt like God and Jesus did not love me or my family—because we had not been protected from harm. That day, I made a decision. I told Jesus I wasn't going to love Him either.

Don't miss the importance of what I just said. *I told Jesus.* To talk to Jesus, I had to believe in him. You see, there is something that happens when you realize Jesus is who He says He is. That happened to me in the week at VBS. I was still very broken and confused by my teacher's words, so I withheld *my* heart and love from Him.

In defense of the young lady who led our VBS class, I know that by no means did she intend to hurt me with her words. She had no idea who I was or what had happened to my family. If she had, I'm sure her words would have come out differently. She would have shared this truth that *is* in the Bible: Jesus loves you unconditionally, in spite of what's been done to you or what you have done. She would have also uttered this truth in God's Word: "I have told you all this so that you may have peace in me. Here on earth you will have many trials and sorrows. But take heart, because I have overcome the world" (John 16:33 NLT).

If I had heard these words, I might have been comforted, and I might not have turned away from God. Instead, because of my brokenness, I grew up with no complete trust for anyone. I got married, had children, got divorced, and finally remarried a fabulous man.

We had been married for about twelve years when he said some interesting words to me: "This is what is missing from our lives."

He said this after we attended a church service where his brother spoke. I didn't know anything was missing from our lives, so this came as a complete shock. But that day, because I was confident in his love and trusted him, I said, "If this is important to you, then it is fine with me."

We had been attending church for just a few weeks when the pastor kicked off a new series about the Ten Commandments. When we came to the week when he would speak about the commandment to honor your parents, I had a few sarcastic words to offer. I said, "I can't wait to hear what he has to say about this."

The pastor started by saying, "If you are a victim of domestic abuse, I have some words for you at the end of the message." The promise of those words was the only thing that kept me in the service that day. I cried all the way through his message, because his description of a loving earthly father was nothing like what I had experienced as a child. The feelings I had about being fatherless were intensified and painful.

As the service came to a close, with a tone of heartfelt sorrow to those who had been abused, the pastor said, "I am so sorry."

No one had ever said that that to me before. Without even knowing it myself, they were the words I needed to hear. In that moment, I wept thankful tears, because those words healed my broken heart.

I wish devastating words and actions did not exist. But because we are sinners, we have those terrible things. If anyone has ever hurt you, I want to share the words that Jesus said to me that day in church.

"I am so sorry."

And you know what? God is sorry too.

God never desires abuse or harmful words for any of us. He gave us all an amazing gift, free will. We have free will to do and say what is right or wrong. Sometimes we do the right thing, and then we sometimes do terribly wrong things. Maybe you've been wronged with words or actions. Or maybe your words and actions have harmed someone else. Either way, here is what we all need to

190

know: We are all sinners. How do I know this? God tells us this in His Word: "For all have sinned and fall short of the glory of God" (Romans 3:23). But He also says He wants us to have a relationship with Him, and He wants us to turn from our sins and receive His forgiveness. And guess what. You can have that today.

The Bible says, "If you confess with your mouth, 'Jesus is Lord,' and believe in your heart that God raised him from the dead, you will be saved. For it is with your heart that you believe and are justified, and it is with your mouth that you confess [your faith] and are saved."

Maybe these words have hit home in your heart today. I hope they have. I would love for you to have that same precious relationship with Jesus that I have.

Who is Jesus to me now? He is my Father. I know there is no perfect father but Him. If you are missing that relationship in your life like I was, consider some of the most loving words I know from God's Word. In 2 Corinthians 6:18, God says, "I will be a Father to you, and you will be my sons and daughters, says the Lord Almighty."

All those years, I thought I was fatherless. But God made me realize I had a Father who was better than any earthly Father. Knowing I was the daughter of God changed how I saw Him. Before I knew the truth in this verse, I saw Him as a distant being, but now as my Father, my relationship with Him is more personal. I now address my prayers to God as "Father God," because He is my heavenly Dad.

I praise God that I am no longer fatherless. I am the daughter of the Most High King.

Hallelujah!

Cecilia Bacon and her husband of thirty years live in Texas, and have a shared love for traveling. Cecilia has a passion for learning and sharing God's Word, and a genuine heart for helping women find themselves within the pages of the Bible. This is evident in her book Going Home, *which is fiction based on the book of Ruth. She hopes her fictional story of Ruth and Naomi spark a desire to open and read the Bible.*

CeciliaBacon@gmail.com

Thoughts to Ponder

from The Power of Words

1. Harsh words can damage our spirit.

2. Words of encouragement and grace can bring peace.

3. There is no perfect father but God.

> ### *For what words do you need to apologize?*

The words of the reckless pierce like swords, but the tongue of the wise brings healing. — Proverbs 12:18

Spirits of Seduction
by Kandi Rose

Is prayer important?

Do our actions and attitudes affect other lives?

Is there a spiritual battle between good and evil that influences our choices?

Do our choices have consequences?

I, Kandi Rose, know firsthand that yes is the answer to those questions.

I want to thank my Lord and Savior, Jesus Christ, for rescuing me. I was lost, but now I'm found. If you had asked me years ago if I was lost, I would have said you were crazy. At the time, I felt that I was a very successful businesswoman doing what I loved: dancing. Prior to meeting my Savior, Jesus, I owned my own Strip-O-Gram business called Kandi Rose Productions. I had twenty-six people working for me, both male and female strippers, and hired other talented people who were choreographed for variety shows in nightclubs. I had advertisements on billboards, in television commercials, on five radio stations, in the Yellow Pages and newspapers—and I made personal appearances at festivals and fairs, signing autographs. You need to know something about my childhood so you can see how I ended up in such an evil lifestyle.

I loved my daddy. Everyone who met Daddy loved his personality. To neighbors and friends, he was a fine family man. Our family *seemed* normal. We did normal family things. We went on outings, picnics, and special-occasion activities. We appeared to be the average American family. My father worked every day and arrived home in the early afternoon. I never saw him drunk. I cannot remember fights or violence in our home, but an evil spiritual force was active in our daily lives.

I was a very affectionate, kindhearted little girl. My mother never had to spank me. I always wanted to please her and Daddy. Back when curriculums were based on a six-month program instead of one year I was promoted in school three times. My mother taught me good morals and manners. I cannot remember being anything but obedient and doing my best to please my parents. I was a very innocent and naïve little girl. I had no idea that my family and I were victims of seducing spirits that would eventually destroy our home.

Sad, but true.

Evil forces lurk behind the scenes in countless homes, tearing lives apart and eventually leaving nothing but painful memories. As I reflect on my life, I am not only aware of these seducing spirits, but I am also intensely aware of the Holy Spirit and angels who intervened on my behalf.

When I became an adult, my mom shared with me that when she was pregnant with me, daddy kicked her in the stomach so hard that it knocked her out of bed. On another occasion, when I was a baby crying in the crib, he slapped my tiny face. From that point forward, mom vowed to never leave me alone with him. I do not remember her leaving me with anyone, not even family members. Little did she realize that the deception of seducing spirits was active right under her nose. Something is very enticing about sin, something so evil that the idea of almost getting caught is exciting.

One of my earliest childhood memories is of Daddy performing a sexual act on me. The horrendous acts that began at the tender age of three continued through my early teens. Years later, I realized that the evil spirit of exhibitionism had become a major factor in my own life.

My father appeared to be a wonderful husband and father. I was an only child and really loved my daddy until I realized he was perpetrating evil acts on me. My mother had no idea, since he was very cunning and sneaky. After years of this sexual and emotional torment, I couldn't take it anymore and let my dark secret out. I told my mom, a kind and loving woman to whom I was very close. I am grateful that she believed me. At that time of my life, lying was not part of my character. Soon after that, with suitcases in hand and no car, we hopped on the bus, moved to another Chicago neighborhood, and rented a three-room apartment. Bitterness and hatred resided in our hearts for years as more heartaches and disappointments piled on.

Mom grieved and fell into depression. I started hanging with the street kids in the neighborhood, and my innocence soon became victim to more evil. Like so many young people and adults do, I began to look for love and acceptance in all the wrong places I became a victim of date rape and gang rape. When I was five months pregnant, I was even kidnapped at knife point. When I was sixteen, I acquired a false I.D. and hung out in bars and nightclubs. This started a life of multiple addictions: alcohol, drugs, gambling, pornography, and many other evils that evolved into an X-rated lifestyle. When I was eighteen, I was introduced to an agent who booked me as a go-go dancer in thirty-three nightclubs in the Chicago area and even in Indiana. Many of the clubs where I worked were in the Rush Street and Old Town areas. My bad choices led to many heartaches and horrible consequences.

At age eighteen, I became pregnant with my oldest daughter. Her father went to jail three days before she was born. A month after she was born, I met a drummer and had a boy and girl by him. He cheated on me with my best friend. Soon after that heartbreaking episode, I met a man just home from Viet Nam. I was quite impressed, because he had a good job. All the other men had been deadbeats. He drove a brand-new car, and he liked all three of my kids. I was infatuated, but not in love. I saw this as security for myself and the kids, a real family situation. After a year living together, this became my first marriage relationship. He adopted all three kids, and we even had a daughter together. We bought a new house in the Chicago suburbs. Instead of a happy home, years of addictions and unhealed brokenness from childhood helped wreck the marriage.

Ten years of marriage ended with domestic violence, and I returned to what I knew would give me lots of money: dancing. I answered a strip club's ad in the paper, which was more degrading than being a go-go dancer. I began the night dressed in beautiful, elaborate costumes and ended up fully nude. The worst was hustling the men in a darkened room to spend all their money and max out their charge cards. I stayed high all the time, and my heart was hardened. I even prostituted myself with men I met in the strip clubs. After a year of that, I quit.

My boyfriend at the time had a friend who was having a bachelor party. He offered to pay me $150 for a half hour if I would come with my costumes and music and end up doing a full strip for the last few minutes. I thought this was awesome, since my boyfriend would be my bodyguard and no one would physically touch me. I'd just *entertain*. I turned this practice into a full-blown business with lots of advertising. I was well on my way to being rich.

One night, I received an alarming phone call. I thought my children were going to a foster home. This was more than I could bear. I needed peace to deal with this, and my mind went to my mom who always had peace and joy, no matter what she went through. About a year earlier, she was born again through faith in Jesus Christ and married a wonderful man who also became a Christian. They were such an *influence* in my life. They not only *talked the talk,* but they *walked the walk.* For years, she suffered with the physical torment of osteoporosis, fibromyalgia, and rheumatoid arthritis. Her attitude was amazing through it all. My stepdad, an awesome father to me, was an amazing man of God who always showed acts of kindness, even though I had such an evil lifestyle. This unconditional love that was extended to me ultimately showed me God's love.

My mind was tormented by the thought of losing my kids, but God was building faith in me to surrender my life to Him. He told me to not worry, but to have childlike faith in trusting Him. My precious Savior was wooing me by His Holy Spirit, telling me to reflect on my parent's lives. He showed me that He made the difference in their lives, and He wanted to do the same for me.

Wow! What love.

I cried and said, "Mom, I want to give my life to Jesus."

She started crying tears of joy. She said she would lead me in a prayer to confess my sins, and I would be saved (Romans 10:9–10). I do not remember the exact words I prayed, but God heard me and knew I meant it. I was crying from the depths of my sinful despair.

When that prayer ended, a peace came over me unlike anything I had ever experienced before. From that day forward, I knew I belonged to God. He was my heavenly Daddy, and everything was going to be all right. Childlike faith was there. Just as a little child does not worry about tomorrow, I had no worries about the future that was now in His hands.

I received the peace I needed and total freedom from all the addictions. Most important of all, I gained a relationship with the One who loves me and died for me. I did not have to lose my kids and went on to follow the Lord for the next three-and-a-half years. That was in 1984. I'd love to tell you that I stayed faithful to the

Lord from then on, but I did not.

I let loneliness overtake me. I didn't wait on the Lord to bring me a good Christian man to marry. I chose my own. Big mistake!

The Bible tells us not to be unequally matched. That command is to keep us from having needless heartache. I learned a great lesson that I now share: Don't spend unchaperoned time with the opposite sex. The devil offers us poisonous promises of happiness, but we can't blame him when we make wrong choices. In my case, God gave me the Holy Spirit to guide me, and I didn't listen. Once I gave in to that first sexual encounter, the mud in that pigpen became quicksand.

To make matters worse, after two weeks I found out my new boyfriend was on angel dust and crack cocaine. I was stuck in a rut. I wanted my pure relationship with the Lord back, but on the other hand, I was giving in to this spirit of lust. Guilt ensued, and I went back to smoking pot and eventually my old nasty attitudes and actions. For two miserable years (yes, they were miserable), I relinquished all the benefits of being in my Father's house, just as the prodigal did. I quit hanging with my Christian friends and going to church. Mental anguish appeared. But the Holy Spirit would not leave me alone. His voice became louder than the devil's. Jesus was pursuing me—to seek and save that which was lost. Oh, I am so thankful He never gave up on me. His love compelled me to return, to "go back home."

God sent so many messages and messengers my way, I finally had to say, "Yes, Lord." The way I got saved was the way I rededicated my life to Him. I confessed my sins and wanted to turn from them. That's repentance. Now I am more determined than ever to never go back to that pigpen. I want to follow the Shepherd's way, not mine. And I want to help others do the same.

I've been clean and free, loving my best friend and Savior for twenty-eight years. I am now a credentialed Evangelist through the Assemblies of God. I am an author of five books, have had a radio program for four years, and host my own TV program called, "Addiction Free," which airs in millions of homes.

If you have not made an all-out commitment to live for Jesus, listen to the voice of love calling. There is peace, joy, and purpose living for Jesus. He has great plans for your life and wants to use you to help others experience His great love, forgiveness, power, and purpose.

Kandi Rose *was a former stripper and prostitute who once owned her own strip business in the Chicago area. She is now a credentialed Evangelist, Producer, and Host of* Addiction Free, *a national TV show, broadcasting on three networks. She had a radio show for three years and has authored five books. She travels across the United States sharing her testimony and ministering the Word. After Kandi ministers in a church or conference, she interviews the pastor and others who have freedom testimonies.*

AddictionFreeTV.com

Thoughts to Ponder
from Spirits of Seduction

1. Evil is real.

2. Right choices are crucial.

3. Belief in Jesus makes us clean and free.

**How has God rescued you
from poor choices?**

---

*Greater is He who is in you, than
he that is in the world. — 1 John 4:4*

The Unsilenced Voice
by Kathy R. Green

When I was a little girl, I loved spending time in my room talking to God and writing in my little diary with lock and key. I never knew this was a clue to my life's purpose, or that it would lead to what I'm doing today. After I got married, I began to seek God through daily prayer, asking what I was created to do. He responded in a unique way while I was attending a women's conference. From that point forward, I studied my Bible and prepared to answer God's call.

In 1996, God gave me a mandate to teach His people how to pray and stand in the gap for their loved ones. I was a stay-at-home mom and church volunteer with a passion for prayer and spending time in God's presence. I didn't realize I would answer this calling in book form, but talking to God and journaling was my way of surviving life's challenges. It was my place of refuge where I always found great peace and comfort despite what was happening around me.

Six months before the release of my first book, I went for a routine colonoscopy and endoscopy. Although all test results came back normal, I began to have difficulty swallowing, which led me back to my doctor. He sent me to an endocrinologist to look at my thyroid. The specialist greeted me and inquired about my symptoms, then said he wanted a sonogram of my thyroid area. A few minutes later, with eyes as large as two saucers, he said, "You have a very large mass on your right thyroid. There is a chance it could be cancer. It must be removed."

Fear attempted to grip my heart. I knew I was in for a fight for my life and health. I had been suffering from other symptoms such as extreme fatigue and anemia, but I had no idea thyroid dysfunction was the cause. After the diagnosis, I consulted two different surgeons. More extensive tests were taken to determine the severity of my condition before other steps were considered.

On the day of my diagnosis, I drove home with tears in my eyes and ran to the secure place where I always went when I was in trouble. As I sat at my desk, I talked to the Lord, asking if I had to have the surgery or if He would supernaturally heal me. By the stripes Jesus bore on His body, we are healed and made whole. I've always believed that healing comes through many avenues. Sometimes it comes through medical intervention, and sometimes God works miracles. I was prepared to do whatever the Lord told me. If He told me to stand in faith, I would have done just that. But He spoke these words to my heart: "I'm going to allow you to be cut on, but I will be glorified in the end." With divine direction, I knew I needed to move forward with the surgery, trusting God every step of the way.

During the months ahead, thoughts were churning through my mind about the surgery. I know it sounds vain, but one of my concerns was having a scar across my neck and needing to wear scarves or turtlenecks for the rest of my life. So I asked God to please not allow me to have a scar, because my skin has a tendency to keloid. God was gracious. He brought me through the surgery just fine. There was no cancer found in my body. Praise the Lord.

But what I didn't expect was what the doctor reported to my husband and me when I came out of recovery. The mass was so large that it had grown into my chest cavity. She had to dig down past my collar bone and into my ribcage to get it all. This surgeon had come highly recommended as one of the top thyroid surgeons in Texas. She had done thousands of these surgeries, but had never seen a case like mine. When she opened me up, she was shocked because there were no outward signs.

When I opened my mouth for the first time, I was surprised that I could barely speak. *What in the world happened to my voice?* My doctor said that was normal for this type of surgery. Months later, there was still no improvement. I had to learn how to swallow without choking. For months, my food or drink wanted to go down the wrong way. I could barely speak above a whisper. At times, my voice was deep and very raspy. I was eventually referred to an Ear Nose and Throat specialist, who diagnosed me with Vocal Cord Paralysis.

After seeing six doctors and enduring many vocal cord examinations, I was tempted to stop using my voice altogether. Everything in me, including the shame that I felt around those who didn't know my situation, wanted to give up on speaking, teaching, and sharing the message of prayer. After all, I couldn't even order food in a crowded restaurant or at a drive-through window, because no one could hear what I was saying.

Most of us answer God's call with a joyful heart, knowing it's a privilege to be called and chosen by God for a specific assignment. But now I was faced with a choice. Was I going to move forward with my life's work, or did I have a legitimate excuse why I couldn't continue?

I soon discovered that God was not going to accept my excuses to get out of what He had called me to do. To the contrary, since I was diagnosed with Vocal Cord Paralysis, God began to open more doors than I would have ever imagined. He wanted me to talk about the power of prayer and share my story via radio and television. For several years, he also blessed me to lead prayer conference calls. God has taken what the enemy used to discourage me to the point of giving up, and he turned it around for His glory. God has confounded the wise by using something foolish.

One woman on my weekly prayer calls was under the impression that I had taken voice lessons to produce the tone of voice with which I spoke. Some said my voice was used as a healing balm to others, because of the peace and comfort they experienced whenever I spoke or prayed. I'm glad I chose to obey God and step out with boldness and courage, depending on Him as I walked through every door He opened.

While I was leading a prayer session at a prayer breakfast, a pastor asked what happened to my voice. When I shared my story, she told me of a similar surgery she had undergone, and her voice was once like mine. She understood what I was going through. Prior to her surgery, she was a singer and worship leader, but her vocal cords had been damaged. As she went—she was healed. She encouraged me greatly and changed the trajectory of my life when she said, "Whatever you do, don't stop using your voice." I took her words to heart, and I continued to move forward by faith. God began to heal me as I went forward. I'm amazed by how He uses my voice to impact the world and awaken the body of Christ to the message of prayer and walking in close fellowship with Him.

I never expected to encounter such a test. I didn't understand why or how this could have happened to me. All I was doing was being obedient to what God called me to do. But we must understand, the calling has a cost. The question is, are we willing to pay the price to follow God and His plan for our lives? Only God and my family really knew what I had to go through. Prior to the surgery, most weeks were spent dragging around the house from room to room, flopping down on the couch, and sleeping an hour here and an hour there. I felt so useless. I was slowly dwindling away as I got weaker by the day. I share this only to expose how the enemy works. He used this time of my life to flood my mind with thoughts of laziness, guilt, and condemnation, because I wasn't doing what I was created to do. I felt like a failure. But thanks be to God, who always causes us to triumph in Christ.

As I continued to walk with God and press toward the mark of the high calling of God in Christ Jesus, I made it to the other side—because I held on tightly to God and refused to give up.

Today, I am healthier than I've ever been before. I fought my way back to good health through exercising and eating healthy. And above all, I never stopped using my voice. I gave God the little that I had to offer, and He made much of it. My voice is completely restored. I don't know the day or hour that it happened, but it's a miracle. One day when I was up early singing and worshipping the Lord, I heard myself reach a range I had not gone to in years. I was singing in a soprano voice, from a place of strength, not weakness. It brought me to tears. I knew that God had worked a miracle in my life. I know it's a miracle, because I went back to my Ear, Nose and Throat doctor so he could look at my vocal cords and give me a written report. To the amazement of both of us, my right vocal cord remained still. Only one of them was moving. Yet the sound of my voice is stronger today than it ever was before.

We may have to walk through valleys throughout our lifetime, but the great news is that God never leaves us or forsakes us. When we stay close to Him and give Him the best we can offer, we are like the boy who offered Jesus his lunch of two fish and five loaves of bread. With that selfless gift, Jesus fed five thousand people. He will take our little and make much of it.

And He gets all the glory.

Kathy R. Green is a prayer author and speaker. She is the owner of KRG Publishing and Consulting. She is an acquisition editor and writing coach for Christian authors. Kathy's books include Pray-ers Bear Fruit *and* Come. *Kathy serves on the Executive Advisory Board for the Christian*

Women in Media Association and Leave Your Beauty Mark Foundation. Kathy and her husband, Cliff, have been married for thirty-two years. They have two adult children married to wonderful spouses and two grandchildren.

KathyRGreen.com

Thoughts to Ponder
from The Unsilenced Voice

1. The greater the battle, the greater the need to call on Christ.

2. Jesus still performs miraculous healings.

3. Most callings of God have a cost.

When have you given up on a promise from God?

Then Jesus said to his disciples, "Whoever wants to be my disciple must deny themselves and take up their cross and follow me." — Matthew 16:24

Choices
by Charlene Sims

Think back to when you were twenty-five. What were you doing? What choices were you making? We make choices every day that shape our future. I invite you to walk down memory lane with me. Imagine slipping the key of your future into the lock of the door of your brand-new printing company. You have just opened the door to one of the best choices you will ever make.

In September 1976, I had the opportunity to unlock that door. This was made possible by the financial backing of a friend as a silent partner. Picture me: single, barely twenty-five, 5 feet 1½ inches, 95 pounds, looking wide-eyed into an industry dominated by men. In 1976, very few businesses were owned by women.

Though I was a hard worker, I had only one year of college and no money, but I loved managing the printing company where I worked and possessed a passion for serving my customers. Still, I knew nothing about owning a business. When my future partner made his offer, evidently based on seeing something in me that I couldn't see in myself, I knew a miracle was unfolding.

Let me take you back even further in my life, at a time when choices were not my own. I was five, and my childhood was stripped away after my parents divorced. The split was devastating. My dad left home. Until I was in my early twenties, I never had the opportunity to have a relationship with him. My mom remarried a man who sexually abused me for seven years. This left me a scarred and insecure little girl full of shame. I had to make daily choices to protect myself and simply survive.

As I grew older, I determined to not let this define my life. However, that process took time. Through the years, my three older siblings moved out to live with my biological father, and my little brother and I stayed with my mom. I became a caretaker nursing my mother, who was sick, while caring for and trying to protect my little brother from our predator stepfather. I was shy and insecure, with very few friends. I never learned how to dress, wear makeup, fix my hair or other things that young ladies did at that age. I became a tomboy and convinced myself that if I had been a boy, what happened to me as a little girl would not have occurred. Little did I know how untrue that was, that my stepfather had abused my brothers as well as my sisters. We all grew up with a lot of pain and turmoil in our lives. Both of my brothers have spent twenty-plus years in prison. One of my sisters committed suicide. The other has had a very difficult life, living in much turmoil.

At the age of fourteen, I was thrust into another life-changing event over which I had no control. I felt abandoned once again as my mother, the only person I felt loved me, died of brain cancer. I was left with no one but my little brother at home, and I was scared and lonely. I did not think anything or anyone could ever fill the big hole in my life.

However, through a dear friend, a pastor told me about someone Who loved me deeply. So much so that He sent His Son to die on the cross for *me*. It was at this time I trusted Jesus Christ as my personal Savior, and when He came into my life I knew He would never abandon me. This has proven to be the most important decision I've ever made.

There were still inner struggles as I wrestled with the pain of abuse, shame, false guilt, insecurities, and yes, hate. I was very unsure of myself. In other ways, I was a fighter and an overachiever. I did well in school, became a master manipulator, and was not going to let anyone hurt or use me again. My stepfather had not touched me in a number of years, so I felt a little more in control. I believed very early in life that *I* had to control my circumstances in order to survive. If I did the right thing and made the right decision, I would receive praise and love, something I desperately craved. With that driving me, I did well in high school. I graduated from high school at seventeen and moved to Dallas to begin a new journey.

I attended a Bible college for a year but ran out of money. I made some friends, but because of my insecurities I would latch on to anyone who would love me or care for me. As I sucked that relationship dry, I felt worse about myself. I was lonely, extremely co-dependent, and still so confused about the things that had happened to me as a child. It was hard for me to believe that anyone could *like* me, much less *love* me.

That summer, God led me to a Christian Youth Camp in the Palo Duro Canyon, close to Amarillo, Texas. I experienced people caring for me and liking me, and I felt like I finally had a family I could trust. I loved that time, and those next few summers at camp signified a crucial period of spiritual growth. I began to understand the faithfulness of God as He brought others to love me.

When I was twenty, I went to counseling for healing from the abuse, hate, shame, and guilt. That's when I realized I could not only survive, I could thrive. I attended a new start-up church, where people loved me and took me in as their family. I started working at a printing company where I felt so insecure it was hard to look a customer in the eyes, much less talk to them. The Christian couple I worked for believed in me and in what God could do in my life. They loved me and mentored me in life as well as in the printing business.

Much to my dismay, they sold the printing company in 1975. The next year, I experienced God's faithfulness again, as I take you back to the beginning of my story. I was sitting across the desk from my possible future partner. I knew that God was blessing me with a miracle, with the opportunity to open my own printing company. My business partner mentored me as a father figure and a friend, teaching me precious life skills of trusting my decisions. In 1987, I bought out his shares of the business.

God showed me His faithfulness again as he brought someone else into my life. Steve was a wrangler I had known at camp when I was in my late teens. I loved horses and hanging around with the boys. To Steve, I was just one of the guys. I was his buddy and would ride horses and shoot guns with him and his brothers. Instead of an insecure tomboy wearing boots and jeans, he found a lady in process, someone God had changed, healed, and matured. After being friends for a year, we realized we had something pretty special. So in April 1988, I married the love of my life. Because of my past abuse, I was unsure that I would ever get married. However, Steve was my friend, and he loved me. That gave me a security I had never experienced before. Even though we had many ups and downs in our growing experiences over the next years, we had a very good marriage.

Life was good.

In July 2001, Steve and I were at dinner and talking about how great our world was at fifty. He was serving as a missionary, my printing business was doing well, and we were attending a church we loved. We felt like God was really using us. Steve was an elder at the church and I was the Finance Director and the Women's Ministry Director. I could hardly believe that God was using *me*, a tomboy in ministry with women.

I *thought* I was in the prime of my life. I did not think I could want or ask for anything more. The Bible says, "Be of sober spirit, be on the alert. Your adversary, the devil, prowls around like a roaring lion, seeking someone to devour" (1 Peter 5:8). He was definitely on the prowl and did not like what was going on in my life, so he launched a full-force attack.

I found myself in a co-dependent relationship with someone who needed me and worshiped me. I liked that feeling. It fed into all my old insecurities of wanting to be needed and loved as a little girl. That feeling was confusing because it fought with the adult, sensible me. I had a good relationship with my husband, so why were these emotions so overwhelming? What was this incredible power gripping me? It was called *temptation*, an opening for Satan to weave his way into my life, set traps, and wreak destruction.

I was listening to the lies of my emotions instead of the truth I knew. One sad weekend in October of 2001, the destruction that Satan had planned for me overcame me. I possessed full knowledge in my brain that it was wrong, but obviously not my senses. Even with the overwhelming consequences looming in front of me, I entered a sexual relationship with this person.

After a few days of torment and hell, I went to my pastor, confessed my sin, and resigned my positions at church. In an extremely difficult conversation, I confessed to my husband, who was in disbelief. He was not alone. I could not believe what I had done. I had made a conscious choice to sin, and the ripple effect was devastating—on my husband, church, friends, business, and most of all, my relationship with my Lord and Savior. I loved my husband. He was good to me and trusted me so much, yet I hurt him tremendously. Everything had been going right, but Satan wanted to take me down. I opened the door for his opportunity. I could hardly live with myself and quite frankly, did not want to live. The next weeks were a blur. The pain moved in slow motion.

I had experienced one of my biggest fears—failure. I felt like the most horrible sinful person who had ever lived. The pain was excruciating. Unlike past sins, this offense was not something I could blame on others. I was responsible. A wise counselor made me promise I would not hurt myself, trusting in my integrity to keep my promise. The alternative was to admit me into a hospital, which scared me to death and spiraled me into a deep black hole of depression.

Early one night in my husband's arms, sobbing, I said, "I promise I will never do anything like that again."

He gently pushed me away and looked at me. Softly he said, "Don't say that, because you might—but if you do, I will be there to walk beside you, just like I will now."

What a picture of grace. He did walk beside me every moment of the way. He was angry and had a hard time with what I'd done, but he loved me and wanted to rebuild our relationship. He was willing to forgive and give me grace like his heavenly Father had offered him.

Slowly, God's grace reached me. I read that there is nothing I could do to make God love me any *less,* but I also had to realize there was nothing I could do to make God love me any *more.* He loves me fully, even in my sin. I realized that *my* sin is why Christ died on the cross for me—so I would never have to be separated from my heavenly Father. The fresh reality of what He did for me on the cross was overwhelming. I realized that He did not see my sin. I was clean, washed as white as snow.

With the help of much counseling, workshops, friends loving us, and studying the Word of God, Steve and I have healed profoundly. I think I will always have this sin as a thorn in my flesh to remind me that I fell flat on my face when I was not looking up and depending on God's power for my growth, recovery, and healing.

There will always be chances to grow and learn in this world. God gives us the strength to cope with what He allows. God gave us that strength a few years later when Steve was diagnosed with bladder cancer. The diagnosis was a shock. We knew we had no choice but to depend on God for what He had in store for us. He enabled a fine surgeon to make a new bladder out of his intestines, giving give him the opportunity to live longer and serve God, sharing the stories of God's Word to people across the world. He is cancer-free and living a healthy life.

In March 2015, another life challenge left us having to trust God. Steve's son died of a gunshot wound to his chest—

devastating for our whole family. This was such a sad way to lose a son. He left behind two little girls and his wife. God was amazing again, as He gave us strength to cope, grieve, learn, grow, and trust through that experience. He is so faithful, and we are grateful.

Romans 5:3–5 says, "Not only so, but we also rejoice in our sufferings, because we know that suffering produces perseverance, perseverance, character, and character, hope." I would not trade these last years, even as hard as they have been, because God has used these things to build character in both Steve and me. As we have healed, we know God *can and is* still using us in even bigger and more-effective ways, enabling us to share His faithfulness, forgiveness, grace, and hope.

I have had many choices to make. Some were not my own, and of those that were, some were not so good. There were hard choices to survive, grow, and be successful, to forgive and trust— and sometimes there were lessons from not trusting. I'm thankful that God continues to work on me during the new choices that He has put before me.

I have worked through a lot of forgiveness issues concerning my stepfather, mom, dad, as well as my own sin. God has clearly shown me some roots are planted deep down, tormenting and controlling fears and trust issues with God. After hearing a "Forgiving Forward" message, I asked God what He had for me to learn. God spoke to my heart, saying, "You need to forgive your stepfather for *using* you." After arguing with God, trying to convince Him that I had already forgiven my stepdad, God persisted. As I opened my heart to what He was telling me, I realized this was *a root* of unforgiveness. I had forgiven him for the overall abuse, but I had not forgiven the specific wound, for the specific pain, for the acts *of using* me. As I realized the difference in naming the specific acts and forgiving each wound, I sobbed. I named each wound, forgiving them all, laying them at the foot of the cross to be covered with the blood of Jesus.

I prayed that somehow my stepfather could experience the same grace from God that I had received. I hoped he would be in heaven when I got there.

I have never experienced such freedom as I have for the last three years. When I get irritated, angry, or frustrated, I know I have a forgiveness issue to look at. It is usually because someone is not doing what I wanted them to do in the way I wanted them to do it. My greatest blessing is my relationship with my Father in heaven— deeper, closer, and better than ever before. I have learned to trust Him much more. The wall of protection I had built around me has been broken down, and I know He has me in His hands.

Allow me to challenge you to make some choices. If you know Jesus as your Savior, what choices are you making in your life? Good ones? Bad ones? Perhaps you are struggling with unforgiveness in your life. Somewhere deep down, it has a strong grip on you, perhaps torturing you. Ask God to open your heart and show you ways you might be hurting because of unforgiveness.

Someone told me once that life is 10 percent of what happens to you and 90 percent how you respond. I have chosen to live my life in the 90 percent. God has given me an incredibly rich, productive, and blessed life. Are you living in the 10 percent or the 90 percent? Live in the 90 percent, and let the lessons of the 10 percent make you stronger. Be a thriver—don't settle for just surviving.

Today I am thrilled to share with you as a thriver. I have just celebrated my company's fortieth anniversary of unlocking that front door to my future.

My life verse is Psalm 40:1–3: "I waited patiently for the Lord and he inclined to me and heard my cry. He brought me up out of the pit of destruction, out of the miry clay, and he set my feet upon a rock making my footsteps firm. He put a new song in my mouth, a song of praise to our God. Many will see and fear and will trust in the Lord."

I can't sing worth a flip, but God has given me a new song to belt out, and it is truly a song of praise. I pray that as He uses me, many will see and fear and will put their trust in the Lord. They will come to understand that their choices have eternal consequences.

Charlene Sims is a successful entrepreneur, businesswoman, and speaker. She brings her encouraging and convicting account of the endless grace of God through her life story. Remarkable in her candor, she shares about God lifting her from childhood sexual abuse, teenage loss of her mother, guilt, shame, and then feelings of worthlessness and despair in the face of her own sin, to the boundless glory of God's redeeming forgiveness, grace, and His constant faithfulness. Char@TheMastersPress.com

Thoughts to Ponder
from Choices

1. Forgiveness is a gift you extend to others.

2. Life is 10% what happens to you and 90% how you respond.

3. Choices can have eternal consequences.

> **How are you responding to life's choices?**

See, I set before you today life and prosperity, death and destruction. — Deuteronomy 30:15

The Over-Doer
by Michelle Bengtson

I've always been a do-er, an achiever, and a go-getter. To say I was born that way might be a cliché for some, but not for me. I was born weighing less than three pounds during an era when babies that small usually didn't live, and if they did, there were severe cognitive or physical ramifications.

At the age of three, I came down with a high fever. The doctors were concerned about the potential for brain damage if the fever was not alleviated. My mother tried everything the doctors advised, from alcohol rubs to ice baths. When nothing worked, they told her to give me aspirin, not knowing that I was deathly allergic to aspirin.

Medical personnel quickly realized the error of their ways when I lapsed into anaphylactic shock They prepared my parents for the likelihood that I would not live. If I did make it, I would be mentally incapacitated and/or physically deformed. The aspirin did cause severe physical deformity of my legs and my foot, and my parents were told I would never walk again. But those doctors didn't know my parents, and they didn't know *me*.

My mother was strong, and she passed that on to me. I was a fighter. I was an achiever. I was a go-getter. And I wasn't a quitter.

I got straight A's in school, sat at the top of my class, and set my sights high. In those respects, I take after my dad. He was driven too. So driven, in fact, that he tended to be a workaholic and suffered his first major heart attack at age forty. But the health crisis wasn't going to slow him down. He was still driven, and determined to beat heart disease. Cold-turkey, he quit smoking, began a "heart healthy" diet, and took up running every day, even on Christmas. He went all out. But it wasn't enough. He died of a second major heart attack at age forty-two.

I was fifteen when he passed away.

My mother was from New Zealand and wasn't an American citizen. She didn't have an education or a trade. One of my first thoughts after my father died was: *What can I do to make enough money to support my family?* And my next thought? *I am going to do whatever I have to do to make sure this doesn't happen to me. If something ever happens to my husband, I'm going to be able to support my family.*

I had the God-given tenacity to back it up. And I did.

I graduated from college. I earned a master's degree, then a doctorate. My husband and I spent four years apart in a long-distance commuter marriage so I could complete my internship and three years of fellowship in a male-dominated specialty of Neuropsychology.

Honestly, I can't tell you of any goal I've ever set that I haven't achieved. Failure has never been an option.

When times got tough, I got tougher. I had developed the coping mechanism of jumping in with both feet and doing whatever it took to handle the demands. I just worked a little harder.

Shortly after I completed all my training, my husband and I were able to reunite under one roof. We both found jobs in our respective careers, and in the same geographic region of the country. I became pregnant with our first baby (my family's first grandchild, the one I think they had all but given up on since we had been married twelve years).

Within months of his birth, my mother was diagnosed with lung cancer. And within the year, my husband was diagnosed with a very rare form of abdominal cancer. He was given two years to live, and a one in four chance of dying on the operating table. While I was nursing my husband and my mother back to health, I miscarried our baby.

People would say to me during this time, "I don't know how you do it. I don't think I could do it." To be honest, I felt like saying, "What choice do I have? I just do the next thing." But then, that was me—the do-er.

As the doctor was telling me I was miscarrying our baby, and that I needed a higher-level ultrasound, I was calling the hospital where I worked to check my schedule, to fit the ultrasound around the patients I was scheduled to see.

What was wrong with this picture?

There comes a point when doing, achieving and performing is no longer productive.

I wish I could tell you that I learned that valuable lesson the day I miscarried our baby. Or when my mother finally succumbed to lung cancer. But I didn't. I was too stubborn for that. I was too busy picking up the pieces of our shattered lives and trying to make a mosaic out of it.

I finally learned the lesson when I was the one whose body gave out and shut down. For almost five months, I could no longer do. I couldn't achieve. I couldn't perform, no matter how badly I wanted to. I couldn't be the doctor treating patients, or the provider for our family. I couldn't even hold down food. I was on home IV fluid and nutrition to keep me alive and out of the hospital. My body said, "No more."

I have never before, nor ever since, felt so weak and helpless. It was such a foreign experience for this achieving, go-getter, can-do woman. I had endless hours when I could do nothing but think, pray, reflect, and read from the confines of my bed. It brought me to the very place I had been running from.

Over time, somehow, I had begun to equate my worth with my accomplishments. The more I did, the better I did, and that led to more self-worth, or so I thought. Unconsciously, I reasoned that the more I did, the better I did, and the more God would love me.

I was raised in a Christian home. We attended church every time the doors were open. I knew that Jesus shed his blood, died on a cross to save me from my sins, and provided eternal salvation. I had that assurance—I had accepted Him as my Savior when I was seven years old. Yet somehow in my go-getter, achiever mentality, I missed a fundamental principle that there was nothing I could do to make God love me any more or love me any less.

It took coming to a place when I was no longer able to do anything—when all I could do for months on end was to "be" in God's presence. I had to realize that what God desires is for me to have faith and believe in a God, who desires a relationship with His children—not for me to spend my life trying to do more and be more in exchange for additional love and approval. He already gave that.

It's up to me to believe it.

"For God so loved the world that he gave his one and only Son, that whoever believes in him shall not perish but have eternal life" (John 3:16).

It's up to you to believe it as well.

Dr. Michelle Bengtson, *an author, speaker, and board-certified neuropsychologist, knows pain and despair firsthand, and combines her professional expertise and personal experience with her faith to address issues surrounding medical and mental disorders for those suffering and those caring for them. She offers practical tools, affirms worth, and encourages faith. Dr. Bengtson offers hope to unlock joy and relief—even in the middle of the storm. She is the author of* Hope Prevails: Insights from a Doctor's Personal Journey through Depression.

DrMichelleBengtson.com

Thoughts to Ponder
from The Over-Doer

1. The "doing" should never override the "being."

2. God will sometimes force us to be still before Him.

3. Illness or physical deformity does not disqualify us from God's service.

> **What unrealistic expectations have you placed on yourself?**

Be still in the presence of the Lord and wait patiently for him. — *Psalm 37:7*

Choose Wisely
by Johnna Howell

My heart raced, drumming rhythmically loud in my ears. My mouth grew dry, and my tongue felt like dehydrated jerky searching thirstily for moisture. I stared at the beautiful young woman sitting across from me at the luncheon table. Was she serious? How did this happen? How was it possible?

My friend saw my discomfort. She leaned back, set her jaw, and crossed her arms, repeating herself. "Yes. I no longer believe in God, Jesus, or the Bible."

I opened my mouth to object, but she held her hand out to shush me.

"You can't change my mind," she said. "I've been researching and studying this for a while, and this is what I believe. Don't try to convince me otherwise. It won't happen."

I felt smacked across the face. Not even a conversation about this? No opportunity for rebuttal? I thought about the years I'd known her and her family, going to church, praying together, and praising God through songs. I thought about the God I love and the overwhelming difference He'd made in my life. How could I live without Him? How could she?

I prayed as I talked. "So you don't believe in a Creator? That all the intricacies of life in the world just evolved from nothing?"

Lips still tight. Arms still crossed. "It's just as easy to believe in that as in a supernatural being doing it."

I sipped my water. Now what? That was my testimony: The belief in God as Creator. The wonder of the complexity of the world. The amazement of every minute detail of every living thing, the beauty of it, and the conclusion of the existence of a divine designer.

I'd been raised in a Christian home, taught stories from the Bible, and attended church twice every Sunday and once on Wednesday nights. In an instant, I flashed back to the moment I accepted Jesus Christ as my Savior. A young child alone in a darkening Sunday school classroom, waiting for my parents to stop talking and go home. The church's neon sign glowed through the frosted windows, providing the only light. I rocked back and forth in the chair, my arms wrapped around my knees, humming Christian songs.

Did I really believe all this stuff, or did I just accept it because everyone in my life did? I thought of the ladybugs and ants I often watched as I played outside. I thought of the birds, dogs, cats, and other animals. Flowers, weeds, and trees were added, along with fish and frogs. These were all parts of my life, of the world I lived in and loved.

Did these things just kind of come together on their own? Did sunlight, lightning, and rain generate them? Who or what created the sun, moon and clouds? I examined the world with the same scrutiny as my friend, but I made a different choice. I chose to believe in the powerful God of the universe, the Creator God.

With my friend, I attempted to use the Bible as a reliable source for belief in God. I pointed out a couple of previously unknown scientific facts contained within the writings and the amazing discoveries, years later, of their truths as well as of the continuity of its content. She brushed these thoughts away and closed the conversation once again.

Time for reaching her was running out. She was making movements like she intended to leave. I needed another approach. I prayed and sought the Holy Spirit's guidance. Where was she coming from? What did she need? What was the one thing *she* most needed from God? What was the one thing *I* most needed from God?

"Where do you go?" I asked.

"What? Where?" She frowned. "If you mean, when I die. I die." She shrugged. "Dead. No more. Nothing."

My stomach lurched. The sharp bluntness of her response again caught me off guard. "No. I don't mean, when you die. I'm talking about when you're upset, afraid, or lonely. When you need comfort or are trying to understand something. Where do you find peace or joy? Where do you go? To your friends? Relatives? Yourself?"

I touched a nerve. I glimpsed it in her face.

"Where do you go?" I said. "I don't know what I'd do if I didn't have God. I truly don't know what I'd do." My mind scrambled for examples. Which ones should I use? What does she need? *Lord, help me say the right thing.*

She picked up her purse, stood, and smiled down at me. "Ready to go?"

The moment was gone. The door was closed—at least for today.

Through the years, I'd had many conversations with people questioning the existence of God or the necessity of following his words in the Bible. A dialogue of discovery easily followed. I'd had time to ask more questions, listen to the person's doubts and concerns, suggest further evidences or solutions, and offer them Jesus, who means everything to me.

This was new. I was not prepared. I was not quick on my feet. My life stories weren't etched firmly enough in my mind to offer them on the spot.

Since that day, I've had many hours of reflection upon the powerful God of universes and his working in my life.

He thunders in the storm.

He whispers in the breeze.

He fills the heavens with his light.

He shows his beauty in a sunset, a flower, an oak tree.

He hates evil and loves good. He is good. He loves completely.

He comforts, heals, helps, fights, counsels, teaches, and shepherds.

He is my hope, my peace, my Savior, my all.

From my office window, I stare out into the trees and think about the many things I could share about a large portion of my life. My childhood, education, marriage at age nineteen, divorce at twenty-five, two children during that time, a new marriage four years later, pursuit of an advanced degree, exciting, adventurous jobs taking me around the world in chauffeured limousines, fine dining, and staying in five-star hotel suites. There are wonderful stories of God's working in my life and many successes I eagerly attributed to him. But these blessed times cannot compare to the blessings that have come to me in the years since.

Life had been good to me. God had been good to me. But worldly success and pleasures are not enough. I wanted more. I wanted to go deeper, to know Him more fully. I prayed. "Lord sift me. Get all the impurities out of me. Draw me closer to You. Make me clean before You."

First came a career transition. I loved my job, but the company I worked for was sold, and I was not interested in relocating to the new headquarters. I gave my notice.

Since people were always asking what books I referred to for doing my job, I decided to write. A few books were out there, but not that many specific to what I was doing. I wrote two nonfiction books (one co-authored with a colleague). I knew the markets and the people controlling them. The opportunity for success was enormous worldwide, but my heart was not in nonfiction. God was calling me to another path—one I'd never considered and would not have chosen on my own.

Fiction writing. If you're a business woman who'd received multiple accolades and awards for years on her direct, organized presentations, proposals, nonfiction writing and speaking, and now you find yourself required to paint a scene and develop a character without *telling*, you're all but doomed to failure. It was foreign to my way of thinking or communicating. It required knowledge of punctuation, proper use of words, and of course, the dreaded metaphor. I was used to saying what I meant with very little drama. Now, my whole writing life was full of drama. It was hard, harder, and hardest. I took classes at writer's conferences and participated in an advanced writers' group. I felt humiliated and humbled in my feeble efforts.

Not only did I struggle with the new way of writing, but I was feeling led to write Young Adult Christian Dystopian Suspense fiction. Try spending a suspense-filled day with a group of evolving young characters. It's fun and exciting and exhausting. Not to mention, stress-filled.

Writing is a lonely business. You spend days, weeks, and months in long stretches of isolation. I sometimes played computer games and listened to talk radio as a distraction. But God had other ideas, and I was not a quitter. Besides, I'd announced what I was now doing to everyone I knew. How could I explain my failure if I gave up?

I also began the pursuit for another job. Since I hadn't worked in a while, I had trouble getting back in, professionally. A temporary job seemed like a good way to get past the recruiting gatekeepers and get to the hiring managers, so I sought out temp agencies. I accepted the same types of positions of people who had worked for me in the past and even reported to managers for which I had more experience. I was a nobody—a nobody who couldn't even write a good story.

I continually questioned God. "Maybe I got the writing message wrong? Maybe you really don't want me to be doing this?" And "What about this job, Lord? Why am I here?" I fasted and prayed constantly and was becoming more and more of a loner.

He answered me more times than I can count. Sometimes, while studying my Bible, a scripture jumped out at me and quickened my heart. Phrases like "fear not," "I go before you," and "be strong and courageous" stirred in my heart and kept me moving forward. Sometimes his encouraging voice came from a sermon. Stories of God's servants, such as Nehemiah trusting God to help him rebuild Jerusalem, Joshua leading millions of Israelites into the promised land of Canaan, or Noah spending more than seventy years building an ark without having experienced a flood or rain. How could I complain when these people trusted God, most often with very little regular feedback or affirmation?

Then a new darkness set in. I was writing the second book and no longer working outside the home. I became distracted by other things that suddenly needed my attention. There were days when my mind became befuddled and confused. I even had spells of feeling overwhelmed, anxious, and fearful. I withdrew even more, asking others to pray for me. Inadequacy and hazy thinking filled my mind.

Who was I to be doing this? Who would buy these books? Who would care? I'm a nobody with no platform to share. My storytelling capabilities are limited.

I clung to God out of desperation. I gripped tightly to His calling and to His promise that He would "go before me." I read His Word and listened to Christian radio stations. My heart was moved when a popular author explained the spiritual warfare he'd endured throughout the writing and publication of his bestselling books. Tears spilled down my face. He'd just described my life.

Spiritual warfare.

It was a part of my story line. I'd fought it before. But it was nothing like what I was experiencing now. Sometimes I felt like I was drowning. A couple of my prayer partners reported that their lives had been turned upside down. The only thing they could figure out was that it all began when they agreed to pray for me and my writing. They withdrew their prayer support, desiring to get their lives back on track.

I took a deep breath, and everything changed. Now I knew what the problem was. Not depression or dementia. It was spiritual warfare. I opened my Bible and began to equip myself with the right battle tools. There was light at the end of this dark tunnel. I stood up and fought this evil influence with God as my Helper. I learned to see Satan's attacks coming, and I called out Jesus' name and rebuked Satan with the power it invoked.

The happy life I'd led for so many years was long gone. God sifted me like I'd asked. He was continuing to do so. But now, things were different. I no longer had a *happy* life. I now had a life of *joy*. I was learning to lean on Him and not myself. The difference between these two approaches was astonishing. My happiness used to be based on my outward circumstances. But now I found the real joy that is only obtained inwardly, through trusting and leaning on him. It's letting go, clinging to Him, and accepting everything that's thrown at you—with a peace that passes all understanding. I was eager to go to the next level.

Wanting my writing to honor God and be entirely from Him, I prayed for humility. I wanted it all. I wanted Jesus, all of Him, and all that He had to do to get me there. Done. Done. Done.

I'm naturally a confident, do-it-yourself kind of gal. I assumed that this new humility goal would hurt a little but be worth it in the end. After all, I could improve on putting others first and maybe keep my opinions to myself—once in a while. I was in no way prepared for what followed.

Things went from difficult to *more* difficult to *most* difficult. My wonderful marriage fell apart, care of aging parents consumed my energy, and strife among extended family members grew exponentially. I silently accepted the blame for something I hadn't initiated in order to protect others and put an end to the drama. A couple who had known me most of my life questioned if I was a different person than they originally thought.

I felt completely isolated in my situation. I had trouble sleeping. I cried. Who could I talk to? Who would understand? Who would believe me? My husband was struggling as I was, and I didn't want to involve my grown children. Church members had lots of pat answers and scriptures to quote at me while making quick judgments.

Fortunately, there was God. Wanting to choose wisely, I chose him by burying myself in scripture and praise songs, fasting and praying. I joined a Bible study group with a wonderful spirit-led leader. They were a safe place. Cool water in the desert. I never explained to them the entirety of my circumstances, but God used them to minister to me anyway. He always gave them the right words at the right time. Soothing ointment to my soul. They believed in me. They valued me. They enveloped me in their love— God's love.

I fell on my face before the Lord and emptied every last bit of my pride at His feet. I humbled myself before my husband and worked toward complete reconciliation. And I thanked the Lord for bringing me to this point. The road had been rough, really rough, but how else do you get to that mountaintop to enjoy the sunrise? How else do you find the joy only He can give? Joy in the midst of overwhelming pain.

I now pray even more for God's sifting and humbling. This truly is where joy and peace are found. This pursuit drives you to the center of God's will.

> "Jesus beckons his followers to a path that's far from the easy road. It's a path filled with adventure, uncertainty, and unlimited possibilities—the only path that can fulfill the deepest longings and desires of your heart . . . to give your heart to the only one who can make you fully alive. To unleash the untamed faith within. To be consumed by the presence of a passionate and compassionate God. To go where he sends, no matter the cost."
> Erwin Raphael McManus, "The Barbarian Way"

I've chosen the more difficult path and found the deep penetrating overflowing joy it provides. That's the choice my young friend has before her too. How about you? What will you choose? Today is the day. Choose wisely.

Johnna Howell is an author, blogger, and speaker who has delivered keynote speeches and been the recipient of many professional awards. Her current work, The Caller Series, *a Young Adult Christian Dystopian Suspense series, challenges readers to find and follow a life of purpose, powered by an eternal God who is calling each of us to Himself. The series currently includes three books. Her latest is* The Caller *with a fourth,* The Calling, *due in 2018.* JohnnaHowell.com

Thoughts to Ponder
from Choose Wisely

1. Rejection of God is deadly.

2. When difficulties come, immerse yourself in God's Word, prayer, and praise.

3. The pursuit of God will drive you to the center of His will.

> **When you're upset, afraid, lonely, or need comfort, where do you go?**

Choose this day who you will serve. — Joshua 24:15

The Perfect Storm
by Sarah Nelson

Have you ever been caught in *the perfect storm?* I live in a place where thunderstorms roll in and out faster than the time it takes to watch your favorite sitcom. In springtime and summer, heavy winds and tornados are commonplace. Every year, homes and towns lose life and incur devastation caused by colliding winds. The force is so powerful, only destruction is left in its wake. Others live in climates that would chill the rest of us to the bone, while some choose to live in warmer temperatures where they face hurricanes and flooding. Regardless of what climate you live in, nature has a way of combining elements that come together at just the right time to form forces that leave destruction.

Equally as devastating are the tidal waves and dark clouds of life's difficulties that often blow in and catch us by surprise. Life sometimes has a way of dealing us a bad hand when we are already losing, or pushing us down when we are already drowning. All at once, a series of problems can come together and cause us to feel the burden is too heavy to carry, as if we were in *the perfect storm*. My family was caught in this type of force

It was a bright, beautiful day in Park City, Utah. Even in the cold, crisp air, the sun was warm, so much so that the snow on the ski slopes was a bit icy. I was uneasy. I had already fallen, sprained my knee, and used my face as a human snowplow, but I knew the apprehension I felt was not because I was unsteady on my skis. I could not stop wondering how my two-year-old baby girl, Adalee, was doing at the base of the mountain, in the childcare center called the "Kid Zone." Earlier that morning, Adalee was unusually quiet. She was not her normal chatty self and gave me a half-smile on the left side of her face, which I had never seen before. Something was off, and my gut was unsettled. I retired early from our first day on the slopes to pick her up. I needed to see how she was doing.

When I picked Adalee up in my arms, I could tell she had a fun time playing on the indoor playground. But when I looked at her face, something was wrong. I asked if she had a good time. Instead of her usual, cheerful response, she silently looked at me and smiled another half-smile. My motherly intuition said she needed to see a doctor right away.

After a brief conversation with our pediatrician's office back home, my husband, Mark, and I left our other two children with family at the lodge, loaded Adalee into the car, and frantically drove to the Children's Hospital in Salt Lake City.

Forty-five minutes later, the ER doctor looked at her face, saw her symptoms, watched her walk, and saw her right leg giving out. He asked if her right hand was weakening. I told him I did not know and had not noticed it. He took Adalee's right hand and had her grip his finger. Her right hand was weakening.

He looked at me with concern. "I am worried about your daughter. I think she is having a stroke."

It was the hardest thing I had ever heard, but it confirmed everything in my being. He saw it too. My motherly intuition was right.

Within minutes, doctors and nurses flooded the room and drew Adalee's blood, poked her for IV's, and prepped her for a CAT scan. Confused and traumatized, she immediately began crying. Mark and I did our best to remain calm and tried to hold her while she was being poked and prodded.

Adalee was losing the ability to use the entire right side of her body. The doctors said the symptoms would worsen within the next thirty-six hours before she stabilized. The next hours were spent answering a multitude of questions and compiling data to eliminate possible causes. I began to understand why I had felt so uneasy back at the ski slopes. My motherly intuitions had been running overtime, which I quickly appreciated. I would never discount that intuition again, or apologize for acting on what my "gut" was telling me to do.

It was confirmed. Adalee had suffered an ischemic stroke on the left side of her brain. She lost her ability to use the right side of her body. Her face was paralyzed on one side, and she lost her ability to speak, walk, and move her right arm, hand, and fingers. For three days, the team of pediatric doctors performed a series of tests to find out why Adalee had suffered a stroke. After reviewing her veins, blood, and heart, the doctors could not find the reason of her "acute situation." They ruled that her stroke was caused by *The Perfect Storm*. A handful of sources had to come together in just the right way and at just the right time to result in this life-threatening

228

situation. We were told that not finding the origin was good, so much better than having a disease or problem with a major organ. We learned to take this as *good news*, yet Adalee's little body was still debilitated. The wake of this storm had already left its damage.

The first few hours in the emergency room were a whirlwind. As the team of nurses and doctors whisked my child away for an MRI, I stood facing a dark, empty corridor in the ER. My heart felt like a bowling ball was pressing down on my chest. My stomach was balled in knots and pulled in four different directions. As I closed my eyes to take a breath, I felt the Holy Spirit speak to me. The voice was not audible, but I heard it just the same. The first thing I heard was from scripture.

The Lord said, "I will never leave you, nor forsake you (Joshua 1:5). I am here, I am God, and I am *constant*."

Time stood still, and I will forever remember what I heard and felt sweep over me. God's peace fell on my head and shoulders like a soft blanket. He draped a cloak over my shoulders, and I felt the peace adorn my neck. The overwhelming sense of peace rested upon the anxiety in my stomach and calmed me. The ache in my stomach didn't go away, but my emotions found composure. In that instant as the Lord spoke, He assured me that He was there by using His own words from scripture:

"No one will be able to stand up against you all the days of your life. As I was with Moses, so I will be with you; I will never leave you nor forsake you" (Joshua 1:5).

These words are also found in Deuteronomy 31:6, Deuteronomy 31:8, and Hebrews 13:5, reminding me of God's promise. He will always be with us. He will never leave us.

God's Word never says we will not endure hardship or that we will never experience tragedy or loss. In life, we can count on bad things happening, but we can also rest assured that when we experience pain and difficulties, He will always be there to give us strength. In that precious moment, God gave me peace, strength, and an eternal perspective. He gave me strength to handle the situation, process the loads of information we sifted through each time we spoke with the doctors, keep a clear mind in order to make the best decisions for Adalee, and be emotionally strong for her.

In a raging instant, our lives changed, and our family livelihood turned upside down. All we knew was that our daughter's life, our lives, might never be the same. We were told she would *never* be the same. Our daughter's normalcy was stripped away. Her abilities, her personality, and her words were deteriorating before our eyes. The rug of normality was pulled from beneath our feet. Mark and I did not know what her life, or our life as a family, would be like from that moment on.

However, through God's Word and the eternal perspective, I felt a peace during a moment when everything about my daughter was being taken away. He gave me an eternal hope, my heart resting on the assurance that God never changes. If Adalee did not recover physically, she would be whole again in eternity. I was reminded of how temporary this life is. Our material possessions and physical abilities here on earth cannot be measured against an eternity with God. It was the presence of God that made Him known to me. I felt Him, and He spoke within my spirit. God was revealing Himself, because He loves me. He loves my daughter, and He wanted me to experience the comfort He alone can give in times of pain and crisis. I was blessed to recognize His presence, and I was simply reminded that He wants us to experience Him.

God wants to comfort us as our Father, just like Mark and I wanted nothing more than to comfort our tiny daughter. Even though it was just a second, I felt like time froze. The Lord breathed through me several lessons with great depth and meaning that I would not only use to deal with this crisis, but I would carry with me forever.

The team of neurologists said children have a good chance at partial recovery from a stroke, but they could offer no guarantees. It was made clear Adalee would not be able to regain 100 percent of the abilities she had lost. She would never have a "full recovery." The best-case scenario would be to regain up to 80 percent. Mark and I were willing to accept Adalee's condition. We resolved to focus on all the information that was set before us in order to make the best decisions for her future. We were willing to do whatever it took, or whatever was needed to care for a child with special needs. We prepared to adjust our mindset to accommodate how different our life would be.

At the same time, I had faith and knew that if it was God's will, He was capable of healing her body and allowing her to have a "full recovery." As Adalee slept, I sat in the Pediatric Intensive Care

Unit and prayed. I told the Lord I knew nothing was impossible for Him. I prayed Adalee would recover 100 percent of what she had lost. I prayed she would talk, walk, and even run again. I prayed out of faith, and then handed it over to our heavenly Father. I gave it all to the Lord and turned my focus to all the information to make the best decisions for her future. I then asked our family, friends, church, and community to pray the same prayer. I specifically asked them to pray that Adalee would talk, walk, and run—to recover all the abilities she had lost—to live a normal life. Our family, church, and community turned into thousands of people across Texas, lifting up our daughter in prayer. My family and friends who live in Indiana, Illinois, California, and other states had their own churches, prayer chains, and Bible studies covering our entire family with prayer. We watched a community of believers turn into a national army of prayer warriors. It was a true testament of how the body of believers can come together to be a powerful force.

Once Adalee was stable, her progress slowly became evident. At every step, she progressed. Adalee learned to eat again. After two weeks, she was released and transferred to Our Children's House (OCH), a children's rehabilitation hospital and recovery center. As we settled into the new facility, the team of doctors said Adalee would likely need inpatient therapy for eight to twelve weeks. We adjusted our life so I could stay in the facility with her while Mark took care of Seth and Hannah Grace at home where he could work and manage our lives.

The next morning was Saturday, when Adalee would begin her three to four sessions of therapy. I awoke with a sore throat that had been festering for days, and it was time to address it. The pain was the worst I had ever felt, so I knew I had strep. I had not had the chance to think about the soreness that had been developing over the last couple of days, but if I did not take care of myself, I could not help my daughter.

My parents arrived first thing that morning and went with Adalee to her first therapy session. I found the closest medical clinic, scheduled an appointment, and within the hour found myself on the doctor's bench answering questions and explaining my situation. I will never forget her sweet words and her gasp when she looked down my throat with her light. We agreed we needed to treat this as efficiently as possible, so she gave me a shot of penicillin and a shot of steroids to help with the pain. I topped it off with a milkshake from the closest McDonalds to sooth the discomfort, and mentally moved on to see how my baby was handling her first session of physical therapy.

By the time I got back to the hospital, the steroids had kicked in and I was met with unbelievable news. My parents were over-the-top thrilled, because Adalee was standing and holding their hands. When I left just two hours earlier, she could not stand or walk on her own. Here I was, watching my daughter regain some strength in her leg. The questions that bombarded my mind were, "Is this normal? Can this happen?" My dad showed me the video he had taken of Adalee's first therapy session. The physical therapist took her into a playroom with slides, swings, and padded contraptions and floors. He sat her down and played chase with her. He turned therapy into a game and somehow got her to run. Not only did my parents witness this taking place, but my dad had the forethought to record it on his phone so I could see it with my own eyes. There was Adalee on the video, sitting on the mat, then in the next instant, running. She was having so much fun playing with this genius of a therapist, she just took off running a few steps, then plopped back on the floor. In the video, you could hear the joyful reaction of my parents. He then stood her up, and she did it several more times. She ran a few steps, then fell back down, giggling and laughing for the first time since her stroke. Tears welled up in my eyes, but then my excitement overpowered them, and I felt the pressure in my heart ease up. By late morning, Adalee was able to walk while holding our hands. She was still a little unsteady and needed help, but she quickly regained strength in her legs.

It was a lot to process. I had no concept of whether this was normal. Based on her diagnosis and on the comments from the staff, I knew that regaining a lost ability that fast was not usual. We had not even been at the rehab hospital for an entire day. When I checked Adalee in, I had hoped that by the time she was released from rehabilitation she would build enough strength to learn how to use a walker. Yet we had not even been there twenty-four hours when she instantly regained enough strength to not only walk but run. My dad told me that the therapist who worked with her was over Physical Therapy for the different centers for the entire health network, which consisted of a very large hospital with multiple locations. On the weekends, various therapists under the health care system conducted the therapy sessions.

If my dad had not captured Adalee's progress on video, I am not sure I would have believed what happened. She was walking with help as if she had been undergoing therapy for weeks. We never had a chance to ask the visiting therapist the questions that would make sense out of what we witnessed. Processing what took place is hard to measure and describe. I can only explain that I felt so much relief. I knew we had an army of prayer warriors praying over Adalee, and I was grasping the fact that what we witnessed was not only an answer to prayer, it was so much more. We witnessed healing and recovery at a supernatural pace. I kept uttering "Thank You, Lord."

Adalee ended up staying at OCH for four weeks. Her progress was so rapid, they released her earlier than the anticipated eight to twelve weeks. By the time we arrived home, Adalee was able to function as a normal child. She began talking just days into our stay at OCH, no longer qualifying for speech therapy. She was an outpatient for two-and-a-half years, undergoing therapy to increase strength in her right leg, arm, and hand. As she moved on, she was a normal child who talked, walked, ran, and participated in gymnastics. We saw her progress occur at an unusual rate. We know the prayer of hundreds of people impacted our daughter.

I share this story because of how the Lord revealed Himself to my family, our community, and me. When we talk about Adalee's testimony it is not about what happened to her as much as it is about how the Lord revealed Himself and ministered to us. God allowed us to feel His calming presence in the midst of the *Perfect Storm*. As we were walking through this crisis, God opened our eyes to see the many lessons He wanted to teach us along the way. We also witnessed how the faith of an entire community was strengthened as they watched their prayers for a tiny girl being answered.

We all can relate to what it feels like when life delivers unwelcome difficulties on our doorsteps. I believe the Lord placed a sense of responsibility on my heart to share how He comforted us through a traumatic situation in order to encourage and remind others that He wants to be our strength in times of hardship. We can all relate to stories, because our lives are made of them. Our chapters may look different in the details, but we all share in love, laughter, pain, and death. The prayer and purpose of my story is to inspire strength and encourage faith to those of you who may be victimized by an unexpected storm.

Know that only God can provide peace when the winds are at their peak, and the devastation is great. He is the perfect comforter in the midst of the *Perfect Storm*.

Sarah Nelson lives in Waco, Texas with her husband, Mark, and their three children. Sarah is a singer with a background in Christian music and worship, as well as a writer. On her blog, she has recently begun a series that focuses on dealing with crisis from a spiritual perspective,

SarahNelsonBlog.com

Sarah is a contributing writer for WacoMomsBlog, has a BBA in Marketing from Baylor University, and is a former business owner in the skincare industry.

http://Waco.CityMomsBlog.com

https://itunes.apple.com.us/artist/Sarah-Nelson/id373073046

Thoughts to Ponder
from The Perfect Storm

1. In the eye of the storm, God remains in control.

2. The Lord reveals Himself to us and others through our difficult circumstances.

3. Allow God to be your strength in times of hardships.

> ## What storms has God brought you through?

He got up, rebuked the wind and said to the waves, "Quiet! Be still!" Then the wind died down and it was completely calm. — Mark 4:39

The Hardest Thing
by Karen Sims

"Accepting that we are loved for no other reason than the
God of the universe loves us—it's in His very being and nature
to do so—is the hardest thing you and I will ever do. Grace is
nonreciprocal." Stephan Bauman

In and out. In and out. Hours at a time. I pushed and pulled the
little pine knot in one of the support boards under the mattress of
my bed. As a child, I lay under the bed for hours when sent
to my room as punishment, my facial muscles clenched with
determination to outlast my parents. Or so I thought. But no one
came to check on me. As I manipulated the tiny piece of wood, I
vowed never to let anyone see what I was feeling—about anything.
The walls of our home could've spoken volumes, but my family of
five silently stewed.

During my teen years, my mom and I didn't converse with each
other for days. We were polite, but only the minimum words were
exchanged. I didn't know why Mom wouldn't talk to me, and I'd
find out later that she thought I was mad at her. The stagnation was
disrupted with my dad's next outburst. The pent-up explosive rage
would eventually erupt, leaving verbal shrapnel embedded in our
souls. I didn't realize until recently that I suffer a form of PTSD
(Post-Traumatic Stress Disorder) and have an abnormally high
startle response.

My mom and brothers strived for calm and normalcy until the
next explosion. Forgiveness wasn't granted. We suffered in penitent
silence. Dishonesty with our feelings prevailed in order to avoid
future eruptions. And so the pattern was formed and repeated into
adulthood. The few times I was asked questions or my opinion
about something, my mind froze and went blank. My typical
response was, "I don't know." That elicited a sharp retort and
ridicule.

I wanted to be like everyone else. I wanted to be American. I
wanted to go to church on Sundays like most of my friends did, but
shame caused me to avoid religious kids at school. On the
television at home, we saw Billy Graham. I went to a Catholic

church a few times as a child. I attended a Catholic service once at the Air Force Academy with some college friends, just to be part of the group. My best friend gave me a King James Bible for my sixteenth birthday. I kept it hidden, but secretively read it when no one was around. God was not mentioned in my family. There were no other Bibles in the house.

Surprisingly, I believed there was a God, but He was distant and angry—just waiting to punish me when I did something wrong.

Mom and Dad were good, moral people who were raised in Catholic homes, but we only practiced our faith by eating fish on Fridays. Dad was the dominant personality, and Mom was passive, gentle, and quietly compliant. Shame and guilt motivated us to behave properly. In a traditional Czech family, we were to be seen and not heard. No praise for good behavior. Intellect was valued. Social interaction was formal and limited. We didn't invite friends over to our house.

Love was not expressed. Conflict was unresolved. We traveled, fished, and camped as a family, but we didn't really know one another.

I didn't go to prom or homecoming, even though I fantasized about attending. I never was asked on a date. I was slender, but perceived myself as chubby. I even bought bigger-sized clothes than was necessary. Finally, in college, I had a few blind dates. I married my third blind date a week after college graduation.

I grew up in Boulder, Colorado, the capital of the hippie movement during the late sixties and early seventies. But I wasn't going to be like one of them. Even without God or instruction from my parents, I vowed to never use drugs or have premarital sex. *Could it be that God, yet unknown to me at the time, was protecting me?* Since the University of Colorado is in Boulder, the town also had a higher than average intellectual community, which further separated my mind from my heart.

College was a lonely time for me. While at Colorado State University, I submerged myself in studying. I was too introverted to engage in the party scene. The only way I knew how to get the approval that I was desperate for was to perform well. And so I did. I was in the honor society, but I didn't have any close friends. My best friend from childhood attended a university a couple hours away.

As a sophomore, I was on the brink of a nervous breakdown from the self-imposed stress to excel. But one evening, a friend in my dormitory asked if I'd like to go to an event in the neighboring dorm—a Christian concert. Even though I was lost in the crowd, I felt uneasy, as if everyone could see my unchurched heart. Yet I was also drawn to the wholesome fun and joy that permeated the room. The evening ended with an invitation to pray for an eternal relationship with Jesus. Truth nudged my spirit, but I didn't pray.

When I returned to the quietness of my dorm room, I cried from the pain of my emptiness. I prayed to Jesus to forgive me and accept me. I thought that was all there was to it. Nothing in my life changed. I still knew nothing of love. I didn't tell anyone for months, not until I met the man I married.

I was nervously standing in the church doorway that led to the altar where my fiancé waited.

"I love you," my dad abruptly whispered in my ear.

What? Had I heard correctly? Dad hadn't uttered those words to me—ever—and didn't again until ten years later, by telephone.

A few months after marriage, I was baptized and my husband and I became active in a local church. We joined a small group that focused on discipleship. I grew in head knowledge and religious performance. I lived in fear of saying or doing the "wrong" things in church groups. When I left services and ladies' Bible study groups, I felt heaped with self-condemnation. I wasn't good enough. I would never measure up.

Insight and understanding never healed a single disease of my spirit. The illuminating light of Jesus shed Truth from the Holy Spirit in my spirit through prayer, but not for decades.

Before we married, my husband and I agreed that we would never utter the "D" (divorce) word. We also agreed not to have children. A vasectomy was our permanent choice of birth control to ensure I'd never become pregnant. We lacked hope of being successful parents since we had both come from unhealthy families.

After three years and growing restlessness, my husband was accepted into a doctoral program at the University of Texas Medical Branch in Galveston. I dreaded what the move would mean for my young faith. I didn't realize then that God had already gone before us. When we arrived in August 1980, without use of the yet-to-be discovered World Wide Web, God led us to a Bible teaching in a Christ-centered church fellowship. The first Sunday we visited, we stepped into the gym of the local YMCA and sat on rolled-up tumbling mats. We worshipped with the small congregation of young medical student couples and their young children.

We worked, studied, and ministered with families. After a few years, we shared our transformed feelings about children with each other. So now what would we do? Using phone books and university connections, we discovered that one of only two micro-neurosurgeons in the United States performing vasectomy reversals was practicing in Houston. After appointments to assess the situation, my husband underwent surgery at no cost, since the surgeon wanted to help a struggling student.

What a huge blessing, and this was the first time I'd ever truly experienced God working personally in my life. Unfortunately, by the time we were ready to have children, the doctor wasn't very positive about the viability and potential success rate for us. He prescribed steroids to be taken at just the right time of month to enhance the probability of impregnation—but not one pill was ever taken. I knew before we could have it verified that I was indeed pregnant. My husband was skeptical until we received the unbelievable news. We had a healthy boy and two years later had no trouble having a healthy daughter. We were thrilled and hopeful of raising a godly family.

Unfortunately, I struggled with chronic depression that I tried to deny and overcome by my own efforts. I failed miserably. I didn't know how to love my husband or my children. I tried to be perfect, but my self-righteousness truly was as "filthy rags" (Isaiah 64:6). Pride in my self-righteousness nailed my defeat as a devoted Christ-follower.

After undergoing multiple Christian counseling for chronic depression, I had a heart-changing encounter with God in the middle of the night when I was eight months pregnant with my second child. God impressed upon my spirit that He loved me. I read and received these words: "So we have come to know and to believe the love that God has for us. God is love, and whoever abides in love abides in him" (1 John 4:16). Soon after that heart-changing experience, I dared to pray a dangerous prayer. It wasn't dangerous because it was harmful. It was dangerous because it was daring, risky, and bold. I pleaded with my heavenly Father: *Do whatever it takes to bring healing to my damaged emotions. Break the destructive patterns and cycles in my family.*

Soon, my life turned upside down. I learned to love my husband more unconditionally, but on my tenth wedding anniversary, he punctured my heart with these words: "I don't love you, and I never have. I think we need to be separated."

Life drained from my being.

Over the next month, through the help of a Christian counselor, my husband admitted that he was having an affair. I was devastated, but my response was not at all what I thought it would be. I chose forgiveness instead of leaving him. But he wasn't interested in staying. After two years of counseling and struggling to keep our family together, he moved out and filed for divorce. He married "the other woman." In spite of being devastated, my relationship with the Lord flourished. God provided for my children and me. I began to genuinely believe that "nothing would be able to separate me from the love of God" (Romans 8:39).

After a few years, I decided to remarry but my rationalization was for the wrong reasons. This time, my young son was the target of verbal and emotional abuse. After seven years, I took my children and left. The only way I could justify my decision to divorce was to remain unmarried. During that time, I bought my first house. But within six months, I was demoted at work, 9-11 happened, my first husband died at the age of forty-five, leaving my teen children fatherless, and my depression medication stopped working.

With so many things pressing in on me, I crashed. I couldn't function at work or at home. The only place I felt safe was in the arms of my comfy blue chair in front on the television. I was in full-blown panic and anxiety. I checked myself into the local psychiatric unit. The only thing I knew for sure was that I still believed in God. He was faithful and patient with me. After intensive therapy and multiple medications for two years, I regained stability. My counselor taught me to pray honestly out loud and to praise God when I didn't feel like it. For the first time in my forty-nine years, I was connecting with God in a real relationship, not just in my mind and good works.

After eleven years, my second ex-husband had remarried. I

accepted God's grace to believe I was free to remarry. I've been married for almost eight years to a godly man. We are growing in love daily.

I recently completed certification in biblical counseling and am engaged in coming alongside young women who have come from abusive backgrounds. I've been ministering to youth for almost thirty years and walk with purpose.

What rules our hearts rules our lives. God now rules my heart in love, which has been the hardest thing for me to accept.

I've read thousands of books trying to find the "key" to freedom.

Multiple Christian counselors. Two failed marriages. Learning that it is safe to confess my pride and self-righteousness through receiving God's grace. Grace will not punish or reject me.

__Karen Sims__ and her husband, Calvin, live in the piney woods near Tyler, Texas. Together, they have four adult children and six grandchildren. Karen engages women with the truth and hope of the gospel through biblical lay counseling. She has been a contributing writer for the first women's online devotional, Encouraging.com *and* God Moments, Too. *Part of Karen's life story, "Faith ... Beyond the Blue Chair," was published in* Dare to Be a Difference Maker, *compiled by Michelle Prince.*

__LiveTheJoy.org__
__KarenDianeSims@live.com;__
__HopenedHeart.com__

Thoughts to Ponder
from The Hardest Thing

1. Even with our mistakes, God still loves us.

2. Let God's light illuminate where change is needed.

3. Generational curses can be broken by God's grace.

> ### *In what ways does God show that He is pleased with you?*

*And the God of all grace, who called you
to his eternal glory in Christ, after you have suffered
a little while, will himself restore you and make you
strong, firm and steadfast. — 1 Peter 5:10*

Unlearning the Lies

by Dr. Lynnette Simm

What memories come to mind when you think of your school days? Did you love school? Did you have a special subject you enjoyed? Can you think of a person, teacher, or coach who changed your life?

School can bring back many memories: good, bad, fun, or horrible. Regardless, I'm sure you learned many lessons both in and out of the classroom.

After spending over thirty years in a classroom, I earned a Doctorate in Education. I loved school, and I loved learning. I've learned about writing, history, psychology, motivation, gender differences, and learning disabilities. But as a dyslexic, obsessive-compulsive, attention-deficit, anxiety filled, abandoned, and abused sinner, I wasn't always an easy student to teach. It took a few special teachers to help me understand some difficult, life-changing subjects.

In *The Acorn Story*, J.K. Montgomery wrote: "The lies I tell myself are true." At least we *believe* they're true. My first lesson was the hardest. I had to *unlearn* the lies that I told myself *and* the lies the enemy used to hold me captive.

At four years old, I was thrown away, discarded by my biological father and his family. Then my new father and other family members sexually abused me for nearly five years, from ages nine through fourteen. Lies permeated my mind, body, and soul.

There were lies like:

I am not worth keeping.
I am not valuable. Nobody wants me.
I am weak and pathetic. I deserve to be abused.
I am ugly, stupid, lazy, fat, and needy.

The lies kept spinning in my mind, so I was in a constant state of confusion. These lies enveloped my soul, crushed my heart, and held my mind captive. They trampled my happiness, my joy, and my peace as they attempted to destroy my life. As the lies kept swirling, they were breaking me down until I nearly ended it all.

My actions mimicked the lies I believed. Feelings of being without value and unworthiness resulted in thinking premarital sex was acceptable. Feelings of being weak and pathetic resulted in thinking an abortion was okay. Feelings of being ugly, lazy, and fat were exacerbated by overeating and weight gain. Feelings of being stupid and needy resulted in constantly seeking validation. And the feeling that nobody wanted me resulted in adultery.

As my life crumbled before my eyes, I was given an amazing Christian therapist. This woman of God worked on each lie, replacing them with truth. She put bandages on every wound and filled me with love and acceptance. She ventured beyond work to care about the little girl whom God loves. As I moved on in my life, I had to continue the fight, sometimes moment by moment, to keep the lies out. I was still fighting two other demons: guilt and shame.

The second lesson I had to learn was that guilt and shame are the enemy's tools. Another Christian therapist walked me through this battlefield. She taught me that the Lord's tools are forgiveness and love.

Daniel 9:9 says, "The Lord our God is merciful and forgiving, even though we have rebelled against him." Luke 1:77 adds, "He gave us knowledge of salvation through the forgiveness of our sins."

I was filled with guilt over the sins I had committed. I was ashamed of being abused. I was confused by the abuse itself. How can someone love you and hurt you? And why was sex so painful, yet it was meant for so much love? I was drowning in anxiety, depression, and pain, like I was in a bathtub with my head under water. Guilt and shame laughed as they held me down, but I faintly heard sweet voices of love and mercy. Grace, salvation, truth, and forgiveness were all around me, but muffled.

I cried out, and the Lord took my hand. He pulled me out of the water—a new person.

I was washed clean.

I was remade.

I walked down the aisle of my newly found church, confessed my sins, and asked forgiveness. God saved me right then and there. He restored me. He renewed my heart for Him. He loved me unconditionally.

The Bible says, "Therefore, if anyone is in Christ, they are a new creation, old things have passed away, behold all things have become new" (2 Corinthians 5:17).

My life changed in many ways. I now had tools to fight the lies. I learned words to command the enemy to let go of me. *Love* protected me. I began to share this forgiveness, love, and joy with my husband, my daughters, and my friends.

Yet there was more forgiveness needed, and the Holy Spirit sent me to work. The Lord pressed 2 Corinthians 5:18 into me: "All this is from God, who reconciled us to Himself through Christ, and gave us the ministry of reconciliation." That's when I began the difficult work of forgiving my parents and biological father. I had to forgive their abandonment, their abuse, and their neglect. As I did, I became more and more free, because forgiveness was cutting through the chains. Truth was shining a light in the darkness.

Everything is not perfect. I still struggle. I am learning that school is never over. I continue in Christian therapy as issues arise. I still fight the enemy, but not moment by moment. Each day I grow stronger in His ways. God is continually showing me new things, increasing my capacity for compassion, and renewing my heart and soul. I find myself seeking His wisdom in His Word, in worship, and from people of wisdom.

I claim Romans 12:2 and Ephesians 4:23: "Be transformed by the renewing of your mind . . . and be made new in the attitudes of your mind." I have also learned the importance of surrounding myself with wise women and men who have gone before me. Job 12:12 says, "Is not wisdom found among the aged? Does not long life bring understanding?"

Scripture reminds us that wisdom originated from God. It is our job to continue to learn, to seek Him continuously, feverishly, and passionately. The freedom of forgiveness is available to everyone. As a student of the Bible, I know and accept John 3:16. I know God loves us all. He sacrificed His Son, Jesus Christ, for *every one* of us. We just need to cry out for Him, and He promised to raise us, washed clean.

I love being engaged in *higher* learning, and I know I will forever be a Doctor of Education for the Lord.

Dr. Lynnette Simm, *with degrees in psychology and education, has been a college professor for nearly fifteen years. She is a contributor for* Focus on Fabulous *magazine and a freelance editor. Married over twenty years, Dr. Simm, her husband, Madison, and their two amazing daughters live in North Dallas, Texas, where she continues working on her writing. She is the author of* And the Day Came, *an inspirational memoir. Contact her on Facebook or by email:* **DrLMS96@gmail.com.**

Thoughts to Ponder
from Unlearning the Lies

1. It's important to be a lifelong learner.

2. Unlearn the lies that have been taught to us.

3. Make God's Word the plumbline of your life.

What lies do you believe?

[Satan] was a murderer from the beginning, not holding to the truth, for there is no truth in him. When he lies, he speaks his native language, for he is a liar and the father of lies. — John 8:44

A Jewish Girl Searching
by Nancy Nelson

I am Jewish. Totally Jewish. Both parents, all of my grandparents, and all of my great-grandparents. Going back many generations, we were all Jewish. So how did I come to spend my Tuesday nights teaching Bible study, my Wednesday nights in choir practice, and Sunday mornings in my neighborhood Baptist church? Good question.

I was raised in a Jewish family in the small East Texas town of Longview. We attended Temple services and celebrated the major Jewish holidays, so I know a little about Jewish history and laws. My religion was cultural, like being one of just a couple of kids in town who got out of school for Easter *and* Passover and celebrated in December with a Hanukkah bush.

For eight years as a child, I spent summers at a *Christian* camp, and on Sunday mornings we went to church in the woods. Singing was my favorite part, and one of my favorite songs was "Onward Christian Soldiers." At Vacation Bible School with friends, I sang "I have the love of Jesus, love of Jesus, down in my heart." I never thought much about the doctrinal content of these songs. They just made me feel close to God. Even as a kid, I never doubted the existence of God or the fact of Creation.

In my pre-teens, I sensed a desire to really know God, but I didn't know how to find Him. It wasn't that I was such a terrible person, although I did feel guilt for childish pranks like taking a pumpkin from someone else's patch without permission and stealing bubble gum from the grocery store (which I later returned and apologized). Truth is, I felt an emptiness, a uselessness, and I had questions about the meaning of my life and why I had been born. I felt separated from God.

Along with the other four Jewish kids my age, I attended Confirmation classes. We learned the Hebrew alphabet, did a little reading of scripture in Hebrew, and studied some Jewish history.

When I was fifteen, my mother passed away. That was a very difficult time that led to even more questions: "Why did she have to die? Would I ever see her again? How could there be a loving God if he let my mother die?" I joined the choir and the youth group, and was superintendent of the Jewish Sunday school since no adult among the forty families of our Temple would do the job, but I still didn't have answers or comfort from my religion.

I was searching.

I dated a young Baptist man and went with him to church several times. In those days, the Baptist Sunday school classes were separated by gender, so I sat in a class of girls I didn't know and listened to a lesson I didn't really understand. Then we sat in the small sanctuary among people I didn't know but who all knew one another. At the end of the service, the pastor gave the invitation. It seemed that every head was turning to see if I was going to go forward, since I was the only one there who wasn't already a believer. Silently they waited. I was embarrassed that I couldn't do what they obviously wanted me to do, but I did go back several times.

I was searching.

After Mother died, we moved into an apartment. Our neighbor was a young woman with a large biblical reference library. Whenever I had a question about religious things, and that was frequently, I went to her, and she helped me look up the answer. She never shared the gospel, but she and her books were always there for me.

I was searching.

Early in college, I drifted away from God. The services in the conservative campus synagogue were all in Hebrew, and I couldn't discern the Shema, the most important prayer in Judaism. So I stopped going.

At that point, I met Ken, the man who would become my husband. He and his family invited me to attend church with them, and I sensed that they had some kind of relationship with God. I wanted what they had.

One sermon was titled, "The Freedom We Have in Jesus Christ." It was an explanation of how the Bible says I come short of God's standard, and it explained the penalty for that failure: eternal separation from God. But God loved me so much that He made a way for the price of my failure to be paid so I could be forgiven and be free to have the special relationship with Him that I wanted. The way for the price to be paid was for me to believe that Jesus Christ was the Son of God and that He died for *my* sins.

Freedom in Jesus was freedom from the penalty of sin, not freedom from sin itself. But what a wonderful freedom.

Ken thought it was just another sermon, and not a very good one. But he could tell by the way my fingernails dug into his hands that it was more than that for me. I felt as if I was the only person in the congregation. God was speaking directly to me. We met with the pastor who preached the sermon and discussed issues like one God versus the triune God. He explained it this way: If you had an urgent message to deliver to a horse, what would you do? The horse doesn't speak people, and you don't speak horse. How could you deliver your message? I answered that if I had the power, I would become a horse. The pastor just nodded. I got it! God had become Jesus to accomplish the necessary payment for sin, but He was still God, the one God of my Jewish prayers.

Before we left his office, the pastor asked us to do a very difficult thing, to get down on our knees and pray from our hearts. Reform Jews never get on their knees, and their prayers are recited straight from the printed prayer book, so this was most unusual, to say the least. But he also did something I really appreciated. He did not pray that I would become a Christian, which might have felt like an attack and very likely would have put me on the defensive. Instead, he prayed that if there was a God, that He would reveal Himself to me.

What a powerful prayer.

For months, I struggled with these issues. My head knew that the biblical explanation of God's plan of salvation was logical, and I believed it intellectually. My heart had a hard time letting go of prejudices built into Jewish people. All I had to do was *"just believe"* that Christ died for my sins, but that was a huge stumbling block for a Jew.

Everything I had been taught told me there was only one God, that I couldn't worship God *and* Jesus as God, and what about the Holy Spirit? Everything I knew whispered, "Traitor," at the thought of going against my culture, which is, I think, much more important to most Jews than the religious aspects of Judaism. In many ways, Jews feel Christians are the enemy, simply out to win converts. Could I join forces with the enemy? Many Jews had suffered physically and socially at the hands of Christians, so how could I even consider becoming one of "them"? And how could a relationship with God come as easily as opening my hand and receiving a gift, simply by just believing?

One night, Ken and I talked about it. He thought I was just being stubborn, that I really believed Jesus had died for my sins but wouldn't admit it. I realized he was right, and that night Ken led me to pray and tell God that I accepted His gift of Jesus Christ's life to pay for my sins.

A few days later, I had the chance to take my first communion. Ken assured me that communion was a private time with God, and that no one would notice if I did or didn't take the elements when they were passed. I had never liked doing anything in front of people, even giving book reports in elementary school. However, with Ken's assurance of anonymity, I decided to take communion that night.

We arrived late and sat in the last row of the sanctuary. When the time came for communion, the pastor announced that we would do things a little differently, that we would go forward row by row to take communion at the front of the church, in front of the congregation. Row after row, people were going forward. I was panic stricken, but we were seated on the aisle, and if we hesitated, we would block the rest of the row from going forward.

When it was our turn, Ken had a strong grip on my hand and pulled me from my seat and into the aisle. We started forward. The pastor at the front saw me coming down the aisle and realized what had happened. He announced to the congregation that I had become a Christian. Then he started to cry, and by the time we reached him, we were both in tears as well. So much for anonymity.

Amazingly, that church had never done communion that way, and they have never done it that way since. Ken and I laughed many times about that night—how God knew I needed to make a public confession of Him early in my Christian walk, before I could change my mind.

I now understand that my life's purpose is, in the words of the Westminster Shorter Catechism, "to glorify God and enjoy Him forever." I no longer feel separated from God. In fact, those who worship with me will sometimes see me singing with my hands raised and tears streaming down my face. When a song really moves me, I will applaud or even stand and applaud. Sometimes, that is the only way to express my deep love for and awe of the

God who loves me.

It's a great story, but changed lives are the evidence of God's work, not just the act of saying we believe. So has my life changed since I made that decision to accept God's gift of salvation?

I now know that He hears my prayers and answers them, even if his answer is no. My life is, in fact, an answer to prayer. After becoming a Christian, I discovered that the woman who never shared the gospel but always made herself and her library available had prayed for my salvation every day for four years. God has since answered yes for many prayers. We've prayed for new friends and jobs, for a way to get out of a destructive business partnership, for freedom from fear, for money to pay bills, even for a new church home.

I now believe in the power of prayer.

I have found new joy in God's creation, and I often marvel that the One who made it all loved this part of His creation enough to send Jesus to die for me—before I ever acknowledged Him. I know God has a plan for my life, even if I don't daily know or understand what that is. So I don't have to worry about what will come next. I just have to keep praying for Him to reveal Himself and His will, and for the strength to do His will, the same as I prayed when I was searching.

God opened opportunities for me to grow and become the woman He wants me to be. I learned to speak in front of large groups, something I had been desperately frightened of. He prompted me to sing in the choir, giving me thirty years of incredible singing experiences. I participated in a large Christmas festival in front of thousands, performances that led more than 1,000 people to accept Christ. Since I am not Billy Graham, and I don't have the voice of Sandi Patti, how else would I have had the chance to impact so many lives?

As a Christian, I still sin. But now, if I repent and ask God's forgiveness, He is "faithful and just to forgive us our sins and to cleanse us from all unrighteousness." I know that sinning as a Christian doesn't make me a hypocrite. It just makes me a human who needs God's forgiveness daily.

As a Christian, I do not have the answers to all my questions. I don't know why my mother died so young or if I will see her again. Before she married my father, my mother had so many questions about her faith that she talked with a minister. She decided her conversion would kill her parents, and that it wasn't that important to her. As far as I know, she never acted on what she had learned.

A strange sequence of events leads me to believe it is possible that my mother did find Christ to be the answer to her questions. I have a book that belonged to my mother. I moved it from house to house for years but never stopped to look at it. When I did, I discovered the book was a devotional with poems about God and scripture verses. It had been inscribed specifically to my mother from its author Raymond Edman's wife, dated October 1966, just a month before my mother got sick. I know that from the time she became ill until she died, she had this book and may have read it and recalled her earlier questioning experience. My mother lived in East Texas. The author and his wife lived in Wheaton, Illinois. How did they meet? The author was president of Wheaton College, and my father-in-law lived in their home when he attended Wheaton College. Was this just a coincidence? The Lord moves in mysterious ways, so we may meet again in heaven.

Now I know that God didn't take my mother away to punish me. He didn't take her for me to "see the light." He did, I believe, *use* the circumstance of my mother dying (as we all must do), to bring about good in my life.

I have an answer now to one question I never consciously voiced: "Where will I go when I die?" Now, I'm not afraid to die, because I know I will spend eternity in heaven, worshiping and praising the one God of Jews and Christians alike. But as someone told me years ago, you can't accept the promises of scripture—that God is love and mercy, the promises leading to a good outcome for you—and reject the promises that say God is just. You can't dismiss the statements indicating God will remove His hand of blessing or that He will punish those who reject Him. While I believe in a literal heaven where Jesus sits on the throne and where I will worship for all eternity, I also believe in a literal hell, where those who reject God's free gift of salvation will live for all eternity, separated from God and His love.

Do I also believe that if my mother did not accept Jesus as God's provision for her sins that she is now in hell? That takes on new meaning when you apply it to those you know and love. The answer is yes. I believe God desires everyone to choose to spend eternity with Him, and that He shows mercy by making ministers, missionaries, and millions of copies of His Word available to us. He looks at us through the blood of Christ if we are Christians. And if my mother didn't choose to believe in Jesus, God saw only her sin and she is in hell today.

Although Jewish funerals don't include viewing the body of the deceased, the family was allowed to see my Jewish stepmother before her funeral. As I stood looking at her body, I was overwhelmed by the knowledge that what I saw was only an earthly shell, and her soul was not there. Most likely, her soul was in hell. I thought, *How can anyone stand next to a dead body and not believe there has to be more to life than that we are born and we die?* Our bodies return to dust, but what about our souls? If this is all there is to the meaning of life, God is a cruel being who gets pleasure from watching us struggle through life, only to return to dust when life ends. I know there is more to life and to God than that.

I do *not* believe my stepmother is sitting on a fluffy, white cloud watching what we do down here on earth, as she suggested when I kissed her goodbye. I believe God would have heard her if, with her dying breath, she had called out to Him for salvation. I believe her heart was hard and that she never accepted His free gift, and sadly, I believe her soul is in hell today.

After all these years, I am still praying for my sister's salvation. She told me that if she believed in God, believing in Jesus would be a no-brainer, but she doesn't believe in God. I did have the opportunity to witness to my dad. He listened to me, then said that even if he believed what I said, he couldn't act on it. His wife would leave him, his friends would desert him, and religion was just not that important to him. Well, his wife died and left him, and many of his friends moved away when they retired. He told me when he had a heart attack that he was afraid of dying, but then said he wasn't interested in more religion than what he already had. I believe he was still a fearful unbeliever when he died.

God used financial and business setbacks to draw Ken and me closer to Him. Then, after thirty-three years of marriage, Ken was diagnosed with a highly aggressive brain cancer. Ken knew God could heal him, but He might not. He repeatedly said that he wasn't different from everyone else, that everyone would die, but he simply had a better idea of when that would happen for him. He was not afraid of death and was a wonderful inspiration to everyone during the twenty months he lived with cancer.

God grew me a lot during that time. Ken's ability to speak and understand language was severely diminished by the tumor, which left me to do all the talking to doctors, insurance companies, and funeral home staff. We declared bankruptcy during that time, and I did all the paperwork as well as talk with the attorney. We also owed money to the IRS, and I worked with the accountant on that. I had never lived alone in my life, but since my daughter was married, one son was in town, living on his own and one son was in college, I had to learn to live alone. The deaths of these loved ones cemented my beliefs about heaven and hell.

God has continued to grow my faith since Ken's death. For years, I participated in the "Precepts for Life" Bible studies, and then God led me to begin to teach the studies. I believe I am using the teaching gift He gave me to help others know Him better. In addition, after being a stay-at-home mom while my children were at home, I was forced to go back to work to support myself, because we dropped Ken's life insurance policy three months before his diagnosis. Since then, God has placed me in one ministry position after another.

God has been faithful since the night I asked Him to come in to my life, be my Savior, and sit on the throne of my life. All His answers have not been yes, but He has walked with me every step of the way.

Nancy Nelson is a mother, grandmother, widow, sister, and friend. She is also a traveler, avid reader, knitter, scrap booker, editor, administrator, gift giver, lover of red in any form, cake decorator, home and dog owner, driver of a red VW Beetle convertible, novice tennis and golf watcher, and chocolate lover. Most importantly, she is a Jesus follower, Bible teacher, choir member, and blessed and highly favored child of the King of kings and Lord of lords. Email her at **NancyNelson909@gmail.com.**

Thoughts to Ponder
from A Jewish Girl Searching

1. Vanity and pride hinder our relationship with God.

2. You, too, can be adopted by God.

3. When we turn our back on God, He anxiously awaits our return.

> **How have you forgotten the King of kings?**

Here my cry for help, my King and my God, for to you I pray. — Psalm 5:2

Diary of a Wimpy Adult
by T. S. May

The movie *Diary of a Wimpy Kid* centers around a preteen named Greg, who in his quest to be popular and suffers one misadventure after another. He devises schemes to win the recognition and status he desires, but all fail miserably.

My adult life followed this pattern. Everything seemed to stem from the one terrible, horrible, and no-good situation I put myself into when I was nineteen years old.

I met a boy and liked feeling wanted. Against my better judgment, I slept with him, after which I barely saw him again. Weeks later, I was in terrible pain, so I went to the doctor. After a few tests, the nurse came back and said, "Well, the rabbit died." Her statement confused me, so she had to explain that I was pregnant. To my horror, my first thought was, *I can't be. What will my parents think of me?*

I knew this news would hit my parents like a boxer's knockout punch. I was born and raised in a devout Southern Baptist family. Despite my parents' divorce early in my life, both of my parents continued to be loyal to the church and active in their respective congregations. So no matter which parent I was with, I attended Sunday school and service in the morning, then returned Sunday evening and sang in the children's choir. On Wednesdays, we shared a meal and attended church again. Sleeping with a boy went against the biblical standards I was taught as a child.

I bawled all the way home to my tiny apartment, then cried some more. Pure fear pulled me into a dark space where there was no logical thinking. Only reactive thinking was going on in my brain, as it seemed my heart had shut down.

While still contemplating whether to tell Mom and Dad, I found the boy and shared with him about the situation. I can't remember who came up with the idea to visit Planned Parenthood, but the father of my child said he would take me there. He then offered to pay the $250 to end a little life. I knew this decision was dreadful and horrifying. I later realized I did not cherish the gift of life. I felt the decision was unforgiveable, and I also feared losing the love of my parents if I told them. So I came to the decision to not inform family or friends. I had to go through this all by myself, completely alone, out of fear of being judged and rejected.

A few days later, I was prepared for the procedure. As I lay on that cold table with fluorescent lighting above, I prayed like I have never prayed before. *Oh, please God, do not let me be the one to make this decision. If you want me to have this child, I will. And if you decide this child is not to be, then you make that decision.*

I left the abortion clinic broken, fearful, and undeniably sad to my core.

When I went back to work, the pain in my belly was unbearable. I went to the bathroom and found myself bleeding profusely. As the blood spilled out, so did a mass. I almost fainted alone in a public bathroom, but I managed to pull myself together. Despite my dizziness, I made it to the hospital, but the pain had not subsided.

After checking me out, the doctor said I had a miscarriage. The baby would not have survived, because it was in my fallopian tubes, a tubal ectopic pregnancy.

I burst into tears, this time mixed with sadness and a revelation that God had heard my prayer. I knew then that God was my Father and Savior. From then on, my loyalty and love never dimmed. In an act of complete desperation, right on the edge of the cliff, I clung to God like no other. He did not spare me the pain, but he did spare me. Meanwhile, the boy who got me pregnant never returned to my life.

Although I was dedicated to God, over the next twenty years, I had an almost bipolar relationship with Him. I loved Him and prayed, but I also begged, screamed, and wept at His feet. At times I could hear Him. I felt His hand on my shoulder and heard His whispering in my ear. That was comforting, but the next moment I was angry and rebellious, acting out and almost daring God, very much like a spoiled, bratty child. I had this bittersweet concoction of humbleness and haughtiness. My relationship with God was stifled through long bouts of depression that affected my mind and heart. I was often accused by friends and acquaintances of being flighty and self-absorbed. They were right. The walls around me were constructed like the barrier around Fort Knox. Only God had the right equipment to tear them down.

I attended church but would often cry. Others offered me

comfort, but I could not allow myself to be truthful about what was really bothering me. For years, I sat in the pew among church family, feeling completely unworthy. I believed I was a traitor and a liar no one could love. I certainly didn't *deserve* their love. It was a running theme throughout my 20s, 30s, and early 40s.

The largest, nearly unscalable wall was unforgiveness. I pointed my finger at everyone else who slighted me, hurt me, or ignored me. Then by the grace of God and a couple of visits to his holy "boot camp," I developed a prism of perception I had not seen before. Self-awareness drifted in and out for a few years, always giving me a chance to grab on and stick to it. It was ever patient with me until I grasped new truths and could adjust the prism to see even more clearly.

I attended a boot camp three times in five years. It was powerful, and I needed it again and again to reaffirm the tools that I use to combat harmful thoughts and beliefs. The first boot camp was simply called "The Road." It was super-scary. Over 300 adults participated in the three-day workshop, where we were first broken down, then rebuilt. Tears flowed, anger diminished, and resolution occurred. The biggest tools I took from "The Road" was tossing my baggage into the pit and releasing the anger. In the beginning, I did not know the training was centered around the Bible. They talked about God in the last hour of the last day. I had a physical sensation that this was where God wanted me. I left feeling better, happier. Yet the tools I brought home were slowly lost, and I resumed the old me, allowing harmful temptations to draw me back.

Four years later, I participated in another "boot camp," where my tools emerged again, a bit stronger and a bit more powerful than before. Again the boot camp broke all 300 of us down, pushed and pulled a lot out of us, and we were taught how to help our peers. Forgiveness was the major takeaway. I still felt unworthy, unlovable, and undeserving, but these tools stuck around a little longer than before.

The healing process has been slow, but God has provided many people to help along my way. They tried to tell me what I needed to do, but I was deaf, my heart was caged up, and my eyes were covered with scales. So God in His patient ways stayed beside me, pushed me, cajoled me, and sometimes stayed very silent. But He never left my side. I was the one who kept leaving when it got too hard. When the temptations won over, I said to myself, *See? I told you that you would mess it up. You don't deserve what God is trying to offer you. You are an unworthy and undeserving spoiled child.* The tapes ran long and loud. But those newly built tools stayed with me, like best friends looking out for one another.

I eventually saw that if I finally forgave myself for my mistake as a nineteen-year-old, I would lighten my burden and receive more joy in my life. I finally recognized my true calling, my true north. I grasped the fact that God forgave me the moment I was on the table, prepared to abort my child. I am the one who never forgave myself.

Through the desert walk of the past twenty years I fell a lot, hurt a lot, and got angry a lot. I turned to self-medication to mask my feelings because I was simply lost, and as a Christian I could not move up the ladder of understanding and deeper relationship till I removed the mask. I needed to unveil the pain, then give myself the reprieve I should have offered myself twenty years ago.

That's what I finally did. Over the past year, I have been on a more fruitful journey. I no longer consider myself the "wimpy adult." One of my friends described my new path as the "sweet Jesus walk." I have developed more strength in my faith and wake each day looking forward to what is in store for me. I see others clearly now, the way God sees them, and I forgive easily. I now possess the gift of grace, ready to offer to someone else who needs it. I unshackled myself from the mental punishment I had placed on myself for so many years.

All my life I thought I wanted to be married and be a wife and mother. After that devastating decision at the age of nineteen, I felt that God punished me and removed any opportunity to fulfill my desires. I blamed him, angrily, tearfully, and pridefully.

However, days after the miscarriage, I had a vivid dream, as alive to me today as it was then. I was in a mall, looking through clothes on circular racks. My friends were with me. Shots rang out, and we all ducked for cover under the circular racks of clothes. One by one, my friends were discovered and shot. Then a light appeared in pristine whiteness. I looked around and saw pearl-like smooth roads and English-architecture grand homes in absolute quiet. No person was in sight. Lampposts lined the street. I walked up to a home that looked familiar and knocked, but no one answered. The door was unlocked so I wandered around inside and found myself staring at the refrigerator. I pulled out the chocolate cake and took a bite. As I enjoyed the cake, I looked out the back windows. Beyond the pier, the lake was calm, smooth as glass. I walked down the pier to see the man sitting there. Who was he? Jesus. He patted His hand on the pier for me to sit next to Him, and I did, completely humbled and awed. We both dangled our feet in the water, and I silently finished the piece of cake. He put his arm around my shoulders and tilted His head toward me to let me know everything was all right. If He said any words, I do not recall. The calm and serene quietness is what I most remember, a friend assuring another who is in pain that everything is "okay."

Jesus was right. Everything is "okay."

What would have happened if I had held on to the immense shame and guilt that I had carried for such a long, long time? The past is the past. The path I was on was constantly erratic because I would give the reins to God, then take them back and stray off God's course.

I have a picture of an angel with her head in her hands, in a show of complete exhaustion. It reminds me how God sent His angels to protect me, but felt sad when I chose to go my own way. On the surface, this makes me smile and quietly laugh, but deeper down I feel deep remorse for not understanding sooner that I had to quit trying to lead. I needed to continue my daily, hourly prayer to God and a life devoted to my faith.

Where paralyzing fear and anxiety encroached before, today it no longer has power over me. Where debilitating depression covered me, it no longer casts its shadow. Where walls were up and not built to scale, they are now demolished. True clear light is shining inward, exposing the corners and crevices of areas that need attention. Obedience to His Word has greater meaning now. I seek to live life abundantly and encourage others. I will always be drawn to the "wall flower," the "shy," and the "unnoticed," because I have been there and know the pain. You are not alone in your walk. Others have traversed a similar path and are eager to help. Your journey toward the finish line is lined with loved ones who challenged you, who envied you, who deeply loved you, and who also may have been helped by you.

During the past year, I have also found my way back to family and no longer fear condemnation. My mom had an accident and needed me. I am proud to be the daughter I was designed to be. I am also evolving into the healthy Christian that God designed me to be, because I finally understand that God forgives our mistakes and never views us as wimpy kids. Instead, we are all his beloved children. Yes, everything is going to be "okay."

"Oh, heavenly Father, please remove the scales from my eyes so I may see the truth. Remove the wax between my ears so I can hear and follow the directions You have laid out for me. Remove the mist in front of me, clearing the path. Prevent me from causing harm to others, and help me see and understand when You are calling me to act. Amen."

*T. S. May is a recovering "people pleaser" and is now living an authentic life, sharing her story with others and leading them to love Christ. Ms. May has many dynamic interests that have evolved from hobby to career level as a fashion stylist, including creating jewelry to developing macro nature photographs. She strives to empower and build confidence in others. Ms. May is quick to respond to inquiries at **TSMCollaborations@gmail.com.***

Thoughts to Ponder
from Diary of a Wimpy Adult

1. Regrets are a waste of time because we can't change the past.

2. Guilt and shame are key weapons Satan uses to separate us from God and others.

3. God sees us as He created us to be.

How would your life change if every day you declared: Today I choose to love God, love others, and love myself?

I have loved you with an everlasting love;
I have drawn you with unfailing kindness. — Jeremiah 31:3

My Gift after the Grave
by Carole Gilbert

My thoughts take me back to days when I was a little girl playing outside. The wind was blowing, and I was spreading my arms to the side and leaning back, just waiting to take off in flight. I stood there waiting and waiting and waiting. I must have been a silly sight as I prepared for the air to lift me off my feet, but of course, I never got airborne or soared "like wings of eagles" as described in Isaiah 40:31. Later, I realized I had a lot of growing up and learning to do before I could soar. There was a way to actually soar and feel like you were living happily in the clouds.

Mama always told me I would understand about this type of "living above" one day. What I didn't know is that she wouldn't be there with me when I did. She told me I would need to pray and ask forgiveness and ask Jesus to live in my heart. I always disagreed and said, "But Mama, Jesus already lives in my heart." She simply said softly, "One day you'll understand."

My childhood consisted of playing and chores, and then came chores and playing. Imagination filled my days—role playing, creating, being whatever came into my mind. Then I was called to do chores and sit with curlers in my hair in preparation for church the next day. It was a wonderful childhood.

I remember running down the long hallway on Christmas morning, anticipating the gifts under the tree. My brother and I were never disappointed. As children, we saw things bigger and longer than they actually were. When I saw the hallway as an adult, it wasn't very long. That hall would later hold a different kind of significance.

My life seemed perfect, and it seemed to me that we were some of the richest people in our small Texas town. My brother and I didn't realize that instead of being rich, we were some of the poorest in town.

In the summer, I spent a week with my grandparents. Sometimes my cousin would be there too. We had such fun. On one particular week, I was alone with my grandparents. One day the phone rang. My grandmother was crying and stomping her foot. Something was wrong. I tried to listen, but I was scared.

This phone call changed my life. It left me in a world of uncertainty, sometimes abandonment and rejection, a world I didn't know existed. You can understand why I wasn't told what happened that day.

I was nine years old when Mama was murdered.

During her afternoon nap, someone came into our house, took a gun from the shelf in her bedroom and shot her. Many questions followed, with not enough answers. After that, going down that long hall left an impression of death and blood. Her unexpected, untimely departure left me naïve and vulnerable, thrust into a world I didn't know about or how to live in it. This world was filled with evil, abuse, destruction, tragedy, and secrets—where children had to be adults and take care of themselves. I learned to cope. I first leaned on God, then learned how to turn away from Him, and finally learned how to turn back. I also learned to sin.

At first, I kept praying for a safe, secure home. Mama would never be there, but surely there were homes that didn't involve all the abuse. Why had God let my perfect, wonderful life turn upside down? Why had he allowed so much pain? Why, God?

I cried and pleaded and sometimes even got mad at God. He must've been crying with me, but I didn't know He saw my sadness and pain. Why didn't He do something? So many times, we ask such questions. It's not that God doesn't hear and answer. He always does. His timing is perfect. However, we are impatient.

Three years after Mama's death, I understood what she had been talking about concerning Jesus and sin. I saw the evil ways in my heart, and I realized Jesus wasn't there. I longed for those simple, sweet days when I would say, "But Mama, Jesus is in my heart." I longed for her. I knew I needed repentance. I needed to pray. Mama had told me how.

One night in the bathtub, I was feeling the effects of a horribly sad day filled with sin and abuse. My sobs were muffled under the water because I didn't want anyone to hear. If I was heard crying, more abuse would follow. I came up to breathe, only to discover my young stepsister at the door, listening. She tried to make it worse by telling her mom. The third time I went under, I cried to God and Jesus, "Please forgive me, and come into my heart." After more words of prayer in despair, peace came over me and overpowered the pain with joy and contentment. Deep inside, I somehow knew everything would be all right. I felt the warm embrace of God that Mama had talked about. Jesus was living in my heart. The abuse didn't stop that day, but I was safe and secure because I was not alone. It was my Mama's gift after the grave.

I later learned about Romans 5:3–5: "Not only that, but we rejoice in our sufferings, knowing that suffering produces endurance, and endurance produces character, and character produces hope, and hope does not put us to shame, because God's love has been poured into our hearts through the Holy Spirit who has been given to us."

At eleven years of age, this verse became my motto. I may not have understood the verse completely, but I knew I had sufferings and had to endure. I understood that this hope was through Jesus *and was* Jesus. The Bible says, "Blessed be the God and Father of our Lord Jesus Christ! According to his great mercy, he has caused us to be born again to a living hope through the resurrection of Jesus Christ from the dead, to an inheritance that is imperishable, undefiled, and unfading, kept in heaven for you" (1 Peter 1:3–4).

Life went on with different stepmoms, various homes, and other types of abuse.

Five years later, my brother was found dead in his bed. My dad and I went to the house as soon as we got the call. As I pushed my way into his bedroom, I thought things didn't look right. With more unanswered questions, another mystery remained, even though his death was ruled a suicide. With Mama's death, my feelings were shock, disbelief, sadness, and despair. With my brother's death came anger. It was extremely hard to think, consider, and especially live out James 1:2: "Consider it all joy, my brethren, when you encounter various trials."

God was gracious to put up with my anger and bitterness at Him. He still loved me. Was this a package deal? If it was allowed by God, I would take it and learn how to have this "joy" through it all and be thankful. After all, God had given me complete joy that night in the bathtub.

However, I didn't keep that commitment. I turned my back on God as I went through my teenage years.

When I was eighteen and had made such a mess of my life, the only way out was to return to God. Again I prayed and opened His Word. I looked at my life and tried to see the way out myself, but I couldn't. The only way to victory would be through God's guidance. Through this realization, God came to my rescue.

Shortly after my turnaround, I met my husband to be. The trials continued though. My suffering didn't end, but it was different. This time, instead of abuse, I became pregnant out of wedlock. We got married, and God blessed our union, but we knew we had to keep our eyes on Him if we were to remain married. Even though we had our problems, we went on to have two more children—for the most part, a happy life.

In raising our children, my husband didn't think my past was something our children needed to hear about. We didn't lie. They never asked, and we never offered. With no example of what a good mother was like, raising children wasn't easy. However, I had God's examples from people around me and from the Bible. He had made me and my husband whole, so God gave us all we needed. He also gave us His Holy Spirit and guidance.

Through the years, we increased in our understanding of God and His Word. When our children were grown, God revealed it was time to tell the lessons I'd learned about all those situations of tragedy, suffering, secrets, and truth. Time to tell how my life of brokenness had been unraveled and restored to a life of inspiration. As Isaiah 40:31 tells us: "But those who hope in the Lord will renew their strength. They will soar on wings like eagles." Yes, it was time to tell how I lifted my arms, this time with my hands together in front of me in prayer. Instead of leaning back in the wind, I knelt forward into the arms of God.

I was soaring, in flight with the love and guidance of my Lord. What a feeling. What peace, joy, and contentment. I was at the point in my life like Jeremiah 20:9 says: "If I say, 'I will not mention his word or speak anymore in his name,' his word is in my heart like a fire, a fire shut up in my bones. I am weary of holding it in; indeed, I cannot." *It was* time to tell, which was such a relief.

When I finished writing my story, I gave each of my grown children and their spouses a copy in a folder. It started as my letter to them. For the first time, they heard about the murders, the mysteries, the abuse, and the pain. They learned about my joy and happiness, how my tears were turned to praise. They learned about God unraveling my life, Jesus saving their mama in a bathtub while sobbing under water, and the Holy Spirit given to me forever. They shared my thankfulness to God for every event in my life and how I wanted to use everything for the purpose and plan we're all given from Him.

My purpose is to give Him all the glory for every moment, taking every opportunity to share what He has shared with me and to help others see and know Jesus. My children learned that they too had this purpose. It was a new feeling of anticipation for me as they took my story, all those secret untold trials and situations, and read it. I was overwhelmed with their supportive love and responses. I've always thanked God for them and revealing these secrets brought us so much more closeness to be thankful for.

Mama left me naïve and vulnerable. She may not have told me a lot about life, but she told me the one truth that will be with me always, on earth and in heaven. She told me the truth of the saving grace of God through His Son, Jesus Christ. I learned to live with the unanswered questions about my mother's and brother's deaths, because I knew what the constant, secure life after this world was. I had the serene, comforting knowledge that I would be in heaven, praising God forever with all the joy I could possibly feel.

I invite you to join me there. I invite you to say the prayer to Jesus, giving Him control of your life. Eternity in heaven was promised to me that day when I came up from under the water in the bathtub. It is promised to all who call on the name of Jesus. And God keeps His promises.

"The Lord is not slow to fulfill His promise as some count slowness, but is patient toward you, not wishing that any should perish, but that all should reach repentance" (2 Peter 3:9).

"But the Lord is faithful, and He will strengthen you and protect you from the evil one" (2 Thessalonians 3:3).

As Carole *"Lisa Lynn"* Gilbert, I am a wife, mother, and "Gma" residing in a small Texas town. I stay busy with church activities, grandchildren, and writing. As a child, my seemingly perfect life was uprooted by my Mama's questionable death, and I was thrown into situations and choices far beyond my nine years. However, later in life, God revealed Himself and His truths through His Word. I now press into my life's purpose of sharing Him through my autobiography, *Unraveled, Time to Tell,* by Lisa Lynn (pen name), and through my writing, Bible studies, and speaking.

Carole "Lisa Lynn" Gilbert is a Christian author who stays busy with church and grandchildren. Her autobiography, Unraveled, Time to Tell, *by Lisa Lynn (pen name) tells of her life, which includes murder, secrets, and abuse all being unraveled by God and filled with hope. Through her book, she shared her story for the first time with her grown children and now shares by speaking to groups. She is currently writing her second book. See more at* **CaroleLGilbert.com** *or*

Facebook.com/Carole.LisaLynn.Gilbert.

Thoughts to Ponder
from My Gift after the Grave

1. When we teach our children about Jesus, they will know where to go in times of trouble.

2. Everyone must make a conscious decision to surrender their life to Jesus.

3. Our testimonies validate the reality of Christ.

How often have you soared to God's throne through prayer?

But those who hope in the Lord will renew their strength. They will soar on wings like eagles; they will run and not grow weary, they will walk and not be faint. — Isaiah 40:31

The Butterfly's Gift
by Linda Hammond

When was the last time you received a beautifully-wrapped present? Didn't the fun moment of holding it generate feelings of wonder and anticipation? In the unwritten rules of gift-giving, if someone who loves you offers you a beautifully-wrapped gift, the first thing you do to make it yours is reach out and receive it. Often you say thank you before opening it, knowing the person who lovingly chose the gift had you in mind when selecting it. To enjoy the gift, however, you must unwrap it and discover what's inside. What a joy to find a present that is perfectly to your liking and meets your needs. Gratitude overflows toward the one who chose the gift for you.

This gift analogy came to me a number of years ago as I attempted to write my personal testimony. It helped me understand my faith journey.

"Write your testimony in less than 300 words." The assignment for my church's evangelism class seemed simple. It wasn't. I grappled with the challenge as I realized something was missing from my story.

Recalling my faith development took me back to age nine after I joined the church. I gave as much of myself to Jesus as I knew how to give during an altar call at the end of a revival. During my growing-up years, the church was the hub of our family. Ours was one of those be-there-every-time-the-doors-were-open families, and our church friends became our extended family. However, in the frenzy of doing church, I soon felt my value was based on the things I did (or didn't do), rather than who God is and who He says I am.

During my childhood and teen years, I learned a lot *about* God yet never really felt I had an intimate relationship with Jesus Christ. I believed in God—that He cared for me. I can even remember making repeated commitments to Him. I felt I had to *do* something to earn God's favor, thus impressing Him and others with my holiness. I carried this attitude into my adult life, striving to do enough good things to merit God's love.

When I married, I believed I was following God's direction to be a minister's wife. With perfectionistic tendencies, I tried to fill the best-minister's-wife-ever role, yet discovered that my spiritual gas tank registered empty when I assumed a leadership role in our Houston church, which my husband planted. My intentions were honorable, but my motives were selfish. I craved recognition and praise more than I wanted to honor God. The job became laborious as I tried to lead in my own strength.

I was ill-prepared when tragedy struck our family. Two weeks after being diagnosed with leukemia, our three-year-old daughter died. My world turned upside down as I struggled to make sense out of the grief, truly pondering the meaning of life and death for the first time, feeling helpless and out of control. I was sad, bitter, and angry at God. I couldn't understand why a loving God would allow our little girl to be taken from us. Gradually, however, as our church family loved and encouraged us, we clung to our mustard-seed-sized faith and cried out to God to heal our broken hearts. We returned to the busyness of our daily lives—my husband to tending to the needs of our growing congregation and I to the responsibilities of our growing family.

Recognizing a need to sink my roots deeper into God, I joined a women's weekly study at our church, which included Bible study, sharing, and praying for personal concerns. For several years, I grew in my faith and was healed from my grief. God used that special time to prepare me for the next and most devastating time of my life—a divorce.

When I said "I do" to becoming a pastor's wife, I never dreamed the marriage would end "before death parted us." Facing a shattered, upside-down world, I had to trust God for strength. Feeling guilty and ashamed, I endured a discouraging time of limbo when at times, the *only* certainty I felt was an inner conviction of God's love for me and His reassurance that He would be with me, no matter what.

Because I had no money, no job, and no place to live, I accepted my widowed mother's gracious invitation and relocated my two young children and myself to live in Waco, Texas. Survival was the name of the game. I felt like I was walking in exile, in a dense fog surrounded by high mountains. I wondered if my pain would ever cease so I might enjoy life again.

I struggled to reestablish personal identity and the self-esteem that had been stripped away by the pain of rejection. Broken marriage. Shattered dreams and hopes. Disconnected family. Lost ministry. During the uncertainty and hopelessness of that time, I cried out to God. "Help, Lord. I can't do this alone." In my weakness, I discovered the sufficiency of Christ to meet my needs.

It had been three months since our move, and I knew I had to find a job. Seeking God's will for my employment, I went forward during a special prayer time with the church elders in a Sunday morning worship service. That evening after church, my children and I were enjoying double-dip cones at an ice cream parlor when I recognized Nancy and Fred Grimes, some friends from my previous Waco church. We caught up on life events since we had last seen each other. The next day, Nancy phoned Lois Marie Freeman, the wife of the senior pastor. (My husband had interned as a youth pastor as part of his seminary work at that church. When I moved back to town, I couldn't bring myself to return to that church where we had served together. It was too painful.)

My phone rang unexpectedly the next day. "Linda, this is Lois Marie Freeman. Nancy called to let me know of your meeting last night. Dick and I were so sorry to hear about your circumstances and wanted to invite you to come back to our church. I'll be happy to meet you next Sunday and show you where the classes for the children are and escort you to a welcoming Sunday school class."

As our conversation was ending, Lois asked, "What are your job plans?" At that point, I had no answer. "Dick is interviewing for a secretary this week. Why don't you come by and throw your hat in the ring? Just call him and set up an appointment." I interviewed on Friday, was hired, and went to work on the following Monday!

In retrospect, I believe the job was a gift from God. It morphed from a means-to-earn-a-paycheck into a ministry. (Three pastors and 34½ years later, in the fall of 2016, I retired from that position.) What a broad lens Dick Freeman used to see more than my brokenness and recognize God's potential in me—potential I could not begin to envision in myself. Very gradually, healing did come as God used my children, my mom, my job, my friends, my church, the acceptance of my circumstances, and positive choices to move on with life.

God also used the time I gave to Him in prayer and Bible study to reassure me of His love and care for me. Isaiah 43:1–3 spoke to me personally: "But now this is what the Lord says—He who created you, O Jacob, He who formed you, O Israel: 'Fear not, for I have redeemed you; I have called you by name: you are Mine. When you pass through the waters, I will be with you; and when you pass through the rivers, they will not sweep over you. When you walk through the fire, you will not be burned; the flames will not set you ablaze. For I am the Lord your God, the Holy One of Israel, your Savior.'"

How awesome to realize that the Creator of the universe knows me personally *by name*. And He calls me by name to be His own and promises to be with me through the floods and fires of life. This realization brought deep peace, comfort, and hope.

At another time, I read Romans 9:16: "So then God's gift is not a question of human will and human effort, but of God's mercy. It depends not on one's own willingness nor on his strenuous exertion as in running a race, but on God's having mercy on him" (Amplified Bible).

Upon reading that verse, I understood for the first time that God's merciful gift of forgiveness for actions that separated me from Him was His choice, not because I deserved it or because I had done enough good deeds to merit His reward. I knew something special had happened to me, because I experienced in the midst of my painful circumstances a joy that had no explanation other than the acceptance of that truth. I felt I had received an emotional healing.

However, after experiencing an emotional high for several weeks, I suffered a relapse to my old ways as I began focusing on my circumstances instead of on God's truth. I began to doubt the validity of my Romans 9:16 experience. During that period of rollercoaster highs and lows, I learned that my feelings cannot be the basis of knowing God's presence. The reality of His presence is based on His unconditional love for me, and my acceptance of that love. It was not until I was writing the evangelism class testimony a year later that I understood what all this meant.

As I continued to do a lot of right things for the wrong reasons, I struggled with lack of assurance in my relationship with God and conviction whether I was heaven-bound. I didn't know that reality could be a part of my life. God put a word picture in my mind that helped me understand:

274

It was as if I had been given a beautifully wrapped gift when I joined the church. As I matured, I carried that gift with me, sometimes holding it up, self-righteously, for others to see; sometimes setting it aside, overwhelmed by my busy activities; sometimes striving by my work, work, work, trying to prove my worthiness of it; sometimes hiding it behind my back when I wanted to make sinful choices. Upon close examination, I discovered a nametag on the gift with MY name on it. God wanted me to OPEN and possess all of that gift, not merely carry it around. I didn't have to earn it. I would never be worthy of it. My part was to RECEIVE what God wanted to give me because He loved me unconditionally and made a way to connect with me through the death and resurrection of His Son, Jesus Christ.

As I studied the materials for the evangelism class that had requested my testimony, I read the statements to guide others in making a commitment to Christ:

- I know that I am a sinner.
- I know that I cannot save myself.
- I know that You love me.
- I know that You died on the cross for my sins.
- I repent of every known sin, especially for running my life without You.
- I invite You personally to come into my heart to dwell and take complete control of my life.
- I know on the authority of God's Word that You have come in and that You will never leave me nor forsake me.

I finally got it!

I knew what was missing from my story. A relationship with God had nothing to do with my performance—doing good things did not equal an authentic relationship with Christ. His offer of unconditional love was a free gift—available if I humbly chose to receive it. I did choose to receive God's gift of forgiving grace. The result? A new, life-giving relationship with the Creator of the universe.

Wow!

What an incredible gift in the middle of my broken world to boost my healing. It did not change my circumstances, but it gave me a new, eternal perspective.

Embracing and verbalizing this prayer of commitment, I recognized Jesus' role in my relationship with God and my eternal destiny. I chose to receive and open the gift God had placed before me.

What did God want me to possess? He wanted to give me a personal relationship with His Son, Jesus Christ, who died on a cross to bridge the gap between an imperfect me and a perfect God. I am so thankful I chose to receive and open the free gift God offered on that pivotal night in my life in January 1983. God wanted me to know Christ in my heart, not just know about Christ in my head.

As I strained to balance the binding daily demands of nurturing my children, adapting to financial constraints, redirecting the self-pity spawned by loneliness, juggling work, health, and self-care needs, the struggle became part of the solution. Little by little, I welcomed God's daily presence and direction, which became like a treasure hunt with many heavenly gifts to discover.

The verse, 2 Corinthians 5:17 (CEB), came alive for me: "So then, if anyone is in Christ, that person is part of the new creation. The old things have gone away, and look, new things have arrived." I saw butterflies as a tangible symbol of what was happening in my life. Captivated by the beauty and variety of these fascinating creatures, I learned that distinct life-cycle stages characterize a butterfly's development. Because of its amazing transformation from a caterpillar, a butterfly symbolizes resurrection and new life. I recognized similarities between the metamorphosis of a butterfly and my own life.

Upon my move to Waco, I envisioned myself as a caterpillar, a fragile little worm, crawling and vulnerable in an overwhelming world. Role models in my church family affirmed, encouraged, and counseled me, offering a cocoon-like shelter for my shaken faith to be firmly reestablished. Just as a butterfly struggles to break out of its cocoon, with God's help I began to break through the challenges that encased my soul, mind, heart, and body.

The struggle played a significant role in my recovery. With a new eternal perspective, I learned to depend on Christ for my strength to face the day-to-day priorities, learn new job skills, build healthy relationships, and embrace a repurposed life. Prayer and scripture nourished my hungry soul and thirsty spirit. Exercise increased my physical stamina. New friendships nurtured my heart.

The process was more than rehabilitation or reeducation. I was being re-created. I learned to love and laugh again. (I have been married over thirty years to the godly man God brought into my life four years after my move to Waco.) Gratitude replaced my inward focus. I discovered new and meaningful opportunities for ministry and service as 1 Corinthians 1:2–4 promises: "Praise be to the God and Father of our Lord Jesus Christ, the Father of all comfort, who comforts us in all our troubles, so that we can comfort those in any trouble with the comfort we ourselves have received from God." Becoming a "re-creation" (new creation) in Christ prepared me to spread my wings and learn to soar.

Assurance comes when we realize and believe that eternal life is a gift—it is not deserved and it cannot be earned. John 3:16 says, "For God so loved the world that He gave His one and only Son that whoever believes in Him shall not perish but have eternal life." Based on that promise, I am confident that my life now and forever is in God's hands. The relationship I currently enjoy with Christ will be extended by my death into eternity.

But that provision is not just for me. Perhaps there is an emptiness in your life that you have tried to fill in ineffective ways. Nothing or no one can fill that vacuum but Jesus. God promises a relationship with Jesus Christ and the gift of eternal life to all those who place their trust in His Son. Just as my name was on the gift, so is yours. John 6:47 says: "Whoever believes has eternal life" (NCV). How simple it is, yet how difficult we make it by refusing to accept the gift freely given.

If God is tugging at your heart, please pay attention, and pray the commitment statements listed earlier. Don't put God off another moment. Eternity can begin for you today, and you can enjoy the present-day part as you grow in a daily relationship with God.

Does this mean life will be problem free if you say yes to Christ today? No! I have experienced many joys and blessings, but new "floods and fires" have impacted my life as well, tempting me to take my eyes off Jesus and focus on the circumstances around me. However, I can testify to God's faithfulness in those challenges. As I have experienced God's presence and leadership in my life, He has expanded my understanding of scripture, "For the Word of God is living and active. Sharper than any double-edged sword, it penetrates even to dividing soul and spirit, joints and marrow; it judges the thoughts and attitudes of the heart" (Hebrews 4:12).

The treasure hunt I mentioned earlier has helped me discover the depth and dependability of God's attributes and His direction of my life. Some of those include:

- **God loves me**. "For I am convinced that neither life nor death, neither angels nor demons, neither the present nor the future, nor any powers, neither height nor depth, nor anything else in all creation, will be able to separate us from the love of God that is in Christ Jesus" (Romans 8:38–39).
- **God strengthens and upholds**. "So, do not fear, for I am with you, do not be dismayed, for I am your God. I will strengthen you and help you. I will uphold you with My righteous right hand" (Isaiah 41:10).
- **God cares**. "Cast all your anxiety on Him because He cares for you" (1 Peter 5:7).
- **God infuses me with hope**. "For I know the plans I have for you," declares the Lord, "plans to prosper you and not to harm you, plans to give you a hope and a future" (Jeremiah 29:11).
- **God is always with me**. "Where can I go from Your Spirit? Where can I flee from Your presence? If I go up to the heavens, You are there. If I make my bed in the depths, You are there. If I rise on the wings of the dawn, if I settle on the far side of the sea, even there Your hand will guide me, Your hand will hold me fast" (Psalm 139:7–10).
- **God can be trusted to guide me**. "Trust in the Lord with all your heart and lean not on your own understanding; in all your ways acknowledge Him, and He will make your paths straight" (Proverbs 3:5–6).

These are but a sampling of the riches I have discovered by searching God's Word. As I have shared my testimony with you, I hope you have glimpsed an ordinary life that has been shepherded and sustained by an extraordinary God.

Physical, mental, emotional, and spiritual conditions surround our lives. Over some of them, we have no control. But many of those conditions present personal choices. The best choice I *ever* made was to receive the gift of Jesus Christ into my life. My acceptance of that gift turned my life around. In the years since that acceptance, my relationship with Christ has grown, as I have nurtured it in the company of other Christians. I've discovered that God's partnership in my life is sufficient as I seek to honor Him and to stand in the strength He gives for purposeful daily living. "And we know that in all things God works for the good of those who love Him and who have been called according to His purpose" (Romans 8:28).

And so, I ask you: Have you received the gift of relationship and eternal life Christ offers you by name? Are you enjoying this beautiful package purchased in full by Jesus on the cross? In Revelation 3:20, Jesus promises: "Here I am! I stand at the door and knock. If you hear My voice and open the door, I will come in and eat with you, and you will eat with Me." Eagerly and patiently, Christ waits for *your* answer. Will you accept and open the precious gift Jesus longs to entrust to you?

Linda Hammond *enjoys writing devotionals about real life to encourage people to trust a faithful and empowering God. Utilizing her writing skills for thirty-four-and-a-half years as the Senior Pastor's Administrative Assistant in a 3400-member church in Waco, Texas, Linda recently retired to concentrate on writing. She serves on the board of the Waco Christian Writers Workshop. Linda is married to C. L. Hammond; their family includes one daughter, three sons, one granddaughter, and eight grandsons. Contact Linda at* **LYHammond86@gmail.com.**

Thoughts to Ponder
from The Butterfly's Gift

1. Salvation is a gift from God, but we must receive it.

2. The Bible says God loves us unconditionally even when we don't feel it.

3. The Christian life is not without problems, but it is a life of solutions.

Do you have a personal and intimate relationship with Jesus?

For it is by grace you have been saved through faith. — Ephesians 2:8

Beliefs from God's Word

We believe . . . that the Bible is the verbally inspired Word of God and without mistakes as originally written. It is the complete revelation of His will for salvation and the only unfailing rule of faith and practice for the Christian life.

We believe . . . in one God, Creator of all things, eternally existing in three persons: Father, Son, and Holy Spirit, and that these three are co-eternal and of equal dignity and power.

We believe . . . in the deity of Jesus Christ; His miraculous conception by the Holy Spirit; His virgin birth; His sinless life; His substitutionary death on a cross; His bodily resurrection; His ascension to the right hand of the Father; and His personal, imminent return.

We believe . . . that man was created by and for God; that by man's disobeying God, every person incurred spiritual death, which is separation from God, and physical death as a consequence; and that all people are sinners by nature and practice.

We believe . . . the Lord Jesus Christ died for our sins and that all who believe in Him are declared righteous because of His sacrificial death and are, therefore, in the right relationship with God.

We believe . . . in the present ministry of the Holy Spirit indwelling all believers and thus enabling and empowering the life and ministry of the believer.

We believe . . . in the bodily resurrection of everyone who has lived, the everlasting blessedness of those in right relationship with God, and the everlasting punishment of those who have rejected God's forgiveness in His Son.

God's Good News for You

Now that you have read these stories of great faith, you may want to know how you can have this same kind of faith. We have Good News for you.

He loves you!
For this is the way God loved the world: He gave his one and only Son, so that everyone who believes in him will not perish but have eternal life. — John 3:16 (NET)

He wants to meet your need.
It's your sins that have cut you off from God. Because of your sins, he has turned away and will not listen anymore. — Isaiah 59:2 (NLT)

For God made Christ, who never sinned, to be the offering for our sin, so that we could be made right with God through Christ. — 2 Corinthians 5:21 (NLT)

He offers you a free gift!
For the payoff of sin is death, but the gift of God is eternal life in Christ Jesus our Lord. — Romans 6:23 (NET)

How to receive this gift:
If you openly declare that Jesus is Lord and believe in your heart that God raised him from the dead, you will be saved. For it is by believing in your heart that you are made right with God, and it is by openly declaring your faith that you are saved. — Romans 10:9 (NLT)

Jesus, I recognize I have sinned and need You. I believe You are the Son of God, that You died on the cross for my sin, rose from the dead and now sit at the right hand of God. I trust You alone and choose to follow You. Thank you for forgiving me of my sin and giving me eternal life. In Jesus' name, Amen.

If you have chosen to receive God's gift or would like more information, please contact us at **info@RoaringLambs.org**. We would love to hear from you!

Share with Us

Roaring Lambs is working on our next volume of *Stories of Roaring Faith*, a book of testimonies designed to lead a nonbeliever to faith in Jesus Christ, and to encourage the followers of Jesus. We would love to consider your testimony. To have your testimony considered, please send us, via email or mail, your typed, double-spaced, approximately 3,000-word story.

Email: **info@RoaringLambs.org**
Address: 17110 Dallas Parkway, Suite 260
            Dallas, TX 75248

We ask that you submit it no later than July 1st for consideration in the next volume. If chosen, you will receive a Release Form giving us permission to edit and include your testimony.

In addition, you will be considered as a guest on our radio show, *A Time to Dream*, which also features life-changing testimonies.

Let God use your story by writing, submitting, and sharing what He has done for you.

Roaring Lambs Ministries is a 501(c)(3), which exists on tax deductible donations. We would welcome any gifts to sustain our ministry to equip believers to better communicate their faith. Donations may be mailed to the address above or be made online at **RoaringLambs.org**.

There are many ways to give to Roaring Lambs: check, credit card, gifts of stock or real estate, or planned gifts by will or trust. Roaring Lambs can help with any of the above by working with your attorney or accountant.

Give, and it will be given to you. A good measure, pressed down, shaken together and running over, will be poured into your lap. For with the measure you use, it will be measured to you. — Luke 6:38

About the Editors

Donna Skell

With a heart for God, people, and business, Donna stays active in the Christian community. She has been involved with this ministry since its inception and came on staff in 2008. Donna oversees all Roaring Lambs events and Bible studies, co-hosts an international radio show called, *A Time to Dream*, on the WRNO Worldwide Radio Network. The program features powerful faith stories. She especially enjoys speaking to ladies' groups, churches, and retreats. Her rich Jewish heritage and her study of God's Word enhance her insight into the issues involved in Christian faith and living.

In addition to her work with Roaring Lambs, Donna serves on the Fellowship of Professional Women Board, the Christian Women in Media Advisory Committee, and the Collin County Christian Prayer Breakfast Committee.

DSkell@RoaringLambs.org

Belinda McBride

Answering God's call at the age of nine to become a "missionary," Belinda's mission was to touch others with the Good News of Jesus Christ. Her passion has been equipping believers to effectively live life with hope, purpose, and strength. She has done this as a pastor's daughter, pastor's wife, administrator, Bible study teacher, speaker, and writer.

She has served in many churches and ministries, including Hope for the Heart, Marketplace Ministries, and Roaring Lambs. Belinda's great joy is her husband, four daughters and fifteen grandchildren. She currently resides in Carrollton, Texas and is Director of Operations with Roaring Lambs Ministries. She can be contacted at **BMcBride@RoaringLambs.org**.

Lisa Burkhardt Worley

Lisa Burkhardt Worley is an award-winning author and speaker, and is the Director of Special Projects for Roaring Lambs Ministries. She is also founder of "Pearls of Promise Ministries." Lisa has co-authored or co-edited six books, the *Pearls of Promise* devotional, *If I Only Had, The Most Powerful P: A Child's Introduction to the Power of Prayer, The Most Powerful P Activity Book and Prayer Journal, Stories of Roaring Faith* and *Stories of Roaring Faith, Volume 2*. She recently completed the manuscript for her seventh book, *The Only Father I Ever Knew*.

Lisa is a former television sportscaster, and now co-hosts an international weekly radio show with Donna Skell called, *A Time to Dream*, on the WRNO Worldwide Radio Network. Lisa earned a Master of Theological Studies degree from Perkins School of Theology.

LBWorley@RoaringLambs.org
PearlsofPromiseMinistries.com

Dr. Sherry Ryan

Dr. Sherry D. Ryan is a retired Associate Professor of Information Technology and Decision Sciences at the University of North Texas. She received her Ph.D. in Information Systems from the University of Texas at Arlington and an MBA from the University of Southern California. Prior to earning her doctorate, she worked for IBM, teaching courses and speaking at national conferences.

She has published numerous academic journal articles, conference proceedings, and is currently working on a book. Sherry has two children and one granddaughter. She is passionate about missions and is on the Board of Directors for "His Appointed Time Ministries."

Ministry@RoaringLambs.org

Frank Ball

For ten years, Frank Ball directed North Texas Christian Writers to help members improve their writing and storytelling skills. In 2011, he founded Story Help Groups to encourage and equip all Christians to tell their life-changing stories. Besides his speaking engagements and writing his own books, he does ghostwriting, copy editing, and graphic design to help others publish high-quality books.

As Pastor of Biblical Research and Writing for three years, he wrote sermons, teaching materials, and hundreds of devotions. He coaches writers and writes blogs. He's a panelist on The Writers' View. His book *Eyewitness: The Life of Christ Told in One Story* is a compilation of biblical information on the life of Christ in a chronological story that reads like a novel. His website is **FrankBall.org**.